Social Work with the Dying Patient and the Family

Social Work with the Dying Patient and the Family

Edited By

Elizabeth R. Prichard
Jean Collard
Ben A. Orcutt
Austin H. Kutscher
Irene Seeland
Nathan Lefkowitz

with the editorial assistance of
Lillian G. Kutscher

New York   Columbia University Press

788-138

Library of Congress Cataloging in Publication Data
Main entry under title:

Social work with the dying patient and the family.

   Includes bibliographies and index.
   1. Medical social work—United States—Addresses,
essays, lectures.   2. Psychiatric social work—United
States—Addresses, essays, lectures.   3. Terminal care—
Addresses, essays, lectures.   4. Death—Psychology—
Addresses, essays, lectures.   5. Bereavement—Psy-
chological aspects—Addresses, essays, lectures.
I.   Prichard, Elizabeth R.
HV687.5.U5S65   362.1′04′250973   77–8679
ISBN 0–231–04021–0

Columbia University Press
New York   Guildford, Surrey

Second cloth and First paperback printing.

Acknowledgment

The editors wish to acknowledge the support and encouragement of the Foundation of Thanatology in the preparation of this volume. All royalties from the sale of this book are assigned to the Foundation of Thanatology, a tax exempt, not for profit, public research and educational foundation.

Thanatology, a new subspecialty of medicine, is involved in scientific and humanistic inquiries and the application of the knowledge derived therefrom to the subjects of the psychological aspects of dying; reactions to loss, death, and grief; and recovery from bereavement.

The Foundation of Thanatology is dedicated to advancing the cause of enlightened health care for the terminally ill patient and his family. The Foundation's orientation is a positive one based on the philosophy of fostering a more mature acceptance and understanding of death and the problems of grief and the more effective and humane management and treatment of the dying patient and his bereaved family members.

Dedication

This book is dedicated with respect and admiration to all those in the profession of social work.

The Foundation of Thanatology

Contents

Preface

Elizabeth R. Prichard

Relevant to the goals of social work are death and its relation to the quality of life. As society aims for a more orderly existence, with its individual members enjoying productive, satisfying and enriched lives, there are reflected parallel concerns for the hopes and despairs, struggles and achievements of the family unit—the basic group of that society. It is significant that the biological sciences are providing new dimensions and widened horizons for exploration and research as the individual seeks to adapt to an increasingly complex society. Social work is committed to the stability of the family and to the individual's development of his particular identity within the family and within society at large. Social work is challenged to provide the kind of support that will facilitate the coping behavior of the significant members of families confronted by the various crises of life.

The most challenging crisis to be confronted occurs when death and its related events threaten the fabric of family structure and the life roles of its individual members. Social work's response to the dying individual's needs, the preparation of the family for loss and its adjustment to the burdens imposed by bereavement has been the development of a comprehensive range of services focused on securing the practical requirements of everyday survival and providing guidance for emotional support.

During the Progressive Era of the early 1900s, when the profession of social work began to take shape, social work, while recognizing the effects of death on a family, concerned itself mainly with social reforms. On an organized basis, social work practice had started during the nineteenth century, based on concerns for widows and orphans and a focus on loss and separation as well as the causes and effects of poverty. Between then and now social work, as a discipline, has amassed vast knowledge of the struggles of widowed parents to maintain family unity, the problems of the bereft child shifted from one foster home to another, the dysfunctional behavior of the delinquent, "acting out" the loss of a parent, the distress of the dying mother as she tried to plan for the future of her children, the abandonment of the aged person who was forced to die alone, the emotional and financial strains imposed by catastrophic illness or long terminal illness, and the emotional maladjustment of the individual who had suffered the shattering effects of unresolved grief. The threat to the stability of the family, often impoverished as the result of death of the husband and father, with either threatened or actual separation of its members and dependence upon charity, led many social workers into the bitter battles for widows' pensions and, later, for passage of the Social Security Act. In 1935, with the passage of that Act, this nation gave recognition to the fact that economic survival of a family must be assured after the death of the wage earner.

Gordon Hamilton gave clinical definition to "widow," "widower," "orphans," "loss of children" as states of bereavement in *Medical Social Terminology,* published by the Social Service Department of Presbyterian Hospital (New York, New York). Gordon Hamilton of the faculty of the New York School of Social Work, now the Columbia University School of Social Work, with the participation of the Social Service staff and cooperation of the medical staff of the Hospital developed a classification of social diagnosis terminology to be used in connection with the medical diagnostic terminology. With the inclusion of social diagnosis in a patient's medical chart we see beginning awareness of the relationship of loss and bereavement with disease. Now, almost fifty years later, we have the benefit of clinical research in this area.

Although the early social work case records reveal the devastating effect of death, the development of clinical concepts and interventive techniques to be used by social workers moved forward slowly. The social work literature, until recently, has not reflected the direction of an action-oriented profession in its commitment to the dying. At the National Conference on Social Welfare in 1959, the Eighty-Sixth Annual Forum, a session on dying—held for the first time—drew an unexpectedly high attendance. Since the late 1950s, concern about the needs of the terminally ill and counseling to families has led to the gradual nation-wide development of agencies and programs both in large cities and in small communities.

The contributors to this book present a view of social work's thanatological tasks, reviewing these from the historical perspective of social work as a profession. In their papers are discussions of the impact of death on the family in its fullest consequences; interventive techniques and practice modalities; preparation methods and aims of research. These are presented also with the hope that the need for further understanding of the dimensions of loss and grief will be highlighted for all allied health practitioners, academicians, and researchers.

The first three-quarters of this century have witnessed many changes in society that have affected the family and life styles. As we start the last quarter, there is hope that the accumulated knowledge from all academic sources will be put to use for society's betterment. Social work practice has reflected changes in society as it moved from concerns about social reforms, incorporated the teachings of Freud that offered new understanding and therapeutic methods, and introduced the information and effective interaction of psychology, sociology, public health, biology, and, more recently, genetics. With the incorporation now of a thanatological approach to care of the dying individual and his family, a clearer perspective of social work's commitment is envisioned. Thanatological research and thinking have added new dimensions to the knowledge base of social work and introduced new directions into its practice.

No other profession has the range of opportunity for knowing and understanding the full effects of loss and unresolved grief; the emotional, and frequently economic, deprivations that death can inflict on the individual, the family, and society. Social work's therapeutic responsibilities are manifold, but they are fulfilled when social work programs provide a comprehensive range of services to meet the total needs of the family unit as well as the needs of its individual members. The full use of social work knowledge and the continuing pursuit of knowledge through practice and research confirm the premise that social-health needs and human values form an interlocking component. It is to the most complete and humanitarian exercise of social-work knowledge and skills that this book is dedicated.

Part I

Introduction

The Social Worker's Role

Leon H. Ginsberg

There is a dual reaction to death. On the one hand we may be astonished at how rapidly we forget those who have died and how rapidly others are likely to forget us. On the other hand dying and death itself have permanent effects—obviously on the person who dies but also on his or her family and others closely associated with the dying or dead person. The role the social worker plays in dealing with the dying and those affected by their deaths is the subject of this discussion.

It seems odd and perhaps anachronistic to discuss this topic. Although most social workers serve dying patients and their families in one way or another, it is clear that most would rather not. Like all the other human service professions (with the exception of funeral service) that ought to confront death and dying forcefully and directly—social work tends to avoid it. And that should not be considered unusual. Death may be viewed as the ultimate enemy of professions such as social work, nursing, and medicine. Admitting that it exists is a kind of insult.

Death does not fit the models for treating social problems most widely accepted in social work theory and practice today. The typical problems addressed by social workers are poverty, disease, crime, loneliness, and interpersonal conflicts—all of which may respond to strategies of elimination or amelioration, which are the usual goals of social workers when they confront social problems. Death, though it may be handled more intelligently and more humanely, is final, non-preventable, universal, and irreversible. It requires a strategy of acceptance and adjustment. Death can be viewed as the ultimate defeat for a social work client, and it is not one taken lightly by the social workers who serve him. The client's defeat is also, in part, the worker's defeat.

There was a time in the development of social work strategies and philosophies when programs associated with death and dying could have been more in keeping with the established ways of thinking. That was during an era when social workers spoke about helping people to accept and adjust to certain conditions such as poverty, illness, and physical handicap. That is, social workers sought ways to enable people to function more effectively within the parameters of certain kinds of problems, among which dying might be included. But that attitude has changed, and social workers are now less willing to help people accept severe personal and social problems. Social workers believe that it is much better, in most cases, to help individuals and families change their situations. It is much more desirable to change the facts of the society so that the situation no longer exists. Such a philosophy helps enormously when dealing with many phenomena. It sees to it that efforts will be made to create lasting changes and to ensure that problems will be finally overcome, not just for the individual but for society as a whole. But death is not one of those phenomena.

When I first studied social work in the late 1950s, we were still learning, in dealing with public assistance clients, to help them prepare reasonable budgets to live within very small monthly grants. But we changed that approach in the 1960s. Although I suspect there remain many workers in public assistance programs who help families with the realities of small welfare grants, the official strategy of professional social workers is to talk about the need for improving the system through programs such as guaranteed minimum incomes, better assistance grants, and social action activities designed to modify the distribution of wealth in the United States. Because of these changes and the new strategies of social change and social develop-

ment, strategies aimed at helping people accept and live with problems are less well accepted than they once were.

Learning to accept and to deal with irreversible problems such as
death and finding ways to make sad and difficult situations less so are
essential in services to the dying and their families. For that reason it
may be that most current social work problem-solving strategies do
not fully lend themselves to this problem, although death and dying
are among the most common phenomena with which professional
social workers must deal.

It may also be true that social workers, like other health professionals, are psychologically set in a manner that makes it difficult for
them to deal with the problems of death and dying, and they may be
psychologically less adequately prepared for such problems than
other professionals are. Social work may be the most optimistic and
future oriented of the human service professions. Social workers
seem to believe that improvement is possible, no matter how pervasive a problem might be; the notion that certain problems have
always existed and will continue to exist is not acceptable. It is one
of the lessons we have not wanted to learn from the sociologists and
anthropologists who provide us with much of our theoretical background. I have encountered this nonacceptance of certain social problems as the normal state of affairs among social workers in this country, among social work Peace Corps volunteers overseas, and among
social work educators. I remember my own experiences in East
Africa early in this decade when I was enraged by the high infant
mortality rate. I could not be comfortable in a situation that found the
majority of children dying before they reached the age of five. A
social worker who had spent many years in Africa responded to my
rage by saying simply that one must learn that all people die, some
young and some old, but they all die. For social workers all social
problems are, by definition, phenomena to be battled and reduced,
not facts to be accepted and dealt with as the realities of the situation.
That may be more true for North American social workers than for
others, but, of course, we are talking about social work in North
America.

Death Prevention

Social workers can be and are effective professionals in death prevention. That is true within a number of institutional frameworks and could be true in many others. In the normal course of counseling and guiding, in helping people with emotional problems, through their work in mental health programs and family service programs, social workers can prevent suicide and the psychological depression that often leads to death from so-called normal causes.

Social workers also play active roles in suicide hotlines and suicide prevention centers around the United States. They take part in providing the 24-hour answering services, referral activities, and counseling programs designed to help those contemplating suicide and to prevent it. Such activities are in keeping with social work philosophy and typical social work practices.

Social workers are also effective in maternal and infant care programs, which also prevent death. They want to maintain life and have skill in doing so through the kinds of programs mentioned here.

Social workers also have a major role to play—and it has not been played so heavily as it might be in the United States—in the prevention of industrial deaths and accidental deaths in nonindustrial settings. It seems clear that accidental death, both on and off the job, has a high degree of social content. That is, death in industry, death on the highways, and all accidental deaths are frequently related to the emotional state of the persons who suffer the accidents, the other relationships among group members on the job, and the social structure of the place where the accidental death occurs.

This is not to deny that many deaths result from unsafe plant conditions in industries, from unsafe automobiles, and from the imprudent use of drugs and alcohol in connection with dangerous work and recreation. But each phenomenon has social components, and social workers can be effective in reducing the incidence of accidental death if their services are called upon.

In some countries large numbers of social workers are employed in accident prevention programs, particularly in industries, and provide major inputs in planning for industrial safety and preventing accidents.

Social workers can, I am suggesting, be highly effective in preventing accidental death within and outside industry.

The Social Worker with the Dying Person

Large numbers of social workers work in hospitals and outpatient programs helping patients with both physical and emotional problems. Many are highly effective, and more could be effective in serving the needs of dying persons, which implies a number of activities—among them the help with the acceptance of death mentioned earlier. That is, an effective social caseworker (or a group worker dealing with groups of dying persons) can help serve the needs of those who face lingering deaths. This service can include counseling that enables people to plan intelligently for the balance of their lives and for the lives of those around them, such as family members, so that they can come to terms with death. It is possible and often desirable to use other resources, including religious resources, for those who need or can use such services.

There appear to be "stages" in the dying process. Kübler-Ross (1969) indicates that the stages—she identifies five—range from denial to acceptance. Anger, bargaining, and depression intervene between the two extremes. There is an obvious role for social work services at each of these stages, and it may be that social workers must learn that there are stages to dying in which they may be helpful, just as there are stages of development during the rest of the life span in which they are of service to individuals and their families.

The dying person has not stopped living. He or she often needs help in planning and coming to terms with reality just as other clients do. Social workers can provide this assistance.

Services to the Families and Other Significant Persons in the Lives of Dying Persons

Death has its personal elements but is also a social phenomenon. That is, whereas it is an individual who dies, his or her death has its effects on family members, employees, employers, and friends. In many situations the needs of those around the dying person for the services of social workers may be as great as or greater than the needs of the dying person.

Again social workers can provide a variety of services, such as casework or counseling with individual family members about their own emotional reactions to the death of a family member, as well as help with practical matters such as future budgeting and living arrangements. Death often brings change in the lives of those around the person who dies. Social workers can provide guidance or at least someone to talk with about whether or not the living situation should be changed, whether or not the work situation should be changed, and the like.

In addition many individuals in the United States are employed by small, individually owned firms. The death of the owner or manager of a small firm creates significant needs on the part of his or her employees. Social workers can counsel and assist these employees, who are significant others in the lives of deceased employers.

In the other direction social workers can work with the employers of employees who are dying. Employers can be assisted in adjusting a dying person's work schedule and assignments as one means of helping him or her adapt to reduced health and the process of dying. The dying person may need vocational rehabilitation services, just as those who are temporarily ill or newly handicapped might.

In such roles social workers can be important mediators between employees and employers when death faces one or the other participant in an employment situation.

Services to the Families of Those Who Have Died

Social workers can also help the families of those who have died. The range of skills and of problems of this group may be larger than those of any of the other client systems social workers might serve in dealing with death and dying. For a variety of probably valid reasons, most discussions of death deal with older people or at least with adults. Of course, they constitute the "normal" dying population, but they are not the totality of that population. Infants, young children, adolescents, young adults die too—anyone may die at any time, an obvious statement but one we are reluctant to make and even more reluctant to accept.

It is likely that the extraordinary death causes the greatest social and emotional trauma to the significant others in the former life of the dead person. How many marriages terminate after the unexpected or accidental death of a young child? What happens to the parents of children who are believed to have committed suicide, an increasingly more common phenomenon and a leading cause of death among young people? How easy is it for them to escape the guilt that may be justified or unjustified but that must always exist? What happens to families who experience automobile accidents in which only some of the family members die? What are the emotional reactions of the surviving family members?

The trauma associated with the deaths of persons who would not normally be expected to die is great and often demands the kinds of services that social workers can provide.

The same kinds of needs for counseling services exist with families of older persons who have died. A 60-year-old widow may face the same trauma at the loss of her husband as a 30-year-old widow would, and the same is true for widowers. Perhaps the shock and change are even greater because of the longer marriage and because of the long years of emotional and economic dependence.

There are also a number of practical matters that many families must face. For example, large numbers of American families have virtually no savings to use in supporting themselves once the breadwinner has died. Social Security is not available to younger widows and older children, both of whom may have been supported nicely but precariously on the monthly income of the breadwinner. These great problems associated with economic and social changes may be reduced by the services of social workers, who can help families locate alternate financial resources or modify their living patterns to conform to reduced incomes.

The Social Worker as a Member of the Team

The best assistance social workers can provide to the dying is indirect. That is, they can serve the dying as members of teams of treatment specialists. While dying in itself is a physical phenomenon, it always has its social components. Physicians, nurses, psychologists, clergymen, and others dealing with the dying patient and his family, as well as the families of persons who have died, need to understand and work with these social components. Social workers can contribute to their knowledge as part of the team effort. Social workers can be an important part of the treatment team dealing with dying persons and with death.

Macroplanning

Much of the foregoing discussion has dealt with the microlevel aspects of death and dying, the ways social workers may serve individuals and their families when death and its consequences are being faced.

There are, however, macrolevel considerations as well. Probably not enough general programs dealing with death are available. Not enough services are designed to provide guidance in dealing with the problems of the dying and those who face the deaths of those around them. There are inadequate resources to which they may turn for assistance and guidance. We need more information on death—not just the simple demographic facts of death but the emotional phenomena and the social problems that arise because of it. There is a need for social research on death and dying and for programs in mental health and family service agencies dealing specifically with death. There could be groups of dying persons and of their family members receiving social work services. Groups of people who have recently experienced death in their own families might also be excellent vehicles for helping with the problems related to death. Broad educational programs on death might also meet major needs. Our social welfare services are willing to prepare parents, through family life education programs, for the births of their children, for the facts of marriage, and for retirement. But few educational programs deal with death and dying. Perhaps such programs of education and service in our communities are needed.

Conclusions

It is clear that social workers have many roles to play in death and dying—from counseling with dying persons to planning educational programs for the community.

It is also clear that more needs to be known to meet the needs of those who are dying and those who play other roles in the lives of the dying. Social workers now make and have additional contributions to make in these areas.

But we need to know and learn more about death and dying. We need to confront the phenomena of death and dying directly because they cannot be neglected in a profession that deals with the social components of human existence.

Reference

Kübler-Ross, E. 1969. *On Death and Dying.* New York: Macmillan Company.

The Expression of Grief as Deviant Behavior in American Culture

Gary A. Lloyd

An assumption is made in this chapter that in the United States, most people do not know what to say about grief. Some of the consequences of this silence for the professional social worker are examined and discussed in terms of a taboo that defines many expressions of grief as deviant behavior. Reference is made to the personal and professional influences of the taboo upon social workers who are in frequent contact with dying patients and their families. Facets of grief—including perceptions of grief expression as pathology, and sorrow for self—are remarked upon, and the social and personal constraints standing in the way of extending help to bereaved persons, and acceptance of aid by them, are briefly reviewed.

Limited Expression of Grief

The taboo is well known and easily discerned, yet curiously and paradoxically ignored. The subject of grief, as well as grief itself, is an unremarked topic. Despite manifold changes in our value system, the fall of many shibboleths of the past, new attitudes and behaviors, and a rhetoric of liberation, most people in this culture appear to support a traditional ethic now more stern in its imperative than the work ethic. Death must be denied. Grief must be proper, contained, attenuated.

Social workers practicing in hospitals, nursing homes, and extended care facilities know the process. A patient dies and his family begins or recapitulates a series of coping responses. The social worker offers support through words and aid with arrangements. The ritual of the funeral is entered upon. Here, in ceremony allegedly designed to express and assuage a sense of loss, bereaved persons are expected to conduct themselves as controlled mourners. Grief fully and openly expressed is viewed at best as unseemly, at worst as pathological. As a result, the crisis resulting from loss may remain alive and unresolved, the necessary grief work incomplete.

Many people are socialized to inhibit the expression of grief and to fear overt venting of that emotion. Social workers are as apt as anyone else to be influenced by culture-bound attitudes toward expression of grief and expressing grief themselves. Seeing grief expressed by others undoubtedly stirs conflicting emotions in professional social workers and laypersons alike. Social workers who are in frequent contact with dying patients and their families need to recognize, before all else, the strength of the taboo and their own feelings about grief. That statement is of course a commonplace, but like all truisms, may be ignored or only casually considered.

Despite the denial of both death and grief, the only recourse is to accept the inevitability of death and the essential healing powers of grief. Helping bereaved persons express grief and reduce the extent of unfinished grief work is a critical social work task. The danger always exists, however, that social workers trying to offer comfort to dying patients and their families may be, in truth, agents of a conspiracy to contain grief. While some may have developed special sensitivities through education or therapy, social workers who in the course of their daily routine otherwise cope adequately with outbursts of anger, sorrow, and tears, become timorous in the face of grief. Why?

A search for an answer to that question may begin with an examination of socially sanctioned expressions of grief. Every society develops "normal," ritualized means of expressing grief. Whether through chants, prolonged ceremony, breast-beating, breaking of fetishes—whatever—individual and collective grief is still observed in many traditional—and some Western—societies. In America, however, the ritual is one of nonexpression. The ritual isolates the mourner within his grief, and enforces control over emotion at a time when body and spirit need release of tension and grief. An etiquette of loss prevails which effectively rules out expressions of intense grief, fear, and rage—all normal reactions to death.

Another answer to the question posed might dwell on the proposition that grief expressed because of death touches a pervasive fear of death and sense of "numbness." Expression of grief by another, itself a taboo, may raise within the social worker fear of violating other cultural taboos (e.g., men do not demonstrate feelings; mature people do not lose control of their emotions; adults should not be physically touched) and professional taboos (e.g., disciplined use of self does not permit full expression of personal feeling; subjectivity is not a desirable trait in a social worker).

If expression of grief is to be a healthy means back to life for the bereaved person, the social worker needs to feel and deal directly with the impact of the taboo upon himself or herself as a practitioner and as a human being. On the one hand, outpourings of grief and anger must be dealt with straight on. Kübler-Ross (1969) has stated that part of the task succinctly.

If we tolerate their [bereaved] anger, whether it is directed at us, at the deceased, or at God, we are helping them take a great step towards acceptance without guilt. If we blame them for daring to ventilate such socially poorly tolerated thoughts, we are blameworthy for prolonging their grief, shame, and guilt which often results in physical and emotional ill health.

On the other hand, the social worker is challenged to deal with his or her own feelings in as direct a fashion, and must have experienced what Lifton, in another context, has called "detechnization" and "breakout from numbing."

Expressing Loss

Although a literature exists on the relationship between grief and anger, social workers may forget that while the relationship is a natural one, the expression of anger may be as frightening to a bereaved person as the expression of grief. Fear of expressing grief, when coupled with guilt about feeling anger, creates an even stronger inhibition. Guilt about expressing emotion, particularly anger at loss, may be so strong that health-giving emotions may not surface.

For many persons in this society, the pain of loss—grief—cannot be articulated without consistently expressed permission from some other being. For most persons, permission to express anger and grief must be given in a direct, persuasive, and protective fashion. Social workers' skill and self-confidence are demanded; they must create an atmosphere in which permission to feel, cry, rage, and grieve can be conveyed and acted upon. That task is difficult at best and impossible for a social worker who is uncomfortable about sharing grief experience, or fearful of arousing personal feelings about grief and death. As with so many things, a social worker cannot effectively ask others to risk a violation of the taboo if he or she has not already taken the risk and come to terms with it.

Even the death of a stranger may bring back memory of past loss. Those memories are more acutely stirred when the social worker offers aid and support directly to a grieving person. Because of the cultural definition of grief expression as deviancy, the social worker's own "unfinished business" or incomplete grief work may give rise to feelings of repulsion when facing the grieving person. Feelings of repulsion are then countered by guilt, and an overly solicitous "I know how you feel . . . I understand you" approach. That cliché mode may in fact be sufficient for a grieving person who is free enough to express feelings openly. It rings false and is useless to the person who cannot risk breaking the taboo. In the majority of cases, the social worker must begin by granting permission to grieve and, by accepting signs of grief as normal, sanction the breach. But if expressiveness is to be sustained, the social worker may need to speak of his or her own past experience, or through expression and touch indicate support nonverbally. The need of the grieving person may be sometimes for "understanding." The need for a presence, for a person who can risk rebuff, retreat, withdrawal, and reawakening of past experience in the self, is universal.

Facets of Grief Expression

While the social worker assists in minimizing unfinished grief work, goals cannot extend to releasing all grief and sense of loss. Fear may lead the social worker to stifle grief, but error can also lie on the side of expecting full resolution of the pain of loss. Grief is of many degrees and varying duration.

The objective of social work with bereaved people is not an all-pervasive catharsis. Many people will—at least symbolically— "weep still" for the rest of their own lives. The objective is to assure that continuing "weeping" follows upon expression of grief and anger. If grief cannot be expressed from the first, and if the harsher feelings attached to grief cannot emerge, the lingering, poignant, healthful sorrow for a beloved person cannot occur, and freedom to take up life once again is curtailed.

The finality of death can render a family helpless with its guilt about things said and unsaid, actions taken and untaken. People grieve for the one who is gone, but also for themselves. Sorrow felt for oneself is, in many ways, as difficult to express as grief. Sorrow for self is defined as selfish and unworthy. Turning inward to escape a reality of loss—or to draw upon personal strength because that of even the strongest friend is insufficient—is a normal part of the grief process. Sorrow for self should concern the social worker only when as a process it appears to be attached to, and reinforce, the taboo on expressing grief. Otherwise, the turning inward may be both a method of renewal and of acquiring self-permission to express anger and grief.

Sorrow for self is one means of coming to grips with the sense of unreality that usually accompanies a death and period of bereavement. "I cannot believe that this is happening to me" is a statement frequently heard, even from persons who have believed themselves prepared for an inevitability. The social worker must balance recognition of a need to help others to express grief with an awareness of a natural need of bereaved people to turn inward, and to place distance between the self and a finality too enormous to accept. The social worker must understand that grieving people, just as dying people, need distance from others, and that establishing distance is a necessary part of the grief process. "Distancing," however, must also be viewed as a way of avoiding expression of grief and denying death. In the latter instance, both professional skill and the interior life of the social worker must be put to the challenge of confronting someone who has suffered loss.

Denial and distance, if prolonged, and suppression of grief have to be countered with the realities of a life changed in all its dimension. The struggle must be for expression of *some* emotion, directed at *some* object. "The discovery that our wishes have little or no authority in the world," wrote Lippmann (1929), "brings with it experience of the necessity that is in the nature of things." That necessity must be brought to the fore. Otherwise, the social worker conspires with the grieving person to embalm emotion.

Paradoxes of Grief

Any emotion or energy which cannot find an outlet is dangerous for future living. Grief unexpressed, or insufficiently dealt with, becomes a deadening force felt in the emotion, intellect, and body. Unfortunately, the most effective means of expressing grief are precisely those which break the taboo: crying, screaming, touching, holding, giving way. Particularly with men, in this instance more than most others trapped by the cruelest of stereotypes, the social worker needs to encourage the breaking of the taboo by creating an environment in which the bereaved man knows he can safely break out of numbness and safely return.

There is, in work with grieving persons, an inherent paradox that creates tension for the helper. On the one hand is the knowledge that grief unexpressed leads to life diminished; on the other, awareness of need for solitary sorrow. The result may be too direct confrontation by the social worker or, conversely, withdrawal. Possibilities of the latter taking place are increased by the social worker's own unfinished business about grief and death, the rather little knowledge about grief obtained through professional education, and fear of doing something "wrong" no matter what action is taken.

Even while being sensitive to the need for helping grief expression to occur, the social worker must understand the crucial fact that grief is essentially solitary, that the taboo has some foundation, and that some portion of grief work will remain intensely personal and private. The social worker can provide an atmosphere of comfort and support, can speak on an intellectual level of the human condition and on the more personal level of his or her own experience. But, in the end, only the grieving person can resolve the grief, either by an entirely solitary working-through, or by allowing someone else to enter into a private world constrained by a powerful cultural taboo. Healthy grief, expressed through support of family and perhaps a professional helper, terminates itself. Life will never again, perhaps, be quite the same, but it will go on and will be lived and confronted.

Unhealthy grief is signaled by continued turning in upon self, and sorrow for self taken to the point of a whining rejection (heard in the voice, seen in the posture) not only of death and the dead, but of present life itself. It is then, when life stagnates, when attention is turned either to an irretrievable past or an unfulfillable future, that direct intervention is required. Distancing cannot obviate the requirement that the social worker point out the realities of self-responsibility and help the mourner accept it.

In the final analysis, social workers seem to risk too little rather than too much. The uncertainties of idiosyncratic expression of grief, and fear about expressing grief, may hold the social worker to an ineffective, superficial level of practice. Social workers must begin work with grieving persons by offering concrete services, and being unafraid to serve as catalysts for bringing to the fore one of mankind's most powerful emotions: grief. Expectations must be realistic, and pathological explanations avoided. Risk of self, of rejection, and of reawakened memories must always be recognized and taken. Most of all the social worker must realize that there is a fine line between grief not expressed because of taboo, and because of a necessity to turn temporarily to oneself. In no other area of social work practice is sensitivity about timing and careful attention to phases of a process quite so critical as in work with dying patients and their families. And, it might be hypothesized, in no other area is the social worker so apt to elect to respond as a lay person rather than as a professional helper.

References

Kübler-Ross, E. 1969. *On Death and Dying*. New York: Macmillan, pp. 158–59.

Lifton, Robert Jay. 1973. *Home from the War*. New York: Simon and Schuster, p. 441.

Lippmann, Walter. 1929. *A Preface to Morals*. New York: Macmillan.

Part II

The Family and Death

3

Stress in Family Interaction When a Member Is Dying: A Special Case for Family Interviews

Ben A. Orcutt

The focus of this chapter is on dysfunctional transactional processes and relationships in families when a member is dying, a time that is crucial for intervention by the social worker. Maintenance of flexibility and openness in communication in such families is essential to a balance of intimacy and connectedness. Distorted, unclear, and disqualifying messages, along with barriers to communication, tend to generate family confusion, tension, distance, and even alienation.

General systems theory is used as a theoretical framework for conceptualizing the family structure and transactional processes (Bertalanffy, 1969, pp. 33–46).* This orientation views the dying patient/family-in-environment as a systemic configuration of different hierarchical orders and levels of system differentiation. The family system, as conceptualized, is an aggregate of mutually interacting parts or members and maintains a dynamic balance in functioning.

---

* The approach is conceptualized as a psycho–familial social systems approach.

The family relational system is more than the sum of its individual member interactions, and changes in any member relationships reverberate throughout the system (Watzlawick et al., 1967, pp. 123–25). To help families facing a catastrophic or terminal illness, it is appropriate to begin with the current state of disequilibrium as expressed by the family system.

In this chapter selected concepts from communication and family relational theory are used. Specific qualities of communication that identify content and relationship, such as agreement, confirmation, clarity, congruence, disqualification, and barriers, are discussed (Watzlawick, 1964). Family rules and decision-making power as critical variables for family system functioning are considered. Satir (1971, pp. 663–64) holds that order and sequence of the system are seen in the decision-making process that is made by negotiations of power and in the communication picture. This can be observed in who speaks, who speaks for whom, and who speaks attributing blame or credit to another. Intimacy and distance within the family relate to the rules in operation. Concepts from family relational theory, such as differentiation and triangulation (Bowen, 1971, pp. 159–92), are used, as well as a concept that I have coined: *relational awareness with empathy*. The latter concept is established as a reciprocal transactional process wherein empathic understanding of another in a relationship is achieved.

Help to the patient and his family, drawing on the selected concepts as identified, can be pursued through interviews of varying combinations of individuals, family subgroups, or the total family as a group. Depending on the way the family and patient are coping with the illness, they may be helped to communicate thoughts, worries, fears, plans, and feelings that they may want to share but feel constrained about doing so. Barriers to communication tend to grow out of a need to protect family members from hurt or sadness or out of accumulated feelings of bitterness.

Clinicians, such as Bowen (1971), Mostwin (1974, pp. 209–15), and others, have observed that the family meeting together can be amazingly effective in improving communication and relationships within a relatively short period. Bowen observes that a slight improvement in communication can produce dramatic shifts in the feeling system and even a period of exhilaration. Mostwin refers to unlocking forces in the family system that release emergent qualities in the form of new knowledge and energy for improved adaptive functioning.

Stress theory implies that the family system has been thrown off its customary equilibrium, and relationships show evidence of strain. Thus goals for families wherein a member is dying may be more circumscribed and devoted to support of adaptive functioning in view of this reality. The supports may be directed toward greater sharing and understanding: toward improving quality of communication and flexibility in family rule patterns, arousing awareness and empathy in relational conflicts, reducing patient–family alienation, and dealing with the pain and grief of feelings stirred up around pending loss and abandonment. This is a time when the mourning process can begin for the family. The processes of grief, anger, remembering, longing, and identification can be worked with, in preparation for the final abandonment and decathexis of the patient that is required (Furman, 1974, pp. 50–68).

With the realistic knowledge of what is happening to the dying member there may need to be readjustments in the family, new household work, new responsibilities, reversal of roles, and increasingly less time available for pleasurable activities. These added burdens pose threats and tend to create emotional overload, or stress, especially when compounded with relational conflicts and dysfunctional communication at a system level. For the individual, anger, fear, or guilt may be a crippling dynamic.

From our current research * with high-risk and dying patients, closure of communication is most frequently observed among families wherein there is the stress of dying. Closure tends to be linked with avoidance as the individual family member's mode of coping. The patient himself tends to know his diagnosis but not its full implications or prognosis. In such cases the family knows the truth but

* Partial Research Grant #CA–13696–01/ Scope U 8/73C, NIMH. Auspices, Jean E. Collard, Director, Social Service Department, Neurological Institute, Columbia-Presbyterian Medical Center, New York, N.Y.

protects him from the knowledge. Even when the patient knows the facts, both the patient and family members often tend to mask the truth with cheerful or unrelated talk, excessive activity, or silence that avoids confrontation with reality. Harkner (1972, pp. 162–71), writing about her own bout with cancer and approaching death, referred to the serious glances and to changed patterns in the communications of others that tended to raise her most ominous fears, with subsequent feelings of agony, alienation, and loneliness. She referred to a "moratorium on communication" and stressed that the patient himself may set the pace. The avoidance tendency observed in patients in our research could have communicated to the family a message that set off reciprocal avoidances in the family members. If the patient seems depressed, withdrawn, or silent or expresses his grief in tears, this usually leads the family and others to avoid these feelings rather than give him opportunity to share his grief.

The following excerpt dramatizes the tension in a family with a dying parent, where there were dysfunctional messages, communication barriers, and closure in an outwardly cohesive family. However, to the clinical observer, the family showed signs that the rules of the system did not altogether meet the children's growth needs for self-differentiation. A combination of individual and conjoint interviews was used to help the family deal with the problem of illness and death and to bring changes in their transactions with relief of subjective pain.

Mr. J. was hospitalized for cancer, and his terminal condition was not divulged to the family. Mrs. J. tried to protect the children and Mr. J. from the knowledge of the poor prognosis. Mr. J. suspected the truth because of his rapid deterioration. The patient initially expressed to the social worker his sense of alienation by saying that "nobody cares." These feelings were expressed in spite of the fact that his wife was overextending herself in daily visiting and assuming caretaking duties. Her coping pattern tended to involve excessive activity, with a tendency to infantilize the patient in ritualistic activity. Resentment of her burdens (also reactivated from earlier life burdens) lessened the affective flow of warmth in the interchange. Interestingly Mrs. J. and the children all tended to use activity to deal with fear and grief. Actually all family members expected the worst, but none of them could speak openly. Tensions in the home mounted, and conflict arose over whether Mr. J. could be discharged to the home.

In an initial interview with Mrs. J., the social worker encouraged expression of her anguish, resentment, exhaustion, and helplessness. She began to explore with her the alternatives of further institutionalization or home care. In the course of the work a conjoint interview was suggested with Mrs. J. and the children, since a discharge plan was of concern to all, and Mrs. J. found it too difficult to bring up the subject of care with the children without intense emotion. Mrs. J. resisted at first, saying that it would be too difficult for the children to come in because of school commitments. However, on thinking it over, she agreed to a conjoint session with her two children, John (age 16) and Gloria (age 20). The purpose of the joint interview was explained as helping the family to share some of their common feelings and worries with regard to Mr. J.'s illness and to include the children in planning for his release. (It is possible that a family group meeting including Mr. J. could have been structured around planning; however in our research we were beginning more cautiously with the family subgroup.)

At the beginning of the interview both children were extremely cautious and nonverbal. They kept looking at their mother to size up her reactions. They were most careful not to say anything to which she might object. It was apparent that, on account of her own anxiety, Mrs. J. talked excessively. She also talked on behalf of John and Gloria, often negating or disqualifying what they had just said or restating a response to infer that that was what they wanted to say. It was clear that Mrs. J. was the decision maker and that the rules of the system rested with her as the power. However, the message was that John was unable to clarify or speak for himself. As this continued, the worker suggested that she was really asking John for clarification of a point at issue, and Mrs. J. readily responded that she had always treated John like "a baby." She asked the worker whether John didn't look much younger than his age. The worker responded that she thought he really did look his age, and she wondered if John really couldn't speak for himself. John smiled broadly at this recognition. Mrs. J. continued in the interchange to undercut whatever John said by referring to him as being too young or not knowing "what was going on." In clarifying the family's understanding of Mr. J.'s illness and the care required, the worker asked John whether he knew what his mother was talking about. It turned out that John had a fairly accurate picture of his father's illness. He said that he wanted to bring his father home, saying he was willing to care for him. At this, Gloria shouted at him, "Do you know he is going to die?" John said, "I know and that's why I want him home." Mrs. J. then again commented that John did not really know the problem. The worker suggested that perhaps John was afraid his daddy would never go home if he were transferred to another institution. John nodded in agreement and began to weep openly. Mrs. J., though self-contained, seemed embarrassed and again said, "John is just a little boy." The social worker supported the release of feeling and John's sense of self by commenting to John that it is really more like a man to be able to cry and share what he feels.

In this family's continued contacts with the social worker, Mrs. J. (the power) was helped to recognize that, where agreements in the family were not reached but disagreement could not be tolerated, she in effect, as leader in the home, was denying the disagreement (disqualifying a message), and the members of the family could not openly express their wishes to find a solution. With help, the family as a group were willing to plan realistically, and Mr. J. did go home, with community supports. When his condition worsened so that home care was infeasible, he returned to the hospital, where he died.

It can be seen that helping a family remove communication barriers and dysfunctional rules is basic to the helping process when there is a dying member. In the cited example it is clear that without help John would have been increasingly vulnerable to restriction on growth and separateness as an individual after his father's death. Accentuated closeness to the mother could bring feelings of rejection and distance for Gloria in a triangular relationship (Bowen 1971, pp. 184–85) and threaten a healthy balance of intimacy and distance in the family relationships.

Grosser and Paul (1971, pp. 119–20) generalize goals for conjoint family therapy that are pertinent, with some modification, to the social worker's intervention with a family when a member is dying. Their goals, as modified, are as follows:

1. to accept the existence of illness, deviance, and differences as they exist and affect the family system;
2. to broaden family capacity for reality testing and consensual validation as a check on projections and distortions by encouraging family members to review the same event from their respective points of view;
3. to encourage family members to share feelings and concerns with each other as emotional release and elimination of barriers in relationships;
4. to encourage each family member to develop a greater capacity for empathy and for observing ego functioning in tolerating anxiety;
5. to increase tolerance of frustration when confronting disappointment, loss, and new burdens;
6. to assist in providing for mutual accommodation and adjustment of role relationships in accordance with newly perceived appreciation of reciprocal needs, perceptions, and feelings;

7. to facilitate object relationships outside the family unit;
8. to foster environmental supports for social roles and material needs.

These general goals are sufficiently extensive to allow for variation in focus and extent of service. Social work intervention may be limited to a crisis period or to more substantive work over a longer time period, depending on the illness and the family problem. It is important to begin contact with the patient and family early, when it is first known that the prognosis is poor. From our research, on which this chapter draws, the social worker's contact with the family system was initiated with the patient at the time of hospital admission and moved to spouse, parent, and other members of the family unit. Short-term work with family members individually, and conjointly as subgroups of the family, tended toward positive reverberations throughout the family system. Even minimal input of the social worker into the family transactional processes tended to unlock the family's own adaptive forces. Opening up communication, appropriate sharing, congruent and clear messages, and greater understanding brought some changes in attitude and behavior, greater empathy, and adaptive processes in mourning. Emphasis on clarity, without disqualification and negation in messages, was used to help families become more flexible in their interactions and deal realistically with their grief and the added burdens in their life.

From our study it became clear that, when the patterned communication in the family tended toward closure, with avoidance of sharing painful thoughts and experiences, this quality was exacerbated with the illness, and dysfunctional behavior could be observed. The avoidance was often associated with verbal or nonverbal messages inherent in the family rules to keep silent and avoid risk taking. Grief, fear, or anger tended to be suppressed or displaced.

Paul (1969, pp. 186–205), using object relations theory, refers to building empathy through conjoint family therapy. His premise is that mourning is a psychological process set in motion by the loss of a loved object and, when complete, is associated with relinquishment of that object. In conjoint treatment sessions, where one spouse exhibits maladaptive responses owing to incomplete mourning of real or imagined object loss, with deposits of anger, grief, guilt, bitterness, regret, and so forth, he repeatedly inquires about recollectable responses to the loss that the patient has experienced and encourages the expression of intense feelings. He also solicits the feelings stimulated in the other marital partner by such expressed grief. Paul sees his own ability as therapist to empathize with patient's receiving and exposing his intense inner feelings about his losses as a critical factor dictating the spouse's ability to resonate empathetically with the belated mourner. The focus is to generate a reciprocating-empathic responsiveness in the couple. This approach has some implications for work with the grieving patient and family, when death is expected.

I have identified a procedure in conjoint work with families that I call "relational awareness with empathy," which bears some similarity to the Paul technique and can be a useful approach when a member of the family is dying. In this procedure the social worker does not focus as Paul does on loss as such but encourages the member's recollection and expression of feeling around a difficult life experience(s) that relates to the current family distress. The listening family members tend to be affectively moved as they grasp an awareness of the meaning and pain of these experiences and how they relate to a piece of current behavior. With this awareness, empathy and warm affect tend to flow, and the relationship begins to take on a different meaning. The spouse who has seen his partner as rejecting and uncaring can link these reactions to an earlier hurt or bitter experience rather than interpret them as directed solely to himself. He also achieves some awareness of how his own behavior can set off these reactions to the earlier hurt. Actually the family or the marital dyad perceives the reality more correctly and with empathy. This procedure can be useful to the family, particularly when there has been conflict or bitterness before the terminal illness.

The following case example of the X family illustrates problems in family relationships and barriers to communication that have evolved over the course of a long illness. At the time of the current hospital admission the patient's illness was terminal. Bitterness in family relationships was consensually validated by encouraging each spouse to express the pain he had experienced. The reality was reviewed from the viewpoint of each spouse, with mutual encouragement of appreciation of their reciprocal needs and feelings. Relational awareness with empathy as a procedure in conjoint session had to be modified under the circumstances, but the thrust of the procedure was the same. The social worker enabled the patient to express anger, resentment, and feelings of inadequacy and rejection associated with his deterioration that tended to trigger his angry outbursts toward his wife and his son, whose responses led to further feelings of rejection. By means of separate interviews with the patient and his wife, the relational awareness that accrued to each spouse as he understood the pain experienced by the other led to a flow of warmth and empathy between them. The patient's wife could experience empathetically the feelings of frustration, fear, inferiority, and inadequacy engendered by his severe handicap and hopeless deterioration.

The interviews with the family in the case were held individually with the patient, with his wife, and conjointly with his wife and children. Marked changes occurred in family functioning with obvious relief from tension, guilt, and bitterness. The process of mourning could be carried through with restitution.

The X family consisted of the patient, Mr. X, 40 years old; Mrs. X, 37; Susan, 16; and David, 14. Mr. X had a terminal condition from infiltration of tumor mass in the brain. He was unable to balance himself, to walk, or to maintain bodily controls. Seizures, both focal and grand mal, impotency, and visual loss further severely impaired his general functioning.

The family interactional processes had been dysfunctional over a five-year period, following initial diagnosis and treatment for brain tumor. The changes in relationship disrupted family cohesion and occurred along with changes and deterioration in the patient's condition. The husband–wife subsystem, as the axis of family functioning, was unable to communicate reciprocally their fears and feelings, becoming intolerant of each other and expressing their hurt in angry explosions. Decision making tended to be centralized in Mrs. X. At the time of the initial diagnosis Mrs. X was told that her husband would probably live only a few months. She kept this knowledge to herself. The patient, however, improved with treatment and was able to return to his sedentary work, though continuing to have seizures, lack of good balance, and poor motor control.

But during his treatment, and approximately one year before his current hospital admission, he learned the truth of his poor prognosis. He likewise kept this a secret. Hence the secret became compounded for the family. Increasing symptomatology tended to be associated with irritability and depressed feelings. Impotency stimulated projections and suspicious accusations toward his wife, whose work schedule conflicted with his and made her less available in the home.

Increasing inability to work efficiently caused his demotion, with loss of income—a fact he could not share with his family. Repeated accidents in the home that stemmed from his poor motor control were construed by his wife as purposeful. Automobile accidents, which appeared on the face to be self-destructive (possibly suicidal), were also perceived as purposeful anger directed toward the family. The emotional distance between Mr. and Mrs. X widened, and each tended to reach for the opposite sexed child for gratification. Attempts by Mr. X to exercise control in decision making were generally aborted by the more aggressive leadership of Mrs. X, who was now placing the large, well-developed David in the husband role. David began to fill the emotional void left by his father and would wait up late every night for his mother to come home from work. He was also asked to do the home tasks his father could no longer perform. This further brought on angry, critical attacks from the patient out of jealousy. Through triangulation of the son there was accentuation of distancing and alienation between Mr. and Mrs. X and closeness between David and his mother. David began to act out in school with angry outbursts and failing grades. Family communications with father, except for Susan, became increasingly limited to fights and explosions, or to the patient's passive withholding of his meager income. This was his only means of being heard or of controlling. Susan, who was the object of her father's attentions, drew anger or indifference from Mrs. X, triangulating their relationship. The adolescent children became deeply involved in adult role tasks in the home, with limited involvement in age-appropriate activities outside of the home. Mr. X became increasingly alienated and withdrawn from the family functioning and was told to move out of the home shortly before his hospital admission.

The social worker, in the initial interview with Mr. X, elicited from him his knowledge and understanding of his illness, its meaning, and its implications for him. She observed the quality of his responses for evidence of stress and his coping maneuvers. Feelings of grief and anger that Mr. X could not communicate to his family easily surfaced. His distortions and feelings of inferiority, with loss of autonomy, loss of balance, impotency, loss of self-worth, and a real caring about his family began to emerge. Having knowledge of his limited life expectancy, he told the social worker that he was holding his last paycheck in the hope that this could bring his family in to see him. He so feared rejection, however, that he could not call to let his wife know that he was in the hospital. He was helped to appraise the situation realistically and rehearsed with the worker different responses in making a telephone call to his wife. The painful rejection that he expected did not occur, and Mr. X wept profusely as he recounted the grief and bitterness he felt, really caring about his family with so little time left.

The following excerpt demonstrates the closure and dysfunctional communication observed in the conjoint interview with Mrs. X, Susan, and David after their first visit to Mr. X in the hospital. The children were generally withdrawn, and had difficulty verbalizing. There was much silence, and their responses were largely to questions only. Their comments about their visit with the patient demonstrated the family's inability to talk to each other and the empty, sterile atmosphere that prevailed.

WORKER: What was it like going up to see your father?
SUSAN: All right.
WORKER: All right? You didn't know he was sick?
SUSAN: (*Shook her head to indicate not knowing.*)
WORKER: Could you talk to him?
SUSAN: I didn't have much to say.
WORKER: After so long a time?
SUSAN: I couldn't . . . (*nodding*).
WORKER: How about you, David—did you talk to your father?
DAVID: No.
WORKER: How come? Hm? . . . How are you feeling?
DAVID: Fine.
WORKER: I don't think that you are feeling too good about it. . . . are you worried?
DAVID: No.
WORKER: Did it upset you to see him?
DAVID: No.
(*To the worker's further questions: "Did he seem sick? . . . He doesn't look sick to you? . . . Do you know why he is here?" David could only shake his head, indicating "no" to all questions.*)
WORKER: It has been this way a long time? . . . (*Silence.*) What are you thinking now? . . . You seem so unhappy.
DAVID: I am tired.
WORKER: Is that all?
DAVID: I am tired.

WORKER: I know, but is that all? (*David is silent.*) That wasn't too good of an excuse, huh? (*David smiles.*)

WORKER (*to both children*): Do you miss your father sometimes? (*Susan nods "yes."*) You do. How about you, David? (*David nods "yes."*) You do, too . . . even though you can't talk with him. . . . He didn't talk to you either? (*David nods "no."*) This morning he told me that he really missed you two, and your mother, too. He felt your coming to get the money might be the only chance he would have to see you all. So that's why he said, "I want to hold it, until I see my kids and my family." It's unfortunate that he couldn't tell you that. . . . Have you thought about what is going to happen to Dad? (*Children nod "no."*) Never thought about that? (*To Susan*): What do you think is going to happen?

SUSAN: I don't know. . . .

WORKER: Do you know what is wrong with him? . . . (*Silence.*) You never ask him? Or Mother? (*Susan nods "no."*)

MOTHER: Oh, they know what is wrong; they know. (*To children*): Don't you know what is wrong with your father?

SUSAN: Not now.

MOTHER: Oh, not now, but you knew what was wrong before.

WORKER: What was wrong before?

SUSAN: He had seizures.

WORKER: Do you know what was causing the seizures? (*Susan nods "no."*) . . . the blackouts and seizures and his not having good balance; it's the same old problem, except worse. . . . (*Silence.*) Is there anything you want to talk to your Dad about? (*Silence.*) You just want to see him and see how he does? (*Silence.*) Do you think that you want to come back again? (*Susan nods "yes," cautiously looking at her mother for approval.*) How about you, David? (*Nods "yes," but also looks at his mother for approval.*) Do you feel bad for him, David?

DAVID: No.

WORKER: No? Just want to see him, but not talk to him? How is it that you don't have anything to say to him? (*Silence.*) Are you angry with him?

DAVID: No.

WORKER: Because I know that he hasn't been paying money and all that. Are you mad with him? (*Silence.*) . . . Would you like to tell him how you are getting on in school?

(This less charged subject brought immediate responses from David and his mother about how well he has been getting along, particularly since his father has been out of the home.)

WORKER: (to David): So you were pretty upset when your father was at home. What was happening at that time?

DAVID: Arguments.

WORKER: Arguments? . . . between whom?

DAVID: My mother and my father.

WORKER: Just between the two of them? Never between you and your father or between your father and Susan? (*David nods agreement.*) Who started these arguments?

DAVID: I don't know.

WORKER: You don't know what they were usually about? . . . hm? Just yelling and shouting? (*David nods "yes."*) That must be upsetting, huh? (*David nods "yes."*) Do you feel the same way too, Susan? Is it better this way, or had you rather have father around, even if he is grouchy? (*Susan smiles, nods "yes."*)

. . . .

WORKER: I know it is sad for you to see your father this way. It's a very unhappy situation for everybody: for your mother, for you, and for your father, too. It happens that people do not always get along together well, and I know this situation has been going on for a long time. Does your mother ever talk to you about your Dad?

WIFE: No, I don't mention it. I don't mention anything.

WORKER: They never ask to see Dad, or anything?

WIFE: No.

WORKER: They might not think that they can. . . . It is all right for them to visit here if they want to.

WIFE: Only if they want to.

The various excerpts from the interview illustrate the mother as controller and as power figure. Her underlying rage was also shared by David, who tended to carry the burden of the spouses' role shifts and the relationship dysfunction. He expressed the family difficulties by failure in school and withdrawal from peer relationships. Both children appeared withdrawn and unhappy. In the individual sessions with both Mr. X and Mrs. X, as indicated previously, they were led to remember and review the painful experiences since Mr. X's illness began and to see the reality of events in perspective, with achievement of some relational awareness and empathy. Their anger and resentment began to be interwoven with memories of affection-laden experiences around pre-illness marriage. Rage at events and interpersonal conflicts were seen and understood. Affectional feelings were "unlocked," and the communication block was eased. The reality of impending loss, feelings of guilt, and burdens in role shifts began to be talked about openly. Eventually the family members all planned together for Mr. X to return home, but death came sooner than expected.

The case example reflects the "wall" or "barriers" to communication, role changes, distancing in family relationships with dysfunctional triangulation, and lack of empathy that emerged dramatically as the social worker made initial contacts with the dying patient and his family. Conceptually the patient was seen as a part of the family system, and the thrust of the work was focused on the family as a unit. The goals for intervention with the family were not dissimilar to those general goals that were modified from Grosser and Paul's formulations for conjoint marital therapy.

The goals for the X family were as follows:

1. to encourage acceptance and sharing around the illness;
2. to improve reality perceptions, relational understanding, and empathy among family members;
3. to reduce destructive triangulation of the children and distancing between the spouses;
4. to permit expression of anger and grief in the anticipation of their loss and disappointment and to offer chances for restitution of guilt for past attitudes and behavior;
5. to facilitate accommodation to changed role relationships;
6. to promote action tendencies in coping that lead to adaptive problem solving, rather than to constriction or angry explosions;
7. to facilitate gratifying object relationships outside the family unit;
8. to provide environmental and material supports as needed.

This case example highlights Kübler-Ross's observation (1969, p. 241) that the dying patient may have unfinished business that he wants to talk about to someone who is not going to run away if dying is mentioned and to whom he feels free to express his fears and worries. It dramatizes the fact that fertile ground may exist for guilt, problems in mourning, and dysfunctional relationships within the family.

References

Bertalanffy, L. V. 1969. "General Systems Theory and Psychiatry: An Overview." In *General Systems Theory and Psychiatry,* eds. W. Gray et al. Boston: Little Brown.

Bowen, M. 1971. "The Use of Family Theory in Clinical Practice." In *Changing Families,* ed. J. Haley. New York: Grune and Stratton.

Furman, E. 1974. *A Child's Parent Dies.* New Haven, Conn.: Yale University Press.

Grosser, G. H. and N. L. Paul. 1971. "Ethical Issues in Family Group Therapy." In *Changing Families,* ed. J. Haley. New York: Grune and Stratton.

Harkner, B. L. 1972. "Cancer and Communication Problem: A Personal Experience." *Psychiatry in Medicine* 3:163–71.

Kübler-Ross, E. 1969. *On Death and Dying.* New York: Macmillan Company.

Mostwin, D. 1974. "Multidimensional Model of Working with the Family," *Social Casework* 55:209–15.

Paul, N. L. 1969. "The Role of Mourning and Empathy in Conjoint Marital Therapy." In *Family Therapy and Disturbed Families,* eds. G. H. Zuk and I. Boszormenyi-Nagy. Palo Alto, Calif.: Science and Behavior Books.

Satir, V. 1971. "Symptomatology: A Family Production." In *Theory and Practice of Family Psychiatry,* ed. J. G. Howells. New York: Brunner/Mazel.

Watzlawick, P. 1964. *An Anthology of Human Communication.* Palo Alto, Calif.: Science and Behavior Books.

Watzlawick, P., H. Beavin, and D. Jackson. 1967. *Pragmatics of Human Communication.* New York: W. W. Norton and Company.

4

Helping Families Cope with Acute and Anticipatory Grief

Hilda C. M. Arndt and Mittie Gruber

It is within the family that individuals first develop the feeling of belonging, a sense of self-worth, the ability to trust others, and a capacity for intimate relationships. It is also within the family that individuals first experience frustration and the agony of loss of a loved object or person. The phase-specific development of frustration tolerance, independence, and identity has been described in detail for the healthy child in the well-adjusted family. Much of the literature on death and dying is predicated on the view that personality development is lifelong, rather than limited to childhood, and is bound to the human processes of attachment and separation within a series of changing family and substitute-family contexts. Individual developmental tasks are paralleled by family developmental tasks (Scherz, 1970). The family, like its individual members, must master the tasks of individualization and interdependence. There are parallel stress points for both the family unit and its individual members that are capable of either constructive resolution or maladaptative outcome.

The family is the primary group that provides preparation for life and for death. The family is an interdependent, interacting open system with reverberating transactions among its members and between the family and other systems. The family structure, with its network of need–response patterns, role assignments, subgroup alliances, and values and rules, is influenced by the personalities of its members and in turn influences their capacities for relationships and their abilities to deal with stress. Stress experienced by one member influences the transactions among all members. It is within the family that individuals first learn to deal with separation and loss, the necessary role reassignments, and the shifts in relationship patterns. The resources of the family system augment those of individual members. Out of the family's integration of loss may come a renewed sense of family solidarity, the sustaining quality of togetherness.

The authors hold that acceptance of and adjustment to death is a family problem and that the family group, including the dying member, should be the unit of attention in providing social work services during the time when a member is dying and at his death. It is generally accepted that the attitudes of family members toward death influence the attitudes of the dying patient. How the family copes with the realization that a member is dying can either ease the acceptance of his impending death, add to his pain, or reinforce his tendency to deny the frightening reality.

A family's attitudes toward death and dying are colored not only by cultural values and mores but also by the nature and strength of the family's values and beliefs, its characteristic modes of dealing with stress, and the established patterns of transactions both among family members and with other systems. The family's adaptability and tolerance for stress influence the manner in which a given family deals with the pressures and strains related to a member's dying. Very often the family feels the pain most deeply the first time death threatens its solidarity. The intensity of feelings the family group experiences may also be influenced by the age of the dying person and the significance of the patient's role functioning within the total family structure but even more keenly by the quality of the relationships between this person and other family members. The special problems of childhood bereavement over loss of a parent have been poignantly delineated in the recent report of the Cleveland Center for Research in Child Development (Furman, 1974).

The careful work of therapists and scholars such as Kübler-Ross (1969) and Lindemann (1965) provides helpful guides to social workers in understanding common reactions to dying and bereavement. These frameworks are useful as a background against which to refine and deepen our understanding of individual emotional reactions and those of specific families. It is imperative to recognize, however, that families differ in their philosophies of life and death and that, even within the same family, various members may differ in their emotional reactions and in the degree of their commitment to certain values.

Family Tasks in Coping with Acute Grief

The family tasks in dealing with acute grief parallel those of individual members, as already noted. The first task, as delineated by Lindemann (1965), is "emancipation from the bondage to the deceased." This emancipation is dependent on family members' ability to experience their feelings fully. While individual reactions will vary, usually the bereaved feel the pain of loss, anger, guilt, and fear. The pain and fear arising from loss of the loved one are eased as all members are helped in family sessions to express their feelings. Some families may be hesitant to share deep feelings, especially those of anger and fear. The worker can gently encourage the family to experience and express their feelings, using universalization and partialization as indicated. As the worker responds empathetically, both verbally and nonverbally, family members are provided a model through which they can give mutual support in sharing reactions. Family members can be encouraged to participate appropriately in planning funeral arrangements, disposing of personal effects, and other such activities that imply acceptance of the finality of the death.

Guilt about attitudes and behavior toward the deceased during his lifetime is reinforced by unconscious hostility over feeling abandoned. The guilt is often projected by blaming others for the death or is experienced as disproportionate self-reproach. If a family member can be helped to express such fantasies of guilt over acts of omission or commission, the others, with guidance and support from the worker, can assist in clarifying the objective reality. The worker can encourage expression and evaluation of any criticism of the deceased and any anger. Emphasis on the love and care the deceased provided the family will encourage identification with a kindly, loving image of the dead member. The positive emotional values in the relationships with the deceased can be recognized, once the negative reactions are accepted. Sometimes the worker can encourage constructive atonement, such as completing unfinished tasks of the deceased or adopting his hobby as one's own. Happy memories of the deceased can be evoked. Sometimes the worker may need to assist the family in making decisions based on realities confronting the present members rather than on assertions about what the deceased would have wanted or decreed if alive.

Another family task is readjustment of the family structure and role network. The family will need to reassign role responsibilities, both instrumental and expressive. Family sessions can be very useful in clarifying the nature of these responsibilities and the abilities of specific members to carry them. For example, there is the frequent tendency to suggest that the eldest son, even if only approaching adolescence, must now be the man of the family following the father's death. Such an assignment places unrealistic demands on the boy, and may impede his ability to deal constructively with adolescence. The worker can assist the family members by involving them in joint consideration of such topics as the appropriateness of a given role responsibility for a specific family member, his preparation and probable rewards in assuming the role, and the congruence of the new responsibilities with existing roles.

In some instances the deceased may have carried an expressive role that was crucial to holding dormant conflicts within family subgroups (marital pair, siblings, etc.). If another member is not able to carry this position, the family may well need professional help in dealing with these conflicts at a time when feelings of abandonment, anger, and hurt are high. Scapegoating may occur either as a way of reestablishing family balance or as the result of displacement of guilt or anger. The worker's sensitive understanding of family transactional patterns will be useful in helping the family develop more constructive need–response patterns.

The third family task is the establishment of new relationships with other systems. For example, the bereaved spouse may find she is no longer included in activities of an intimate group of couples. She may turn to an organization such as Parents Without Partners or may become active in supporting an organization in which the spouse was keenly interested or that is related to the cause of the deceased's death (cancer research, volunteer work in a hospital ward, etc.). The worker may need to encourage the extended family or significant others to provide concrete evidences of supportive interest and attention so that the family appreciates that the care and affection necessary for life can come from other sources. The greater the solidarity of the family and the more resilient its adaptability, the greater the likelihood that the family can deal constructively with its mourning tasks.

Conferences with individual members may be held as indicated, and family sessions may draw on dormant family strengths and assist in restructuring the family. Especially when the surviving spouse finds it difficult to express his or her own grief and yet provide essential loving care to the children, the worker's participation in family sessions can complement the parent's efforts and sustain the family group in partializing and undertaking their mourning tasks. The worker can provide a model of how family members can confirm each other, develop more effective modes of communication, and "negotiate the autonomy and interdependence of the psychodynamic turf" of each member and each subsystem (Minuchin, 1974).

Helping Families with Anticipatory Grief

Anticipatory grief peaks when a family member is dying. During this time of stress the strength and resilience of family relationships are severely taxed. The stress is heightened when the dying process is prolonged. The uncertainty about when death will occur leaves the family with the feeling of being in limbo, enduring the strains of current hardships while attempting to prepare for painful changes, knowing neither when these changes will occur nor exactly what sequence of events to anticipate. The family faces dual tasks that always are painful and sometimes make contradictory or incongruent demands. The family must care for the dying patient and continue to interact with him. Simultaneously, the total family attempts to prepare for the final separation that death will bring and for a future from which this family member, now the focus of everybody's concern, will be missing.

At such a time, fatigue and resentment will increase, but the resulting guilt may lead to denial or displacement of angry feelings. Care of the patient, whether at home or in the hospital, requires the assumption of new responsibilities. Simultaneously, the caregiving family must assimilate reassignment of an adult patient's role responsibilities. Economic pressures may also burden the family as expenses are increased and income reduced. Both physical and emotional fatigue may result, while anger at the dying person and the attendant guilt add to family members' mounting frustrations at demands that threaten to become intolerable.

The task of caring for the patient becomes even more stressful if the family and patient cannot interact in an open, honest way. The dying member who supposedly does not know he is dying cannot participate in family planning and role reassignments. He is likely to feel depressed and bewildered by the loss of emotional harmony with family members, if this had existed before the expectation of death intervened. Equally serious is the strain placed on family members when they must withhold knowledge of a poor prognosis from the patient. Both the patient and other members are weakened by this isolation of the patient and fragmentation of family unity.

Even when the patient is aware that he is dying and feels a need to talk about it, some families hesitate to interact honestly, feeling the patient must be protected from the family's worries. The tendency is to underestimate the patient's capacity to care, plan, and participate. Especially when the dying person is an adult on whom other family members have depended, the latter's feelings of being left alone, unprotected, and subjected to overwhelming demands are likely to intensify their helpless rage. One familiar pattern is that feelings of anger toward the dying person are avoided by overprotecting him.

This mechanism reinforces the culturally prescribed care that infantilizes sick people. Another pattern is family withdrawal from the patient, who is thus isolated at the time of his greatest need. The use of family group treatment to assist a family in moving from such destructive and distressing interaction to inclusion of the dying patient in the sharing of deep feelings is illustrated in the following case.

The wife of a patient in the terminal stages of cancer was at first reluctant to accept the worker's proposal of family rather than individual sessions. She finally acceded, on the basis that she and her husband were a loving couple and loving parents whose shared concern was that the children be fully informed of their father's condition but encouraged to continue their usual school responsibilities and activities insofar as possible. In the second family session, while maintaining her brittle facade of serenity and competence, she evidenced irritability in subtle ways. The patient asked her what was wrong. She said everything was okay—she was just tired, and a little extra sleep would correct that. The worker quietly commented that, although she seemed reluctant to admit it, she appeared tense and angry. With a trace of bitterness in her tone she replied that her husband should not worry. Everything was all right except for the pain he suffered. As the 10-year-old daughter slipped her hand into her mother's, the worker spoke sympathetically of how hard it is to see a loved person suffer and be helpless to bring him relief. The patient also observed that his wife seemed angry. He was sorry the family had to struggle with his illness and the extra work and frustrations. When the wife still did not speak, the worker observed that the patient knew his wife well after 12 years of happy married life and wanted to share her problems as she wanted to share his. He agreed firmly. "We've shared the same bed and I know you as you know me." Trying to choke back tears, the wife reported that all the relatives had persuaded her that it was her duty to shield her husband from unpleasantness or worry. The worker started to speak but then looked encouragingly at the husband. He assured his wife he knew how she felt, whether she put it in words or not. The worker said that it was unfair to the patient not to share feelings with him, and besides, bottled-up feelings only increased the wife's anger and frustration and made it harder to give him the help she so much wanted to provide. At this point she openly sobbed, and the older daughter commented that her mother did not want to cry before daddy. The 6-year-old child went to the bed, searching her father's face earnestly. He put out a hand to his daughter as both he and the worker verbally reassured his wife. With strong feeling she told of frustrations and tensions that mounted and felt as if a balloon were blowing up inside her body, getting so large it was about to burst. One of the hardest things to bear about her husband's illness was the pressure from everyone not to let him know of any troubles. They had always talked things over before his illness.

By now the patient looked tired and as if in pain. He feebly reiterated that he wanted her to tell him. The worker elaborated that this effort to help the husband really hurt both of them unnecessarily. He felt less helpful to his family and less needed. The tension of keeping secrets from her husband drained the wife of energy she needed to care for him. With deep feeling she said to the worker, "You do understand, don't you?"

The wife went on to discuss a number of specific frustrations and concerns with which the worker was able to give some practical help. Before the session ended, the wife again checked out whether it really was all right to share worries with the patient. This time he replied, "She [worker] said it. It makes me feel less of a man when you don't let me share." Both daughters were now at the patient's side. The older girl looked at her mother and said, "Look at her, Daddy. She looks like she used to without all those frown wrinkles."

At the next session the feeling of relief for all family members was discussed, now that the wife could share her moods and worries with her husband. He was proud that even now he could help his family, and both girls told him their mother no longer had "black days." A month later, when the patient's condition had markedly worsened and he was in constant pain unless sedated, the wife asked the worker to see her from time to time so that she could unburden to someone now that her husband was in such pain. "It's a help to deflate that balloon before it gets too large." She thought the girls seemed "more at peace within themselves" since everyone shared feelings and when possible helped in deciding what to do.

In the last family session in which this patient was able to participate, he reflected on his earlier feelings. "I knew Jennie had lots of problems while I was lying here. When she wouldn't share them, I felt belittled and useless. At times I felt guilty, knowing how my illness burdened her." His self-esteem and sense of mastery were heightened when his wife and children shared daily events with him, including troubles. The children were pleased to talk over minor hurts with their father and told him how a comforting pat or smile made them "feel warm inside." Once worries and small concerns were shared, the family found increasing solace in recalling earlier happy occasions. One day the 6-year-old child spontaneously said, "Daddy, we'll remember these talks with you and how you loved us when you were hurting."

In this strong, loving family, once daily interaction with the dying husband and father was reestablished with some semblance of its accustomed mode, the patient and family members sustained and guided each other in the sad task of achieving acceptance of the impending death. Not all families can achieve this outcome of anticipatory grief. "How can we live in the present with all its worries and troubles," one husband of a dying patient asked, "and at the same time prepare for a future when my wife has no future?" Some families are hampered by preexisting problems, such as personality defects in family members or any of the myriad deficiencies that may occur in the structure and functioning of the family.

Family members must provide care for the dying patient, assume the additional responsibilities imposed by changes that reach into every area of family life, perhaps carry on duties at work or school, and interact daily with the dying person. They must also anticipate and begin preparation for the final separation. The social worker needs to help these burdened people be in touch with their feelings and ventilate them and then actively assist in locating resources or imaginatively devising ways to ease daily pressures. Sometimes families can be encouraged to live one day at a time, seeking to achieve immediate goals. To live in the present can keep tensions at manageable levels, but it is difficult simultaneously to prepare for the uncertain future. If the dying patient has been able in any small way to participate in planning for his family's future, not only may it be easier for him to move through the process of dying but also the family's mourning later may be helped by carrying out plans in which the departed member participated. If patient and family can accept together the reality of impending death, they are then free to enjoy together whatever time is left. The worker's realistic reassurance, based on knowledge of the family's past experiences and their current functioning, can be an important sustaining factor. When a family's emotional reserves are limited, the social worker may be helpful by encouraging the extended family's interest and support, which can continue after the professional relationship is terminated.

Preparation of Social Work Students

Studies have demonstrated that many professional persons find it very difficult to tolerate the pain related to helping the dying patient and his family (Brim, 1970; Group for the Advancement of Psychiatry, 1965; Lester, 1969). In a recent master's thesis (Brown, 1974) social workers were found not to differ significantly in their attitudes toward death and dying from physicians, nurses, or graduate students in other than the helping professions. The degree of religiousness and the ability to discuss and plan for one's own death seemed significant in influencing the attitudes of the pooled professional sample. An interesting finding was that those professional respondents who believed their professional education had prepared them adequately to help dying persons seemed freer to admit fears related to the dying of others. This suggests that self-awareness, coupled with assurance of adequate preparation to help, would permit the blending of deep empathy with a disciplined use of self.

Social work students need understanding of the usual stages of the dying process and of grief work. In addition they need to develop tolerance of the impact of both their clients' strong feelings and those engendered within themselves on an emotional plane and to prepare for the tasks of assisting the dying and bereaved. These students can be encouraged to examine their own perceptions of death so that they can achieve objectivity and acceptance of ideas that to them may seem dissonant. Some may need assurance that they can help their clients even if they have not experienced the loss of a loved one. Others may need help in understanding the fallacy of generalizing from their own experiences. The instructor needs to express confidence in the student's ability to feel deeply with his clients and yet retain his own sense of identity. Perhaps the necessary professional help to grieving families is hardest for those student workers who are anticipating the death of a member of their own families. In these instances the instructor's faith in the student's concern for the clients and in the student's ability to endure suffering may be especially sustaining. The reward for the student may well be not only the progress his clients make but also the discovery of his own untapped potential and the deeper realization of the sustaining and facilitating power of the professional relationship. If family interviews are used as one way of helping family members share their feelings and support each other, the family may emerge depleted in number but with a quickened sense of solidarity. The deceased lives on in memories of family members who, having coped with their grief, can accept the finality of this death while treasuring the experiences and relationships in which the lost loved one also participated.

References

Brim, O. G., Jr. et al. eds. 1970. *The Dying Patient*. New York: Russell Sage Foundation.

Brown, T. B. 1974. *Attitudes toward Death and Dying in Professionals: A Comparative Study*. Master's thesis, Louisiana State University.

Furman, E. 1974. *A Child's Parent Dies—Studies in Childhood Bereavement*. New Haven: Yale University Press.

Group for the Advancement of Psychiatry. 1965. *Death and Dying: Attitudes of Patient and Doctor*. New York: Mental Health Materials Center.

Kübler-Ross, E. 1969. *On Death and Dying*. New York: Macmillan Company.

Lester, D. 1969. "Studies on Death—Attitude Scales." *Psychological Report* 24, February.

Lindemann, E. 1965. "Symptomatology and Management of Acute Grief." In *Crisis Intervention: Selected Readings,* ed. H. J. Parad. New York: Family Service Association of America.

Minuchin, S. 1974. *Families and Family Therapy*. Cambridge: Harvard University Press.

Scherz, F. H. 1970. "Theory and Practice of Family Therapy." In *Theories of Social Casework,* eds. R. W. Roberts and R. H. Nee. Chicago: University of Chicago Press.

5

Evaluation of Family Care in Terminal Illness

C. Murray Parkes

The history of man's social evolution is dotted with "great discoveries," usually taken to be the product of certain "master minds" without whom they would never have occurred. But I am inclined to favor the school of thought that sees evolution as having discovered Darwin, rather than Darwin evolution. Anybody who studies the history of science must realize that it is usually not a matter of "Who will discover electricity?" but "Who will discover it first?" One step follows another with remorseless inevitability, and individual human enterprise only determines where, how, and when a particular change will come about.

Reasons for Increased Interest in Death and Dying

The increased interest in our subject seems to me to stem from the concurrent flowing together of several tendencies that have become matters of concern in recent years. The first has been an increasing awareness of the limitations of modern medicine. Having passed through a phase of extraordinary success in the endeavor to cure disease by scientific means, we are faced by the unalterable conclusion that, no matter how hard we try, 100 percent of people still die. It has been very hard on the proponents of scientific medicine to accept this fact, and even now many practitioners are determined to use every means at their disposal to postpone death at any cost. But the very single-mindedness of their onslaught against the tide of death has itself provoked a reaction. While they are developing new machines to resuscitate the elderly, transplant wornout organs, and slow the growth of malignant tumors, others are appalled by some of the suffering that the blind pursuit of longer and longer life can inflict and have begun to ask whether a longer life is a sufficient end in itself. This at once raises important philosophical questions about the purpose and value of life that are hard to answer.

Another, related tendency is the increasing success of some of our efforts to relieve physical pain. When anesthetics were first introduced, they were often accused of depriving men of the opportunity to grow spiritually by accepting the pain that flesh is heir to. But we use anesthetics, and we have abolished corporal punishment and those forms of torture that produce physical pain and mutilation. Perhaps as a consequence of this success, however, more and more people are expressing their reluctance to accept psychological pain, in particular the pain of grief and the emotional distress of dying. With the discovery of new ranges of psychotropic drugs we find ourselves faced with a new version of the old problem. Is suffering good for the soul or not? Is it truly necessary to experience the pain of grief to prevent the pain of delayed grief? So far as I can discover, nobody has yet produced scientific evidence for or against the use of psychotropic drugs for grief, but the current consensus warns us to be careful.

Another tendency is expressed in what has been termed the grassroots revolution. The decline in respect for hierarchical systems of social organization has penetrated all sections of society and allowed those of low status to question the assumptions of what were once called their "betters." I became acutely conscious of this a few years ago when I found myself the only physician at a conference for nurses on the care of the dying. Now I know that physicians are alienated from their patients and particularly bad at coming close to a dying person, and I know that we have always tended to pass the buck to the nurses and expect them to cope with our patients' suffering, but that has been the case for a great many years, and nobody dared to complain about it before. But at this conference I found myself taken to task in no uncertain fashion for the failings of my profession by speaker after speaker. In Britain, where the social workers are no longer organized in a way that makes them dependent on the medical profession, we are beginning to run into the same trouble with them.

A different aspect of the grassroots revolution is the increased interest at all levels in the multitude who make up the bulk of the communities we serve but who lack the power to mold the social systems in which they live—the poor, the old, the young, the racially different. This tendency is reflected within American psychiatry in the swing from private psychoanalysis toward community mental health with its related technique of preventive psychiatry. In Britain the development of community medicine has become accepted as a part of National Health Service policy, and attempts are being made to integrate hospital and community services.

In both countries the time is ripe for the initiation of preventive services aimed at helping people in the community cope more effectively with family crises, be they the crises of bereavement and loss or other life events that constitute a threat to physical and mental health.

Need for Scientific Evaluation of Methods

If my analysis of the situation is correct, we can expect the developments in thanatology we are witnessing to continue; they are more than a passing fad. This is very encouraging, but one aspect of these trends gives cause for some anxiety. I have spoken of the extent to which interest in death and bereavement reflects a reaction against some of the uses of scientific medicine; what I fear is that some of us may be tempted to avoid scientific method altogether and imagine that we can develop our own discipline without it. To do this would, in my opinion, be a classic example of throwing the baby out with the bath water. Already we can see some of the problems that result from the introduction of new approaches without any attempt at scientific evaluation. Take the conflict between the proponents of professional and lay bereavement counselors. Already there are two schools of thought: One school holds the view that the best person to visit a bereaved person is a specially trained and experienced caseworker who will be able to understand and assist with the complex psychodynamic problems that arise in the course of grief; the other school regards professional qualifications as a barrier to communication and insists that the best person to understand a widow is another widow. The only satisfactory way to resolve the conflict, or at least to provide the opponents with something more effective than their own preconceptions to throw at each other, would be to undertake a systematic comparison of the effectiveness of the two approaches on two comparable populations of bereaved people. Ideally one would set up services of both types in the same area and randomly assign bereaved people to each group. The outcome might show a clear preference for one approach, or it might indicate that there are some people who benefit from one approach and some from the other. This in itself would be knowledge that could be put to use in deciding where to refer particular cases.

Another important reason for us to adopt scientific methods of evaluating our work at this stage of its development is the certainty that within a few years it will be unethical to do this at all. When introducing a new service where none existed before, there can be no ethical objection to withholding the service from some while offering it to others. This means that we have the opportunity to carry out random allocation studies in which the only difference between the two groups is that one receives the help of the service and the other does not. By comparing these groups we can then discover whether or not our service is having the effects we hope of it.

But within a few years of the introduction of a new service we shall find that the people giving the service have invested so much of themselves in it that they are very reluctant to withhold it from anyone. Furthermore the clients are themselves likely to learn about the service and to demand it and thereby put aside any chance of obtaining an adequate control group.

In many ways death and bereavement provide us with unique opportunities for scientific research. Deaths are remarkably unambiguous events; they occur at particular times and places that are recorded, and the records are available for statistical study; they cause people to seek help from members of the caregiving professions, and because of this there are many situations where death can be anticipated and its effects mapped over time. Short longitudinal studies of bereaved people enable healthy and unhealthy types of reaction to be identified and followed up. Preventive intervention programs can be introduced at any point in the sequence of adjustment and offered either to total populations or to selected "high-risk" groups. If we view grief as an emotional disturbance that may result in lasting handicap, we have the perfect paradigm for the development of preventive psychiatry. In the circumstances one can only deplore the fact that so little systematic research has yet been carried out.

Survey of Literature on Evaluation

Evaluation has not been totally lacking. Probably the first systematic evaluation of a bereavement counseling program was done at Fort Logan Mental Health Center in Denver. Polak et al. (1973) provided intervention, much of it by means of telephone interactions, over a period of 1 to 10 weeks after bereavement for 37 families who had suffered a sudden bereavement that had been reported to the coroner. They compared these with a control group of 65 similarly bereft families who were not supported. The groups were matched for age, socioeconomic status, education, and location of residence. Both groups were followed up for 6 months after bereavement. At that time the supported groups were apparently more disturbed than the control group on several measures of outcome. Some of the failure to show a positive effect from intervention may be explained as a result of a higher refusal rate among the disturbed respondents in the control group. Even so we cannot pretend that this study supports the notion that a service of this type is of very much value. Whether this is due to the special problems of the suddenly bereaved, to the inadequacy of the telephone as a means of nonverbal communication, to the inexperience of the intervenors, or, as the investigators suggest, to the fact that the people who most needed help were the ones least likely to accept it we cannot say.

Equally disappointing were the results of a study by Kincey (1974) in Manchester, England. Surviving spouses of 30 patients who died in two hospitals during April to July 1973 were supported by a social worker or volunteer counselor. Most counseling took place in the patient's home about four weeks after the death. Five to eight months later, a research interview revealed no significant differences between this group and a control group of 55 spouses of patients who had died during December through March.

The defect in this work would seem to be the inadequacy of the counseling. In only 6 of the 30 cases was more than one interview performed and in 6 other cases only telephone contact was made.

A particularly well conducted evaluation of a service for the bereaved was done by Gerber et al. (1975), who randomly assigned widows and widowers of patients dying at the Montefiore Hospital and Medical Center to two groups. One group was offered no special help, and members of the other were supported by a psychiatric social worker or psychiatric nurse who were themselves under the supervision of a psychiatrist (Gerber et al., 1975).

Research interviews made 2, 5, 8, and 15 months after bereavement revealed significant differences between the groups on a number of indices of health. These included physician contacts, consumption of tranquilizers and other drugs, and self-assessments by the respondents of feeling sick without seeking medical help. Each of these was significantly worse in unsupported than in supported groups during one or more of the follow-up periods. These effects were not demonstrable, however, after the eighth month of bereavement.*

* At press time, one additional major study, by Dr. Beverley Raphael of Australia, is still unpublished. This shows highly significant differences between supported and unsupported widows 13 months after bereavement.

Research at St. Christopher's Hospice

A series of studies was performed at St. Christopher's Hospice in London. The aims of this unit are to relieve suffering and to provide opportunities for growth in a psychological and spiritual sense among patients with terminal illness as well as to minimize the painful and damaging effects of the death of a family member on the family.

To achieve these aims a small inpatient unit containing 54 beds has been set up in Sydenham in South London. As well as providing inpatient care for 14 men and 40 women the hospice has an outpatient clinic and home care service for families who are caring for a terminally ill person at home and a family aftercare service for bereaved family members.

The hospice is best seen as a therapeutic community in which close support is provided for patients and family members by nursing staff and doctors who must have the time to get to know the families and patients they serve. There are no impressive operating theaters or radiotherapy equipment, but the principal item of expenditure is on

Photo 1. St. Christopher's Hospice.

people. By maintaining a nurse/patient ratio equivalent to one full-time nurse per patient, Dr. Cicely Saunders, St. Christopher's Medical Director, attempts to ensure that no nurse is "too busy" to talk to a patient. Since half the patients will die within 11 days of admission, the hospice can be said to provide intensive care of a very special kind at a crucial point in the lives of patients and families.

The families themselves are encouraged to visit as much as possible and to undertake those items of patient care that can be left to them. In addition the nurses are supported by 120 volunteers who are under the direction of a paid volunteer organizer. There are four physicians, a chaplain, two part-time social workers, a part-time occupational therapist, two part-time physiotherapists, and a part-time psychiatrist (myself). Add to this the stewards who man the reception desk and have an important role in welcoming family members, the catering officer and her staff, ward orderlies, the staff of the pre-school playgroup and old peoples' wing, and the teaching staff of the study center, and you will have some idea of the overall picture.

Following is a summary of the main principles of care as the staff attempt to apply them.

1. *Provision of a high standard of physical care.* This includes the relief or prevention of pain or other causes of physical distress by whatever means are needed. For cancer patients with pain the physicians prefer to give four hourly drugs in sufficient dosage to prevent the pain from ever becoming severe. Ninety-two percent of cancer patients receive diamorphine at some time, but it is seldom necessary to prescribe massive doses if this is combined with a tranquilizer such as prochlorperazine.
2. *Maintenance of a close relationship between staff and patient.* As a result consistent reassurance and support can be given by both verbal and non-verbal means of communication. When the patient begins to feel safe, he may begin to ask questions about his illness, and staff are expected to be willing to go as far as the patient in looking at what is happening to him. But no attempt is made to force patients to confront the facts of their diagnosis and prognosis if they are not ready to do so.
3. *Family, including the patient, as the unit of care.* The identity of all relevant family members is recorded on the front page of the case notes, and staff are expected to get to know the family and to take every opportunity to support them. The hospice sets out to be an extension of the patient's home, and anything that might give it the aspect of a "machine to die

in'' is rigorously excluded. Patients are invited to bring in favored possessions, and a nicely furnished sitting room is a territory that family members can call their own.

4. *Extension of the service beyond the walls of the hospice by means of the Home Care and Family Services.* The Home Care Service comprises four nurses who visit families of patients being cared for at home. They provide advice and emotional support to the patient, to the family, and to the general practitioners and community nurses responsible for the day-to-day care of the patient. They also provide emergency support at any time of the day or night so that the family members know that they have only to lift the telephone for a nurse to come out to them without question. Sometimes the service facilitates admission to hospital, but more often the assurance of support and the standard of care that can be provided at home enable the patient to remain out of hospital. In fact the mean length of stay on the wards at St. Christopher's has dropped by 12 days since the Home Care Service was introduced.

Relatives of patients who die on the wards are invited to keep in touch and to come back if they have any problems. Some of them join the volunteer service, others come back to monthly meetings of the Social Club. Occasionally this enables staff to spot people in need of help. In addition

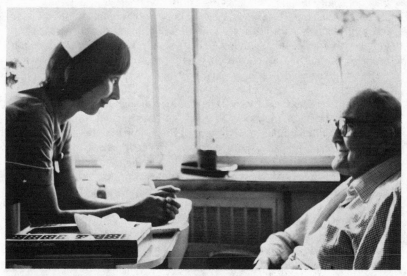

Photo 2. The Hospice provides intensive care of a special kind at a crucial point in the lives of patients and their families.

every family receives a card from the hospice on the anniversary of the patient's death reminding them that they are not forgotten.

But the principal form of bereavement support is provided in the form of a visiting Family Service organized by the social workers. This is provided to about one family in five whenever the nursing staff indicate that the family member is likely to be at risk. Visits are made to the home 7 to 10 days after the funeral by a person who may be a member of the nursing staff, one of the social workers, or occasionally a volunteer. Normally the social worker sends someone already known to the family, but if nobody has had much contact with them, as sometimes happens if a patient dies within a day or so of admission, then the visit is made by one of the two volunteers who give regular help to the service. I meet once a month with the visitors to discuss their visits and to work out a plan for support to each family as required. Typically not more than two to four visits are made to each family during the first few months of bereavement, but occasionally very much more support is needed.

The visitors are not highly qualified case workers, but they do all have experience of coming close to patients and family members at a time of crisis in their lives and are not afraid of grief or inclined to encourage denial. With very few exceptions their visits have been welcomed by the family. We try to make the visits as informal as possible and to avoid the danger of labeling the surviving family members as "sick."

5. *Support to the staff themselves.* Any person who attempts to get close to others in distress will, at times, find himself in need of support. It is all too easy to overidentify with a patient or spouse who is, perhaps, similar in age or social background to ourselves or to find ourselves hurt when we become the object of aggressive grieving. In such circumstances it is important for staff to form a supportive network for each other and, in particular, for senior staff to recognize where problems are likely to arise and give anticipatory support. As consultant psychiatrist to the hospice I spend more time talking to staff members than to patients—not because I regard the staff as particularly weak but to feed back to them my appraisals of the patients and families and to help them develop their skills in human relations. Much staff support comes from the various types of group meeting. Some of these focus on psychological issues and others on spiritual matters. Dr. Saunders believes it is only a community in which a large proportion of staff members have a religious faith enabling them to accept death that can be expected to cope effectively with the fears of the dying. Consequently a part of the support system is found in the religious community and in the services and prayers that are shared by many of the staff. But it is emphasized that the role of the staff does not include proselytizing or persuading patients out of one set of beliefs and into another.

St. Christopher's Hospice is situated in a densely populated part of south London between the boroughs of Lewisham and Bromley. As a preliminary to our attempts at evaluating the service at the hospice we decided to review the patterns of terminal care for cancer patients in these two boroughs as seen through the eyes of surviving husbands or wives of people who had died of cancer. We were assisted by the Registrar General's Office, which provided us with the names and addresses of surviving spouses, and we then contacted all who were under the age of 65. We excluded the older age group for fear that their memory for the period of terminal care would be inaccurate.

Altogether we wrote to 459 persons and asked them to help us with our research; 64 had moved away and could not be located, 12 were too ill or dead, and 107 preferred not to be interviewed. This left us with 100 men and 176 women who were visited in their homes by our research interviewer. This may seem like a large refusal rate, but we must remember that the interviewer was a stranger who was attempting to obtain information about a very distressing period of the respondent's life. In the circumstances it would have been unethical to press people to participate if they were reluctant to do so. Most other studies of bereaved people have similar rates of refusal.

The respondents were visited on average 13 months after bereavement (± 2 months). Questions were asked in a systematic manner about their view of each phase of their spouse's illness but in particular about the period of terminal care, that is, the time from the end of active treatment to the patient's death. Questions covered the patient's pain, distress, mental state, and degree of insight under each type of care, as well as the respondent's own feelings and reactions.

(To test the reliability of our assessments of pain, 15 of the assessments were repeated by an independent interviewer who attended the same interviews and made her own assessments. These were quite satisfactory.)

There was, of course, considerable variation in the duration of the terminal illness. Some patients spent most of the time in hospital, others were mostly at home, others had a number of admissions to hospital. Only 49 (18 percent) were still under active treatment at the time of death, and we naturally had to exclude them from our assessments. Of the remaining 251, 53 percent had been cared for at home during the last 6 weeks of their life, but only 20 percent had died at home.

A full analysis of the different types of care will not be done, but I point out one important finding. We subdivided the group into three, the "home centered," the "St. Christopher's centered," and the "other hospital centered." Anybody who died at home or had spent less than a week in hospital before death was included in the "home-centered" group, and the rest were subdivided according to whether or not they had died at St. Christopher's.

Figure 5.1 shows the most important finding, the number of patients in each setting who were said by their spouses to have suffered severe and mostly unrelieved pain. I would say that any patient with cancer whose pain is severe and mostly unrelieved is probably receiving poor terminal care. Home-centered patients were less likely than hospital-centered patients to have been said to have suffered pain prior to the terminal period. This is probably why they remained at home whereas others were sent into or kept in hospital. During the final phase, however, the home-centered patients seem to have suffered more unrelieved pain than either of the other two groups. No less than 29 percent were said to have had severe and mostly unrelieved pain (an increase in pain that is significant ($p < .002$).

In comparing the other two groups, it can be seen that patients admitted to St. Christopher's are likely to have had more unrelieved pain before the terminal period. This is probably because many patients are referred to the hospital for treatment of intractable pain. During the period of care at St. Christopher's the proportion with severe unrelieved pain dropped ($p < .01$), whereas that of patients dying in other hospitals apparently underwent little change (not significant).

Adequate palliative symptom relief is the first essential in terminal care. The elation that arises when a patient who has been in pain for months suddenly discovers that he does not hurt any more is one of the most gratifying things for any doctor or nurse to witness and goes a long way to build up a relationship of trust.

Despite these findings I am not opposed to home care. It seems to me that home is often the best place to be when one is dying. This study was carried out before the Home Care Service at St. Christopher's Hospice was operative. We are now repeating our evaluations on families who have been supported at home and hope to find that the proportion reporting unrelieved pain will have fallen. Three requirements need to be met: (1) The symptoms of the illness must

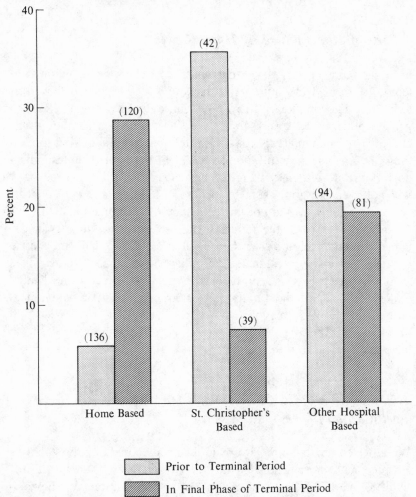

Figure 5.1 Proportions of patients with severe and mostly continuous pain.

not be of a type that cannot be adequately relieved at home; (2) the family must be able to cope with the situation; and (3) the local community health services, in particular the general practitioners and district nurses (who are our "visiting nurses"), must have the knowledge and be willing to give the needed time.

Reasons for Failure of Home Care

Looking more closely at 35 patients whose care was "home centered," I formed the impression that only 10 fulfilled all these criteria. And the commonest reason for failure was the reluctance of the general practitioners to prescribe adequate amounts of narcotic drugs at regular 4-hour intervals. In Britain today, where addiction to hard drugs is nowhere near the problem it is in the United States, many doctors are nevertheless so reluctant to use narcotic drugs that they will not even prescribe them for people in the later stages of cancer, at a time when it would not matter if they did become addicted.

Another reason for the failure of terminal care at home is inadequate communication between patient and doctor. This may arise because general practitioners are reluctant to make home visits (which is much less of a problem in Britain than it is in the United States) or because the family fail to ask for his help when it is needed. Some of the people we talked to seemed to have been told that there was nothing that could be done to help the patient and to have given up asking for help.

Comparison of St. Christopher's Hospice with Other Hospitals

When we compare the patients who received care at St. Christopher's Hospice with those who died in other hospitals, we run into a difficulty—the two populations are not strictly comparable. We have already seen that patients admitted to St. Christopher's were more likely to have had pain problems, and there may well have been other features that distinguished them from patients who were sent to other hospitals.

To try to counteract these differences, we selected two subgroups for further study. These were matched case for case on each of the following criteria: severity of pain before the terminal period, duration of illness, age, sex, place of dwelling, and socioeconomic status. We were left with 34 in each group. Further evidence for satisfactory matching comes from the fact that there were no significant differences between the groups on any of the 31 questions that referred to the period before hospital admission for terminal care. For this part of the study both groups were reinterviewed and additional questions asked about details of hospital care.

Focusing then on the final period of care in hospital, we can start by comparing the hospitals themselves. Most of the patients who died in St. Christopher's Hospice had never heard of the place before they arrived there. (At that time the hospice had not received very much publicity.) Patients dying in other hospitals had usually, however, been sent to a district general hospital with which they were already

Photo 3. Patients in this ward are enjoying visits from friends and relatives, with nurses in attendance.

familiar. Most of them entered wards containing 20 to 30 beds that were usually identified as "general wards." This meant that most of their fellow patients could be expected to leave the hospital alive. Even so 32 percent of spouses reported that another patient had died on the ward during the period of the patient's admission.

At St. Christopher's Hospice most patients were nursed in partitioned areas containing four to six beds. Families were aware that this was a unit specializing in the care of terminal illness, although, at the time of admission, this was not usually true of the patients. Subsequently, 44 percent of patients were thought to have been aware of the death of another patient on the ward, but they were no more likely to be upset by such deaths than patients in other hospitals. I mention this because some people dislike the idea of putting patients with a poor prognosis together on the grounds that they will be upset by the death of other patients. In fact this does not seem to be the case under the circumstances of care that obtain at St. Christopher's. Only two patients (14 percent of those who were aware of the death of another patient) were said by their spouses to have suffered more than "slight" upset at this event.

Patients at St. Christopher's who are on the point of death are not removed from the ward or hidden from view. Curtains may be drawn around the bed at the moment of death, but fellow patients usually have a very good idea of what is going on, and the nursing staff talk about the death with them quite openly. Far from aggravating fears this aims to get across the notion that it is "all right" to die. Assessments made from the nurses' reports on the mode of death during 1974 indicated that 83 percent were "peaceful," 6 percent "unconscious" at the time of death, 9 percent "drowsy or blurred," .8 percent "alert," and only .6 percent "distressed." Bearing in mind the horrific fantasies that most people have about death, we suspect that, on the whole, patients are as likely to be reassured by the deaths of other patients as they are to be upset by them.

Despite this, there are still many patients who give no indication that they want to be told their diagnosis or prognosis. The case notes at St. Christopher's contain a special "pink sheet" on which staff are expected to record any statements made by patients about their illness. A careful scrutiny of these sheets and of all other notes made by doctors, nurses, and social workers about 480 of our patients during 1972 revealed that 51 percent never raised the issue with a member of medical or nursing staff. Of course this does not necessarily mean that these patients did not know their true prognosis, and it is reasonable to suppose that in many cases they strongly suspected that they would die but preferred not to run the risk of testing this assumption by asking leading questions. As long as they had not actually been told that the condition was incurable they could always retain the hope of cure as an "escape route" if it were needed.

Among those who gave some indication of their views about their illness, 51 percent showed quite directly that they were fully aware of their diagnosis and prognosis. There were 10 percent who made indirect statements that were taken by those around them to imply that they understood their true situation. In 14 percent there was evidence that, during the last two weeks of life, the patient expected to die but retained some hope of recovery. Fifteen percent indicated their suspicions but actively avoided knowing the truth, and there were only 10 percent who gave some indication, during the last 2 weeks of their lives, that they expected to improve or recover from their illness.

The assessments made by the patient's spouse in the matched comparison study reflected a similar degree of uncertainty about the patient's degree of insight into his prognosis (Table 5.1). Twenty-nine percent of the spouses of patients dying at St. Christopher's said that they did not know how much insight their spouse had had into his prognosis at the time of his death. Moreover this proportion was not

TABLE 5.1. PATIENT INSIGHT INTO PROGNOSIS (SPOUSE'S VIEW) IN MATCHED GROUPS

	n	St. Christopher's 34	Other Hospitals 34
Doubtful or not known		10	13
Unaware		5	6
Partially aware		7	9
Fully aware		12	6

significantly different from the 38 percent at other hospitals who said that they did not know how much insight the patient had.

Although twice as many patients at St. Christopher's were said to have had full insight into their prognosis (12) as at other hospitals (6), this difference does not quite reach statistical levels of significance. But further confirmation comes from Professor Hinton's study, described later.

The main conclusions to be drawn from these figures would seem to be that, although patients who die at St. Christopher's are rather more likely to have full insight into their prognosis than those dying elsewhere, there is still a sizable proportion who give no indication that they want to discuss their prognosis at all.

A young sociologist who visited the Hospice once expressed to me his surprise that the staff did not take more active steps to promote what Glaser and Strauss call "open awareness." But I think we are still a long way from knowing how much open awareness our patients are able to bear, and I, for one, would hesitate to force my patients to face the fact of their prognosis unless they had given me a clear indication of their wish to do this.

On the matter of pain our matched comparisons confirmed our earlier finding that patients who die at St. Christopher's are less likely to suffer pain than those who die in other hospitals (Table 5.2). Asked to assess the intensity of the worst pain that the patients had suffered at any time during their period in hospital, 18 percent of spouses of St. Christopher's patients rated this as severe or worse compared with 48 percent at other hospitals ($p < .05$).

TABLE 5.2. PAIN, CONSCIOUSNESS, AND MOBILITY DURING TERMINAL PERIOD IN HOSPITAL (MATCHED GROUPS)

		St. Christopher's	Other Hospitals	
	n	34	34	p
Severe pain at some time		18%	48%	<.05
Some confusion		56%	68%	N/S
Mostly confined to bed		59%	85%	<.05

In case it is assumed that this degree of pain relief is obtained by "slugging" the patient with huge doses of diamorphine, we can also show that patients dying at St. Christopher's were no more likely to be confused or unconscious during the major part of their admission than were patients at other hospitals. Moreover, St. Christopher's patients were significantly more likely to remain mobile and to spend some part of the day out of bed than those dying elsewhere.

No less than 53 percent of the patients' husbands or wives reckoned that they had spent 6 or more hours each day at St. Christopher's, whereas only 9 percent spent that amount of time at other hospitals ($p < .002$). Probably because of this, spouses of St. Christopher's patients were more likely to get to know and to talk with relatives of other patients than were spouses at other hospitals (35 and 3 percent spent "much time" in this way, $p < .01$). They got to know the doctors and nurses quite well, as revealed by the fact that 68 percent of the spouses of St. Christopher's patients could recall a doctor's name compared with only 25 percent elsewhere ($p < .002$). And they were significantly less likely to perceive the staff as "busy" or "very busy" (Figure 5.2).

They were also much more likely than at other places to have talked to other hospital personnel such as reception staff (56 and 0 percent), volunteers (56 and 0 percent), the matron (47 and 3 percent), ward orderlies (32 and 9 percent), and the chaplain (15 and 3 percent).

Although 68 percent of the spouses of patients dying at St. Christopher's reported they had "great" or "very great" anxiety during this period and this was only slightly less than the proportion complaining of similar anxiety at other hospitals (82 percent, not significant), there was evidence that the strain on the spouses of St. Christopher's relatives was less than that in other settings.

Thus, using a checklist of six common somatic accompaniments of severe anxiety—anorexia, weight loss, trembling, insomnia, tiredness, and forgetfulness—we found (Table 5.3) that spouses of patients dying elsewhere reported twice as many of these symptoms as spouses of patients who had died at St. Christopher's (Wilcoxon Test, $Z = 2.7, p < .01$).

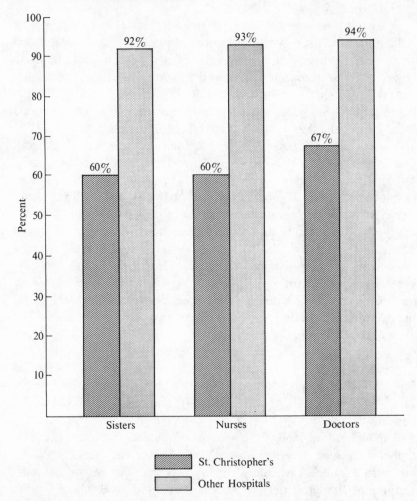

Figure 5.2 Proportion of staff members seen as "busy."

We asked the respondents how worried they had been by each of a series of seven matters that are common sources of anxiety to the relatives of dying patients. Spouses of St. Christopher's patients were significantly less likely than spouses of other patients to be worried about pain (9 and 33 percent expressed "great" anxiety about this, $p < .05$); about fears of others' hurting or harming the patient (7 and

TABLE 5.3. SYMPTOMS RATED AS "GREAT" OR "VERY GREAT" IN PATIENT'S SPOUSE DURING PERIOD OF TERMINAL CARE (MATCHED GROUPS)

	n	St. Christopher's 34	Other Hospitals 34	p
Anorexia		36%	70%	<.05
Weight loss		33%	52%	N/S
Trembling		14%	30%	N/S
Insomnia		39%	62%	N/S
Tiredness		50%	73%	N/S
Forgetfulness		29%	27%	N/S
Mean score		0.38	0.68	<.01

38 percent expressed "some" anxiety, $p < .02$); about revealing their own fears to the patient (9 and 33 percent expressed "great" anxiety about this, $p < .05$); and about fears of being unable to go on (19 and 43 percent expressed "moderate" or more anxiety about this, $p < .10$). There were no significant differences between the two settings with respect to the expression by respondents of worry about their own future, the future of children or dependents, and separation from their spouse if he should be moved elsewhere (seldom a source of anxiety in any setting).

St. Christopher's has been described as a "religious and medical foundation," and we were concerned to see how the religious aspects of the institution were perceived by the respondents. Patients admitted to St. Christopher's were from denominations similar to those admitted elsewhere and were no more likely to have been regular churchgoers. In other words there was no evidence of any tendency to select more "religious" members of the community for admission.

Two out of three spouses were aware that prayers are said on the wards each day, and 62 percent of these thought that the patient had been glad of them. None thought that a patient had been opposed to the saying of prayers. Nearly all were aware of the existence of a hospital chapel, and in 26 percent of cases the patient had been to a service there. Sixty-one percent knew that the patient had talked with a clergyman, and there was only one person who claimed that no clergyman had visited. Such visits were regarded as definitely helpful by 56 percent, and only one person regarded clergy visits as unhelpful. Others expressed no opinion. In general neither patients nor relatives expressed negative opinions about the religious aspects of care at St. Christopher's Hospice.

Religious practices at other hospitals were conspicuous by their absence. Seventy-nine percent of relatives were unaware of the existence of a hospital chapel, ward prayers were rarely mentioned, and only a third of patients were thought to have been visited at any time by a clergyman. When such visits were known to have been made, however, they were generally regarded as helpful.

It is one thing for doctors and nurses to set out to create a place that has the efficiency of a hospital and the security of a home and quite another to achieve this aim in the eyes of the families served. To assess the overall attitudes of spouses to the hospital or hospice, we asked relatives in pilot interviews to describe to us the characteristics of the hospitals where their spouses had died, and we finally formulated six slogans or sentences that seemed to express the principal characteristics of these places. Twenty-seven of the matched pairs of respondents were then asked to indicate which of these sentences could be said to characterize the hospital where their husband or wife had died.

On the whole, respondents had a positive attitude to the hospitals, but there were five, none of whose spouses had died at St. Christopher's, who said that none of these sentences could be said to apply.

The most popular descriptive sentence for both groups was "Nothing is too much trouble" (Table 5.4). This was checked by all of the spouses of patients dying at St. Christopher's and by 59 percent of those dying elsewhere ($p < .002$). But the sentence that best distinguished the two types of care is "The hospital is a family." In agreement were 78 percent of the spouses of St. Christopher's patients and only 11 percent elsewhere ($p < .001$). The only other sentence that distinguished the two was "Don't worry"—checked by 41 percent at St. Christopher's and 11 percent elsewhere ($p < .05$).

TABLE 5.4. ATTITUDES TO HOSPITAL IN 27 MATCHED PAIRS OF SPOUSES

Attitude	St. Christopher's	Other Hospitals
Nothing is too much trouble	100%	59%
The hospital is a family	78%	11%
Don't worry	41%	11%
Leave it to us	26%	33%
Efficiency comes first	22%	37%
We never give up	22%	15%

There were no significant differences between the two settings with respect to the proportions who checked "Leave it to us," "Efficiency comes first," and "We never give up" (Table 5.4). Each of these was reported by a fifth to a third of respondents regardless of the setting in which the patient died.

The picture of St. Christopher's that emerges from this research is of a caring community in which great emphasis is placed on the involvement of the family in the life of the hospice and in which patients receive close attention and satisfactory relief of pain. St. Chris-

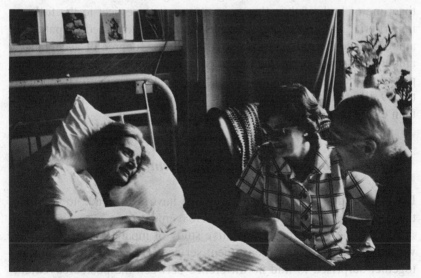

Photo 4. Many patients feel visits by clergymen are helpful.

topher's is not seen as being more efficient than other hospitals, as taking the patient out of the hands of the family, or as being more or less inclined to "give up."

These findings are, of course, biased by any distortion that may have been introduced by the respondents, and we cannot exclude the possibility that a "halo effect" may have colored some of their assessments. It is obviously unfair to compare treatment in a small modern hospital with a large staff and good facilities with that in the average local hospital with all of the chronic shortages of staff and other resources, characteristic of the tottering economy of Britain.

It is therefore reassuring to find confirmation of some of these findings in Professor Hinton's research (personal communication). There is no space to give full details of this study here. Suffice it to say that Hinton was able to interview staff, relatives, and patients with terminal cancers in St. Christopher's and two other hospitals that could be expected to provide above-average standards of care. One of these was a small independent terminal-care unit, similar in size to St. Christopher's; the other was a cancer ward of a university teaching hospital. St. Christopher's emerged as significantly more favorable than one or both of the other two settings with respect to the following criteria: amounts of anxiety and depression expressed by patients, amount of concern expressed about the illness, degree of acceptance, amount of active participation, approval of the treatment given, approval of the staff, and approval of the hospital in general. In none of the 39 different assessments did St. Christopher's have a poorer score than either of the other two hospitals.

Study of Postbereavement Adjustment

Let us consider briefly the attempts that have been made to evaluate the support given to families after bereavement.

At the time when the comparative study of inpatient care was done we had not started our bereavement service. Hence, we were not altogether surprised to find no difference between the postbereavement adjustment of spouses of patients who had died at St. Christopher's and that of spouses of patients from elsewhere.

Our evaluation of the Bereavement Service contained two components. First, we set out to test the effectiveness of our method of identifying "high-risk" bereaved subjects. Second, we evaluated the effectiveness of the service itself.

To measure "risk," the nursing staff made their own assessments of the person most affected by the bereavement at the time of the patient's death. They used a short Predictive Questionnaire derived from the Harvard Bereavement Study (performed at Professor Gerald Caplan's Laboratory of Community Psychiatry in Boston). The questionnaire consisted of 8 five-point scales covering such issues as age, socioeconomic status, duration of preparation for death, observations of the family member clinging to the dying patient, anger, guilt, and lack of a supportive family (since this version of the questionnaire has now been superseded, I have not given these questions in detail). In addition the nurses are invited to use their own intuitive judgment of risk. Family members receiving a score of 18 or more are followed up, but nurses can overrule this score if they think there is a special risk not covered by the questionnaire. About 20 percent of families contain a member who falls into the high-risk group.

For research purposes a series of 182 have now been interviewed on average 23 months after bereavement ($\pm$ 4.5 months). An additional 61 had moved away or could not be located, 11 had died or were too sick or disturbed to be interviewed, and 41 declined an interview. A further 21 were thought by the nursing staff to be in urgent need of support, and since it would have been unethical to refuse help to these people, they were not included in the random allocation study but are called Group A (Table 5.5).

TABLE 5.5. DESCRIPTION OF STUDY GROUPS

		n
Group A.	Imperative need	21
Group B.	Predicted "high-risk" group	
	BH. "Supported" group	32
	BT. Control group	35
Group C.	Predicted "low-risk" group	94
	Total	182

Group *B* were the high-risk group—that is, persons whose questionnaire scores indicated the likelihood that they would have lasting difficulties but who had not been included in Group *A*. They were subdivided into two subgroups by the toss of a coin. Subgroup *BH* were given support in the usual way by the Family Aftercare Service and Subgroup *BT* were not offered support (although help was not refused if they took initiative in asking for it).

Group *C* were the low-risk group, that is, people who had been given a score of 17 or less on the questionnaire and who had not been placed in Group *A*.

At the research followup interview a number of outcome assessments were made. These were derived from the Harvard Bereavement Study and included four symptom scores derived by factor analysis from a total of 54 questions. The first of these, termed "autonomic symptoms," includes 13 questions about the incidence during the preceding year of the psychosomatic symptoms that accompany anxiety and commonly take people to their doctor after a bereavement (palpitations, sweating attacks, and so on); then there are "depression," which includes 24 questions about the subject's general level of contentment or sadness at the time of interview; "worry," which includes 10 questions about externally directed anxiety; and "general health," a miscellany of seven other common symptoms experienced during the past year. In addition two other types of question were grouped for analysis—"habit change," four questions concerning changes in consumption of alcohol, tobacco, tranquilizers, and sedatives; and "health systems utilization," derived from a count of health consultations, visits to general practitioners, and hospital admissions during the year preceding the interview. We also used a weighted system of scoring to obtain an "overall outcome" score that gave approximately equal weight to each of these outcome measures. (See Parkes and Brown, 1972, for further details of these measures.)

To test the efficacy of the predictive questionnaire, we focused on Groups *BT* and *C*, neither of whom received support. By plotting the score on the predictive questionnaire against the overall outcome score, we can see how accurate a prediction of outcome is given by that questionnaire (Figure 5.3). The mean overall outcome score for

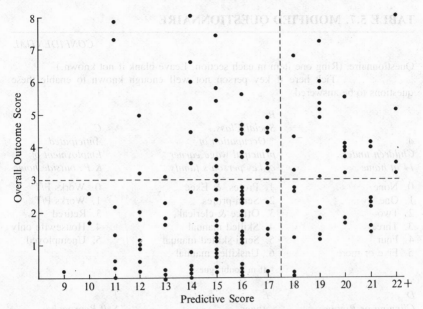

Figure 5.3 Predictive score × overall outcome score 18 to 27 months after bereavement (*n* = 128 Groups *A & BH* excluded).

the high-risk group (*BT*) was 3.24 compared with a mean score in the low-risk group (*C*) of 2.39 (*t* 2.15, *p* < .05). Taking a mean score of 3 or more as indicating "poor outcome," we find that 42 percent of subjects having a poor outcome and 79 percent of those with a "good outcome" would have been correctly identified by our predictive questionnaire (Table 5.6). Clearly there is room for improvement here, and we have carried out a stepwise regression and have now

TABLE 5.6. PREDICTION AND OUTCOME 18–27 MONTHS AFTER BEREAVEMENT

	Outcome	
	Good	*Poor*
Prediction	*(0–2.9)*	*(3+)*
Good (0–17)	59	30
Poor (18 +)	16	22

TABLE 5.7. MODIFIED QUESTIONNAIRE

CONFIDENTIAL

Questionnaire: (Ring one item in each section. Leave blank if not known.)
. . . . Tick here if key person not well enough known to enable these questions to be answered.

A
Children under
14 at home

0. None
1. One
2. Two
3. Three
4. Four
5. Five or more

B
Social Class.
* Occupation of
principal wage earner
of key person's family

1. Profes. & Exec.
2. Semi-profes.
3. Office & clerical
4. Skilled manual
5. Semi-skilled manual
6. Unskilled manual

* If in doubt, guess.

C
Anticipated
Employment of
K.P. outside home

0. Works F/T
1. Works P/T
3. Retired
4. Housewife only
5. Unemployed

D
Clinging or Pining

1. Never
2. Seldom
3. Moderate
4. Frequent
5. Constant
6. Constant intense

E
Anger

1. None (or normal)
2. Mild irritation
3. Moderate—occa-
   sional outbursts
4. Severe—spoiling
   relationships
5. Extreme—always
   bitter

F
Self Reproach

1. None
2. Mild-vague &
   general
3. Moderate—some
   clear self reproach
4. Severe—Preoc.
   self blame
5. Extreme—major
   problem

G
Relationship Now

0. Close intimate relat. with another
2. Warm supportive family permitting expression of feeling
3. Family supportive but live at
   distance
4. Doubtful
5. None of these

H
How will Key Person cope? †

1. Well. Normal grief and recovery
   without special help.
2. Fair, probably get by without
   special help.
3. Doubtful, may need special help.
4. Badly, requires special help.
5. Very badly, requires urgent help.

† All scoring 4-5 on H will be followed up.

modified our questionnaire in the hope of improving its predictive power. The modified questionnaire is shown in Table 5.7.

The Aftercare Service is evaluated by comparing Groups *BH* and *BT*. During the first 16 months of the service (June 1970 to October 1971), when we were all learning how to counsel the bereaved, our results were not very good. There were some differences between the two groups in favor of the supported group, but these did not reach statistical significance. During the next 13 months three out of our five principal measures of outcome showed significant differences (in favor of the supported group) between 15 supported and 19 members of the control group. In the last 7 months of the study (November 1972 to May 1973) a further four supported and three control subjects were added to these, and sadly, on the last analysis, two of these three significant findings had slipped below the 5 percent level again.

At the last analysis (Figure 5.4), the 19 supported subjects had significantly fewer "autonomic symptoms" than the 22 who made up

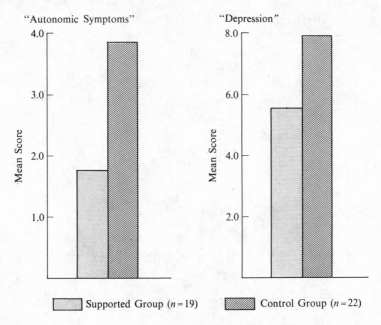

Figure 5.4 Mean symptom scores in "high-risk" bereaved groups.

our control group ($p < .01$). Supported subjects also differed from the controls in having less "depression"; less "worry"; fewer increases in consumption of alcohol, tobacco, and tranquilizers; and a better "overall outcome" (Figure 5.5). But none of these differences quite reaches statistical significance.

There were no appreciable differences between the groups with respect to the "health care utilization" score and the "general health" score. A problem here is the possibility that the Aftercare Service may actually have brought about some use of health services by urging the bereaved to get help with problems that they otherwise would have neglected.

To conclude, it would seem that the research done at St. Christopher's Hospice supports the general conclusion that the hospice is meeting the expectations of its founders that it would provide a form of care for the dying and for the families surviving them that is better than the care currently provided in the area served by the Hospice.

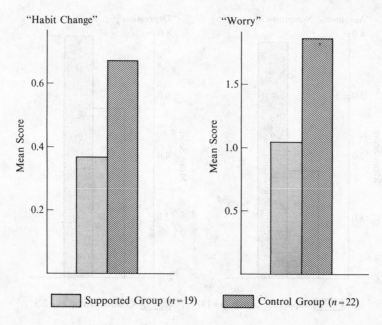

Figure 5.5 Mean outcome scores in "high-risk" bereaved groups.

Acknowledgments

The studies reported here were carried out with the assistance of grants from the Department of Health and Social Security. Thanks are also due to Cynthia Coleman, Margaret Boait, Margaret Napier, John Bowlby, John Hinton, Irwin Gerber, and Mrs. D. M. Stobart for their help and advice.

References

Gerber, I. et al. 1975. "Brief Therapy to the Aged Bereaved." In *Bereavement: Its Psychosocial Aspects,* eds. B. Schoenberg et al. New York: Columbia University Press.

Kincey, V. 1974. *The Evaluation of a Bereavement Counselling Service.* M. Sc. thesis, Manchester University, England.

Parkes, C. M. and R. J. Brown. 1972. "Health after Bereavement: A Controlled Study of Young Boston Widows and Widowers." *Psychosomatic Medicine* 34:449.

Polak, P. R. et al. 1973. *Crisis Intervention in Acute Bereavement: A Controlled Study of Primary Prevention.* Draft paper from Fort Logan Community Mental Health Center, Denver, Colorado.

Clinical Observations on Bereaved Individuals

Delia Battin, Irwin Gerber, Alfred Wiener, and Arthur Arkin

As part of the Montefiore Hospital and Medical Center's prospective controlled investigation on bereavement [1] we studied 58 key family members [2] who received unsolicited psychotherapy [3] for six months immediately after the loss of a close family member.

The authors express their gratitude to Alice Harrell and Elinor Lawless for their helpful suggestions on development of the Clinical Evaluation Form (CEF).

The data for this paper are from an investigation entitled, "The Aged in Crisis: A Study of Bereavement." This program was supported by USPHS Grant MH–14490 and Grant 93–P–57454/2 from the Administration on Aging, Social and Rehabilitation Service, Department of Health, Education and Welfare.

[1] This investigation has been studying bereavement in the aged and evaluating the effects of a 6-month therapeutic intervention offered to them.

[2] The key family member (KFM) is the surviving figure who was the chief authority and who assumed the major responsibility and leadership for keeping the family functioning as a unit. It was assumed that his (her) continued health, ability to "carry on," leadership, and support would "seep through" to the other family members.

[3] Treatment was geared to using the therapeutic relationship in assisting the grief-stricken person to live through the full recognition and conscious experience of object loss, to emancipate himself or herself from strong emotional bondage to the deceased, to readjust to the environment in which the deceased is missing, and to form new relationships and patterns of conduct.

By doing a content analysis of initial clinical interviews, we singled out feelings and behavior specific to intrapsychic, social, and somatic problems that seemed related to bereavement. We decided to study the prevalence of these feelings and behavior at different time periods after the loss: during the first three months (T_1); after six months, the time of termination of treatment (T_2); and three to five years later (T_3). To do so we set up a clinical evaluation form (CEF). We categorized the above-mentioned feelings and behavior into four major areas: (1) relationship to deceased; (2) pathologic change to include (a) intrapsychic state, (b) relationship, and (c) functional problems; (3) somatic problems; and (4) social activities and productive use of time (Table 6.1).

We discuss our findings in terms of significant changes in symptomatology over the timespan mentioned and analyze the meaning of these observations.

Findings

Fifty-eight families were seen for treatment by one clinician during the study. This constituted a 95 percent acceptance rate of the unsolicited service.

Among the 58 KFMs there were 46 women and 12 men, 44 women and 11 men having lost their spouses, and the others having lost a parent. The average age was 63. The religious ethnic composition was 43 percent Catholic, 48 percent Jewish, and 9 percent Protestant. Among the Catholics 72 percent were of Italian background, 20 percent Irish, 4 percent Puerto Rican, and 4 percent American Black. Among the Protestants 60 percent were of German descent and 40 percent of American Black. In the Jewish group the background was 100 percent Eastern European. The total population was in the lower middle-class range.

At followup 51 KFMs were seen: 3 of the initial population had died and 4 had moved away. This reduction in numbers did not significantly change the sex and socioethnic composition of this population.

TABLE 6.1. CLINICAL EVALUATION FORM

	Applicable follow-up contact		T_1		T_2	
	N	%(N=51)	N	N=58	N	N=58
A. RELATIONSHIP TO DECEASED						
1. Anger at deceased for leaving	1	2.0	16	27.8	9	15.5
2. Anger at deceased for past events	2	4.0	19	32.8	16	27.6
3. Feelings of worthlessness without deceased	0	0.0	31	53.4	24	41.4
4. Sense of freedom without deceased	8	15.7	8	13.8	11	19.0
5. Acceptance of death of deceased	44	86.3	26	44.8	14	24.1
6. Involvement with suffering of deceased during illness	0	0.0	6	10.3	6	10.3
7. Taking over role of deceased	—	—	11	19.0	9	15.5
8. Dependency upon deceased	—	—	5	8.6	2	3.4
9. Independency from deceased	2	4.0	3	5.2	4	6.9
10. Emptiness without deceased	0	0.0	47	81.0	41	70.7
11. Helplessness without deceased	8	15.7	23	39.6	10	17.2
12. Concern with deceased's missing life enjoyment	19	37.2	35	60.3	21	36.2
13. Dreams of deceased	2	4.0	13	22.4	4	6.9
14. Feelings that deceased's spirit is around	0	0.0	8	13.8	4	6.9
15. Hallucinations of deceased	2	4.0	17	29.3	3	5.2
16. Wish to believe deceased is not dead	4	8.0	35	60.3	9	15.5
17. Feelings of relief at death of deceased	50	98.0	11	19.0	7	12.1
18. Happy memories of deceased	44	86.3	48	82.8	48	82.8
19. Sad memories of deceased	1	2.0	52	89.6	45	77.6
20. Guilt about death of deceased			21	36.2	12	20.7
21. Visits to cemetery			4	6.9	13	22.4
B. INTRAPSYCHIC STATE						
35. Hallucinations [a]	1	2.0	18	31.0	2	3.4
36. Fears	17	33.3	47	81.0	40	69.0
37. Anxiety spell	0	0.0	33	56.9	27	46.5
38. Feelings of worthlessness	4	8.0	40	69.0	27	46.5
39. Difficulty concentrating	1	2.0	23	39.6	7	12.1

40. Hopeless feeling	1	2.0	31	53.4	11	19.0
41. Dreams	32	62.7	20	34.5	7	12.1
42. Self-blame	3	6.0	28	48.3	16	27.6
43. Worried feeling	22	43.1	49	84.5	40	69.0
44. Depression	3	6.0	53	91.4	46	79.3
45. Sadness	13	25.1	55	94.8	53	91.4
46. Discontentment	5	10.0	44	74.9	33	56.8
47. Relative contentment	50	98.0	5	8.6	39	67.2
48. Relative cheerfulness	24	47.0	3	5.2	20	34.5
49. Uncertainty about doing things	3	6.0	32	55.2	16	27.6
50. Crying	5	10.0	46	79.3	23	39.7
51. Obsessive compulsive behavior	1	2.0	4	6.9	1	1.7
52. Obsessional thoughts	2	4.0	17	29.3	8	13.8
53. Extreme sensitivity	6	11.8	50	86.2	43	74.1
54. Suspicions	3	6.0	44	75.9	9	15.5
55. Paranoid delusions	0	0.0	2	3.4	0	0.0
56. Feelings of isolation	0	0.0	11	19.0	7	12.1
57. Wish for death	0	0.0	9	15.5	2	3.4
58. Wishes of being violent						
59. Anger	5	10.0	48	82.8	35	60.3
60. Anger at self	3	6.0	17	29.3	11	19.0
61. Anger at God	0	0.0	17	29.3	12	20.7
62. Anger at medical personnel	4	8.0	23	39.7	15	25.9
63. Anger at the world	1	2.0	33	56.9	19	32.8
64. Preoccupation with guilt feelings	0	0.0	21	36.2	11	19.0
65. Tendency to feel numb	0	0.0	22	37.9	0	0.0
66. Helplessness	1	2.0	30	51.7	7	12.1
67. Thoughts about previous losses	37	72.5	37	63.8	16	27.6
68. Suicidal thoughts	0	0.0	2	3.4	1	1.7
69. Self-pitying thoughts	9	18.0	33	56.9	22	37.9
70. Fatalistic outlook	5	10.0	21	36.2	20	34.5
73. Reactions to pathological bereavement in another family member	1	2.0	5	8.6	4	6.9
74. Superstitious thoughts	0	0.0	7	12.1	4	6.9
75. Egocentricity	15	29.4	18	31.0	14	24.1

TABLE 6.1. CLINICAL EVALUATION FORM (Continued)

	Applicable follow-up contract		T_1		T_2	
	N	%(N=51)	N	N=58	N	N=58
B. INTRAPSYCHIC STATE						
76. Hopeful about future	45	88.2	8	13.8	41	70.7
77. Reactions to additional loss or losses	15	29.4	3	5.2	10	17.2
C. RELATIONSHIP						
78. Loneliness	17	33.3	51	87.9	42	72.4
79. Complaining attitude	7	13.7	14	24.1	11	19.0
80. Mistrust of people	3	6.0	18	31.0	6	10.3
81. Tendency to feel that people are not understanding	4	8.0	13	22.4	8	13.8
82. Tendency to feel that relatives are not understanding	5	10.0	13	22.4	9	15.5
83. Tendency to feel that people are not helpful	4	8.0	11	19.0	6	10.3
84. Tendency to feel that own relatives are not helpful	2	4.0	11	19.0	7	12.1
85. Tendency to feel that relatives of deceased are not helpful	4	8.0	12	20.7	6	10.3
86. Tendency to annoyance or irritation	3	6.0	34	58.6	20	34.3
87. Tendency to criticism of others	3	6.0	18	31.0	10	17.2
88. Inability to get along with people	0	0.0	2	3.4	0	0.0
89. Arguments with in-laws	—	—	—	—	2	3.4
90. Irritability with children	1	2.0	8	13.8	2	3.4
91. Good relationship with doctors	45	88.2	38	65.5	37	63.8
92. Bad relationship with doctors	3	6.0	7	12.1	5	8.6
93. Use of telephone	49	96.1	43	74.1	42	72.4
94. Loss of interest in things	2	4.0	20	34.5	3	5.2
95. Loss of interest in people	0	0.0	4	6.9	1	1.7
96. Interest in sex	—	—	4	6.9	6	10.3
97. Tendency to feel unloved	1	2.0	15	25.9	9	15.5
98. Fear of criticism	2	4.0	26	44.8	22	37.9
99. Envy of couples	7	14.0	12	20.7	7	12.1
100. Tendency to feel considered "less" by people	0	0.0	8	13.8	2	3.4
101. Tendency to feel abandoned by people	5	10.0	11	19.0	4	6.9

	N	%	N	%	N	%
102. Feelings that religious beliefs help	0	0.0	9	15.5	10	17.2
103. Feeling needed	47	92.1	25	43.1	33	56.9
D. FUNCTIONAL PROBLEMS						
104. Dislike the job	1	5.0(N = 20)	1		1	N = 18
105. Poor work performance	0	0(N = 20)	2		1	N = 18
106. No interest in household	0	0(N = 40)	11	5.2	2	N = 46
107. No interest in looking for job			3		0	
109. Fear of new responsibilities	1	2.0	31	53.4	25	43.1
110. Fear of losing job						
112. No interest in career						
113. Accident prone	1	5.0(N = 20)	1	1.7	1	1.7(N = 18)
114. Excessive involvement with work	3	6.0(N = 51)	24	41.4	11	19.0
115. Financial difficulties	2	4.0(N = 51)	3	5.2	1	1.7
116. Sought welfare	30	100.0(N = 30)	5	8.6	3	5.2
117. Sought Medicaid or Medicare						
E. SOMATIC PROBLEMS						
118. Presence of symptoms of deceased	1	2.0	3	5.2	2	3.4
119. Disturbed sleep	5	10.0	37	63.8	21	36.2
120. Use of Psychiatric medication	3	6.0	4 + 7	6.9	4 + 3	6.9
121. Use of hypnotics			4 +	1.7	1	1.7
122. Fear of using hypnotics			7	12.1	3	5.2
123. Use of sedatives			5	8.6	3	5.2
124. Fear of using sedatives	0	0.0	14	24.1	3	5.2
125. Loss of strength	2	4.0				
126. Change in appetite	4	8.0	27	46.6	17	29.3
127. Tendency to be easily tired	6	11.8	27	46.6	9	15.5
128. Tendency to be keyed up and jittery			40	69.0	27	46.6
129. Loss of weight			0	0.0	0	0.0
130. Neglect of medical care	1	2.0	7	12.1	4	6.9
131. Minimization of symptoms	1	2.0	1	1.7	1	1.7
132. Hypochondriasis	2	4.0	8	13.8	4	6.9

TABLE 6.1. CLINICAL EVALUATION FORM (*Continued*)

	Applicable follow-up contract		T_1		T_2	
	N	%(N=51)	N=58	N=58	N=58	N=58
F. SOCIAL ACTIVITIES AND PRODUCTIVE USE OF TIME						
133. Outings	51	100.0	31	53.4	48	82.8
134. Use of TV	51	100.0	23	39.7	30	51.7
135. Movie Attendance	28	55.0	3	5.2	8	13.8
136. Meetings with friends	47	92.1	26	44.8	42	72.4
137. Work	18	35.3	18	31.0	28	48.3
138. Successful management of financial difficulties	19	37.0	4	6.9	24	41.4
139. Club attendance	23	45.1	7	12.1	14	24.1
140. Visits	50	98.0	34	58.6	48	82.8
141. Wish to meet opposite sex	15	29.4	3	5.2	12	20.7
141.b. Wish to remarry Realistic Assessment	8	16.0	14	24.1	32	55.2
142. Plans for trips, etc.	38	74.5				
143. Interest in appearance, etc.	39	76.5	31	53.4	43	74.1
144. Offer of food to worker, etc.						
145. Has new friends	21	41.2	5	8.6	7	12.1
146. Plans involvement with old and new hobbies	29	57.0	4	6.9	16	27.6
147. Has new hobbies	8	16.0	1	1.7	5	8.6
148. Has new job	2	4.0	3	5.2	6	10.3
149. Plans to work	1	2.0	5	8.6	8	13.8
150. Has new pets	2	4.0	3	5.2	1	1.7
151. Joined new organizations	12	23.5	0	0.0	2	3.4
152. Resides in new abode	15	29.4	—	—	7	12.1
153. New sharing of living accommodations	4	8.0	1	1.7	2	3.4
154. Has remarried	7	14.0	0	0.0	1	1.7
155. Has been on a trip	36	70.6	2	3.4	26	44.8

[a] Owing to omissions of certain items, the entries do not always follow in exact numerical order.

CEF data are presented for those feelings and behavior that seemed most significant for these treated bereaved, at T_1, T_2, and T_3.

In the first major area, "relationship to deceased," during the first three months of bereavement the most prevalent behavior and feelings were the following: worthlessness without the deceased (noted for 53 percent of the treatment population); emptiness without the deceased (81 percent); wish to believe that the deceased was not dead (60 percent); happy memories of the deceased (82 percent); and sad memories (89 percent). The prevalence of the first two feelings, usually illustrated by sentences like "Now I am nothing," "It's like a piece of me that's missing," "I feel empty inside," with detailed elaborations, brings under scrutiny the issue of grief's involving loss of self-esteem. Freud (1917) contrasts normal grief and melancholia by emphasizing how loss of self-esteem is involved in melancholia but not in a "normal" grief reaction. We consider this differently: Loss of self-esteem is involved in the bereavement process; the intensity of the loss of self-esteem, its persistence in time, and the degree to which it affects functioning might determine whether the reaction is melancholia or so-called normal grief. We touch on this idea at various points here but discuss it in greater detail in another article.

The same attitudes were present during the second half of the clinical contacts in a smaller percentage of the population. The largest percentage differences were noted for "concern with deceased missing life enjoyment" and "wish to believe deceased is not dead," indicating, we believe, how survivor's guilt (e.g., "I am here not deserving to be alive while he is dead unable to enjoy this beautiful day") and the need to deny the loss (e.g., "It is a dream, he will be back tomorrow") are relinquished by a high percentage of the treated individuals four to six months after the death has occurred. It is also meaningful that during the first three months only 13 percent disposed of the belongings of the deceased, whereas 55 percent had done so by the end of treatment. Increasing ability to relinquish the bond to the deceased may be responsible for this. On the other hand this could also be interpreted as a compulsion to "do away" with the pain evoked by the clothing of the deceased that reminds of his absence.

Examining the same items at T_3, we note that feelings of worthlessness without the deceased are down to zero and emptiness is present for only 4 percent of the KFMs, as is the wish to believe that the deceased is not dead. If we again link worthlessness and emptiness to self-esteem, we can assert that self-esteem seems "repaired" by T_3; this is supported by evidence of good reality testing as shown in the giving up of the wish to believe that the deceased is not dead.

It is meaningful that the anger toward the deceased for leaving and for past events was not expressed as much as we had expected and that the sense of freedom without deceased was expressed by the same individuals at T_1 and T_3, and helplessness without deceased was true for 40 percent of the KFM initially and decreased extensively by T_2 to 17 percent and to zero by T_3, a decline supporting our ideas on self-esteem in bereavement.

A low percentage reported dreams of the deceased: From 22 percent at T_1 the percentage went to 7 percent at T_2 and increased to 37 percent at T_3, as if the pain involved in unconscious thinking about the deceased was seeping through at T_1, repressed at T_2, and tolerable enough at T_3 to allow recollection of dreaming.

Guilt about the death also seemed to be expressed less than expected. And the lowering of the percentage of people in treatment discussing it is impressive: 36 percent at T_1, 21 percent at T_2, and 2 percent at T_3! This observation also supports our view on self-esteem, taking into consideration the role of feelings of guilt on self-esteem.

Visits to cemetery were apparently infrequent. By T_3 it was observed that the same individuals who went at T_2 kept on going on specific occasions (Father's Day, religious holidays). There seemed to be no correlation between this occurrence and religion or ethnicity.

Mourning attire was worn by only 29 percent at T_1, diminished to 3 percent by T_2, and was nonexistent at T_3. The majority of the individuals observing this practice were of Italian–Catholic background.

As one sees in the CEF, we coded some concrete information on the relationship with the deceased. Most items applied to 100 percent of the population. This was to be expected, since the great majority of the population were widowed after marriages of more than 20 years' duration.

As for disposal of body, only two had been cremated whereas everyone else had been buried according to religious–ethnic traditions.

As to intrapsychic state, the following are the feelings experienced in varying intensity by a great majority of the population during the first three months of bereavement, and the percentages of incidence in parentheses: fears (81 percent, including mainly fear of death, fear of going crazy); anxiety spells (56); hopeless feelings (53); self-blame (48); worried feelings (85); uncertainty about doing things (55); feelings of worthlessness (69); depression (84); anger (82); discontentment (74); extreme sensitivity (86); suspiciousness (75); helplessness (51); self-pitying thoughts (56); and loneliness (87). Most of these feelings can be interpreted as indicative of lower self-esteem. Obviously, sadness was also intense for most individuals (95 percent) at T_1. All these feelings were experienced considerably less by T_2 and T_3. Most striking is the marked decrease for suspiciousness (16 and then 6 percent), hopeless feelings (19 and 2 percent) and helplessness (12 and 2 percent). This would imply that regression to using primitive defense mechanisms (e.g., projection as related to suspiciousness) and to feelings of passivity related to the wish to be taken care of is probably not pathologic during the first 6 months of bereavement, as is demonstrated by the striking remission of these symptoms. The concomitant increase at T_2 in the percentage of individuals feeling needed (from 41 to 56 percent and then to 92 percent), relatively contented (from 8 to 67 percent and then to 98 percent), and hopeful about the future (from 13 to 70 percent and then to 88 percent) would confirm this contention in spite of the fact that the other feelings described have not diminished markedly. This would support the notion that the feelings of hopelessness and helplessness decrease as one starts meaningful activity (this shows in the later section ''Productive Use of Time'') and feels needed, and concurrently a hopeful view to the future is encouraged by the increase in self-worth fostered by feeling needed and not helpless, and this increase in turn may foster meaningful activity. The assertion that feelings still present at T_2 are probably not pathologic is further supported by the evidence that the great majority of the population no longer seems to experience them at T_3.

It may be meaningful that the experience of hallucinations (both auditory and visual) by 31 percent of these treated bereaved is limited to 3 percent by T_2 and 2 percent by T_3. This causes us to question whether hallucinations at the time of bereavement indicate malignant pathology. A study done in Wales shows that hallucinatory experiences are common among bereaved individuals. We are referring to hallucinations as defined by Karl Jaspers (1963), not illusions as defined by the same author. We stress this point because illusions are well known to be a common experience for bereaved individuals.

"Difficulty concentrating" and "obsessional thoughts" were present for 40 and 29 percent of the population, respectively, at T_1. These experiences decreased to 12 and 14 percent at T_2 and then to 2 and 4 percent at T_3. Even though not so prevalent as other experiences at the beginning, these may still be significant symptoms.

Dreaming is resumed by 35 percent of the KFMs at T_1, by 12 percent at T_2, and by 63 percent at T_3. We can interpret this phenomenon in the same way we did for dreaming of the deceased: Unconscious material becomes more or less accessible, depending on the stage one is at during bereavement.

We see how crucial anger is in bereavement. Anger at the world is the feeling most people experience (57 percent at T_1). It becomes limited to 33 percent at T_2 and then to 2 percent at T_3, showing how it is specifically related to the bereavement process. The same is true of anger at self and anger at God, both experienced by 29 percent of the KFMs at T_1 and by 19 and 21 percent of the population, respectively, at T_2. Whereas anger at God seems to disappear completely by T_3, anger at self is still present in 6 percent.

As for crying, 79 percent of the population were observed to do so at T_1, 40 percent at T_2, and 10 percent at T_3. However, a majority of those reported as crying at T_3 were "touched" by a memory or event connected with the deceased: "It comes on like a wave," said one individual; others made similar comments.

Preoccupation with guilt feelings is true for 36 percent at T_1, for 19 percent at T_2, and for none at T_3. *Preoccupation* with guilt feelings is represented with varied symptomatology. The tendency to feel numb, so much described in the literature for people at the initial phase of bereavement, was observed for only 38 percent of the KFMs at T_1

and was gone by T_2. One could speculate that treatment encourages the individual to be in touch with his feelings, and the initial attempt at denial is therefore obviated.

As we expected, thoughts about previous losses are common: 64 percent of the treatment group experienced them. It seems logical that people who experience a loss would reminisce about other, previous losses not necessarily resulting from death. This is a natural association with beneficial implications in some cases: Reviewing how one has mastered a loss gives a perspective on the fact that one can master another loss, even though its meaning might be different. Ultimately any reaction to separation, whether by death or not, seems linked to early separation experiences.

For this population suicidal thoughts were not common: Only 3 percent experienced them at T_1, 2 percent at T_2, and none at T_3.

Egocentricity seemed to be related to character rather than to bereavement: Almost the same population showed this at all three time periods.

Additional loss was experienced after treatment began by 5 percent of the individuals at T_1, 17 percent at T_2, and 29 percent at T_3. But judged from our observations at T_3, this did not seem to have a pathologic effect on this population.

Loneliness seems to be a very important issue at T_2 and T_3. At T_1 only 33 percent experienced it, but at T_2 88 percent complained of it and 72 percent still had a great deal of trouble with it at T_3. This may be related not so much to bereavement as to living alone. It did not seem so prevalent at T_1, which may be due to the willingness of relatives and friends to be with the bereaved right after a loss; by T_2 this is no longer true, and the contrast is felt quite keenly.

A tendency to annoyance or irritation seemed significant at T_1 for 59 percent of this population. By T_2 only 34 percent showed this symptom, and by T_3, only 6 percent. This clearly seems related to their bereavement process.

Relationship with doctors was tapped to determine how the family physician was viewed at the various time periods in light of the common experience of anger toward doctors after a loss and also to determine if the family physician could be of help in bereavement. The results showed that the relationship appeared to be "good" for 65 percent of the individuals in treatment at T_1, for 64 percent at T_2, and for 88 percent at T_3. These results may imply that the individual might maintain a positive attitude toward his physician even when projecting feelings of anger onto him. Treatment might have helped these individuals to handle their ambivalent feelings.

Use of the telephone seemed important in terms of people's ability to maintain communication with relatives and friends. Seventy-four percent were able to use the telephone at T_1, 72 percent at T_2, and 96 percent at T_3. This means of communication was highly valued by this population: Statements like "When you cannot go out evenings because of the crime rate, you can still visit by phone" were heard over and over.

For this population, loss of interest in people was minimal (7 percent at T_1, 2 percent at T_2, and zero at T_3), and loss of interest in things seemed applicable to 35 percent of the KFMs at T_1, 5 percent at T_2, and 4 percent at T_3. This suggests that withdrawal from the world was minimal for this treated population.

Tendency to feel unloved was also not a major issue: Only 26 percent spoke about it at T_1, 15 percent at T_2, and 2 percent at T_3. This aspect of self-esteem seemed to remain unaffected for a majority of the treated individuals. One wonders if unsolicited treatment would by itself influence the perception that someone cares.

Fear of criticism seemed meaningful for 45 percent of this population at T_1, 38 percent at T_2, and 4 percent at T_3.

Negative perceptions related to attitudes of relatives and friends also did not seem to be of major importance, although they were present at T_1 for 19 to 22 percent of the treated bereaved, at T_2 for 10 to 13 percent, and at T_3 for 4 to 10 percent, showing a correlation with the bereavement process.

Mistrust of people, present in 31 percent of the KFMs at T_1, was experienced by only 10 percent at T_2 and 8 percent at T_3. This feeling seems also to be directly related to the bereavement process of the majority of this population.

These reactions might imply again that, right after the loss, a regression occurs to more primitive defense mechanisms like projection (e.g., feelings of guilt → self-criticism → feelings that others might criticize → feelings that others might withdraw their love → negative perceptions and mistrust → tendency to stay away from activities and people).

There do not seem to be other common clinical observations.

The experience of envying couples seems to apply to almost the same number of individuals at all three time periods (21, 12, and 14 percent, respectively): This may be related to character for certain individuals, when single. Tendency to feel one is considered "less" by people, was experienced by only 14 percent at T_1, 3 percent at T_2, and none at T_3. Therefore, this seems related to the bereavement process for a minority of the population.

Regarding "functional problems," only fear of new responsibilities seemed significant: 53 percent of the KFMs experienced it at T_1, 43 percent at T_2, and 2 percent at T_3. In part this seemed to be a realistic apprehension in view of the financial complications after the loss of a spouse; this apprehension was, however, probably accentuated by the general feelings of loss.

As for somatic problems the most significant symptoms appeared to be disturbed sleep for 63 percent at T_1, 36 percent at T_2, and 10 percent at T_3. A tendency to be keyed up and jittery was also considered a problem by 69 percent of the KFMs at T_1, 47 percent at T_2, and 12 percent at T_3. Both symptoms are clearly related to feelings about the loss in view of the marked decrease in the number of individuals experiencing them at T_3. Change in appetite was also meaningful for 47 percent at T_1, 29 percent at T_2, and 4 percent at T_3. This too seems to be a symptom closely related to bereavement. Tendency to be easily tired was also part of the depressive reaction to the loss for 47 percent at T_1, 16 percent at T_2, and 8 percent at T_3. And so was loss of strength for 24 percent at T_1, 5 percent at T_2, and none at T_3.

The other disturbances in this area seemed to be present for a very low percentage of the population.

Involvement in activities and productive use of time seemed to increase steadily during treatment and at time of follow-up, implying the lifting of the depressive reaction to the loss.

Outings, use of television attendance at films, visits, and meetings with friends became progressively part of life for an increasing number of treated bereaved during the three time periods.

	Percent participating at		
Activities	T_1	T_2	T_3
Outings	53	83	100
Use of TV	40	52	100
Movie attendance	5	14	55
Meetings with friends	45	72	92
Visits	59	83	98

It is remarkable how many individuals went on being involved with these activities even at T_1 except for going to the movies. And even more remarkable is the increase in time of this population's involvement in these activities, particularly the ones outside the home, including club attendance (12 percent at T_1, 24 percent at T_2, and 45 percent at T_3).

There is a striking decrease in the number of individuals wishing to remarry from T_2 to T_3 (55 to 16 percent). This might indicate resurgence of good reality testing on the part of widows in particular: Some talk about how they have become aware of the difficulty in meeting available single men after "middle age" (this is supported by statistical studies); others mention their unwillingness to become involved with men whom eventually they might have to "nurse" and lose because of their being older and therefore more likely to become ill and die.

On the other hand eight individuals did remarry by T_3, two women and six men. There was a seventh gentleman who died after three years of "marital bliss" with a new partner. If we take into account that in this population there are only 10 men, by T_3 the remarriage statistics for these widowers is a rather high 60 percent. Of the remaining four widowers who have not remarried, one is about 81 years old and is suffering from a heart condition, another is living with a woman, the third is a highly disturbed individual who seems pathologically involved with his teenage daughter, and the last one is actively searching for a partner although in his late seventies.

Moreover, judging from results in another paper (Gerber et al., 1975) indicating poor outcome for widowers whose spouse died after a terminal illness of long duration, we can speculate that men feel very keenly the deprivation of a "normal" relationship to a partner who is physically well and able to fulfill whatever emotional and physical needs are important to the man.

Interest in appearance, planning for and going on trips, and planning involvement with old and new hobbies are common experiences for this population. The contrast between T_1 and T_2 and then between T_2 and T_3 is remarkable. Involvement in these interests seems to be an important indication of good outcome in adjustment to a loss.

Summary

In summary we have presented a statistical analysis of clinical changes observed over a three- to five-year period in 58 bereaved individuals who received brief psychotherapy.

The analysis appears to show how specific feelings and behavior that would be considered pathologic under different circumstances (e.g., hallucinations) are not to be considered so in the bereavement process of this population.

References

Freud, S. 1917. *Mourning and Melancholia.* Standard Edition, Vol. 14.

Gerber, I. *et al.* 1975. "Anticipatory Grief and Aged Widows and Widowers." *Journal of Gerontology* 30:225–29.

Jaspers, K. 1963. *General Psychopathology.* Chicago: University of Chicago Press.

Lindemann, E. 1944. "Symptomatology and Management of Acute Grief." *American Journal of Psychiatry* 101:141–48.

Rees, W. D. 1970. *The Hallucinatory and Paranormal Reactions of Bereavement.* M.D. thesis.

7

Competence or Crisis: The Social Work Role in Maintaining Family Competency during the Dying Period

Marion Wijnberg and Mary C. Schwartz

Dying is life's most solitary experience; it is also exquisitely transactional. The dying patient leaves to his family the accrued meaning of his life. Identities of family members must often be reconfirmed and self-esteem restructured. Participating in the dying seems to heighten one's sensory perceptions; the memories of the dying period linger and take on particular meaning to the bereaved family.

In this chapter we have chosen to focus on one component of the interactional set: the family members. To do so is in line with traditions in social work. We are concerned with helping the family member maintain his sense of competence in the face of severe stress and the dismemberment of the family system during the time that the patient is dying (Hill, 1965).

Maintaining the sense of competence for the family member involves two different sets of tasks. The first set revolves around the challenge of being helpful to the dying patient. Our concern is with those people whose sense of general well-being will be enhanced by feeling some competency in helping the dying patient and whose self-image will be damaged if some help is not given. Obviously different degrees of motivation around needing or desiring to be facilitative exist among individuals during this period. Section I of this chapter addresses itself to how to make this motivation operational, in whatever degree it appears.

The second set of tasks revolves around enabling the family member to cope with the disruption of his own personal life. Section II explores those tasks along with the common confusions, uncertainties, and concerns that occur during this period. The ways that social workers can help family members cope constructively with the strain of the disruption are described.

It is our assumption that there is a period before and after the death of a family member when the bereaved's feelings of competence are severely taxed. R. W. White (1963) has illuminated the close relationship between feelings of competence and feelings of self-esteem.

Self-esteem has its tap roots in the experience of efficacy. It is not constructed out of what the environment provides gratuitously. It springs rather from what one can make the environment do . . . by coordinated acts of competence.

Two feelings usually aroused in family members are a sense of powerlessness against the inexorableness of the outcome and the sense of helplessness that make "acts of competence" within the framework of the burden of patient care hard to achieve. Feelings of shock, exhaustion, horror, irritability, loneliness, loss, anger, guilt, and sheer boredom are continually aroused during the period of dying. Frequently, they all combine to bring about a self-definition of impotence and lowered self-esteem.

During periods of severe stress, resolutions to earlier psychosocial crises are reopened and old vulnerabilities are exposed. Erikson speaks to the delicate balance of each maturational crisis and to the misuse of his conception of development as achievements secured once and for all (Erikson, 1956).

The assumption that in each stage a goodness is achieved which is impervious to new inner conflicts and to changing conditions . . . can make us inept in a heightened struggle for meaning in a new industrial era. . . . The personality is engaged with the hazards of existence continuously. . . . As we come to diagnose a state of relative strength and the symptoms of an impaired one, we face only more clearly the paradoxes and tragic potentials of human life.

Considered alertness to the newly aroused vulnerabilities of the bereaved family members becomes an important consideration for the social worker who wishes to use these differential strategies for enhancing competency.

A family member is asked to perform certain specific tasks to be helpful to the dying patient and to achieve competencies that need to be supported, encouraged, or developed by the social worker. The list presented here does not purport to be exhaustive.

I. Role of the Family Member in Helping the Dying Patient

PHYSICAL PRESENCE

To feel helpful, in most cases the family member must be able actually to visit the patient. This may seem obvious until one realizes how many family members are afraid to visit because of what they may have to face. Presence does not mean continuous bedside presence, but it is represented by the act of coming face to face with the dying patient.

The social worker can do a number of things to make it easier for that member to "meet" the dying patient (Buber, 1955). From the beginning the social worker should speak to the development of competence in this task.* She can telephone the family member to explore with him the ways he might be helpful, while at the same time she offers the physical presence of her own protection and authority in this frightening situation. She indicates that she is not asking for

---

* For clarity the social worker will be referred to as "she," and the family member as "he" (Schwartz, 1974).

what cannot realistically be given; she asks the member what he thinks is realistic in the way of time and so on. Clarity about the meaningful though limited role each member can play is essential.

The social worker can also help with information about reality factors, transportation, the general needs of the patient, the location of the specific floor, visiting hours, places where children can be left, and so forth. If she feels the member is particularly frightened or inadequate, she may offer to arrange transportation or pick him up personally. In short the social worker mobilizes all the professional skills she would use with any client who is frightened about taking a new step into an unknown situation.

HELPFULNESS WITH THE INTERVIEW
Most family members need to feel that they are actually being useful to the sick patient. Too often they feel confused and incompetent. If the visitor feels rejected or inadequate during the visit, this will lower his self-confidence and decrease the probability that he will visit again. Here the social worker can perform the following services.

Reacting to Stages of Dying. If, for example, the patient is railing at the visitor and using him as a way of projecting all the anger at the situation, it is helpful to talk with the member about the stages of dying (Kübler-Ross, 1969). The social worker might indicate that the angry interchange was actually helpful to the patient, for it helped him release his frustration and feel less alone in his despair. The family member is thus helped to feel that he has, in fact, facilitated a crucial psychic process for the patient.

Teaching Listening Behaviors. We subscribe to the general rule that it is the patient's right to decide what he wishes to talk about. This requires that the social worker help the family member become particularly sensitive to the patient's signals and cues, his need to talk, and his need to remain silent. That is, the patient may or may not be ready to talk about his dying, or to plan for his family after his death, or to discuss his fear of pain, and so forth. In the past we have erred in not hearing the patient's readiness to talk about these subjects, because of our own fears or our anxiety that such a discussion may undo the patient's defensive structure. It is important that we help the family member not to err in either direction, that is, not to push the dying patient when he is unready to talk about certain issues and not to cut off the dying patient from reviewing and completing his life cycle.

Interpreting the Patient's Coping Pattern. It is often difficult for a family member who feels upset, guilty, and tired to respond in an acutely sensitive manner. It becomes the role of the social worker to help interpret the patient's coping behaviors in this situation. The social worker may, for example, have noticed that the patient wants to talk about his fears, and she can help the family member to understand this need. It cannot be emphasized enough that for most family members this is "no man's land," without familiar signposts that have allowed them to know how to be helpful. Thus information about what might be useful to the patient gives a focus to their visits, builds their sense of competence, and makes them less wary about "saying the wrong thing."

The social worker may elect to ask the patient if there is any special way he would like to be treated by particular family members. This helps develop in the patient more control and initiative over at least part of his life; it recognizes that we all have special friends for special moments and gives the patient an exit to use that he might not otherwise have. It also gives valuable information to the social worker that can help with her strategies with family members. As suggested the patient will probably want different emotional responses from different family members, and we need to know these different expectations if we are to perform our interpreter role successfully. The patient may wish to talk about dying with his wife but keep up a cheerful front with his sister; clearly this is valuable information to have. Of course, it is up to the patient to choose whether he wishes to tell the individual family members himself how he would like to be responded to or whether he would like to use the social worker as a mediator.

It is not our intention to give the impression that the social worker has superior knowledge of the dying patient. Rather we see an exchange process taking place—one in which information is exchanged between the family member and the social worker.

Dealing with Patient Pride. For some dying patients the humiliation that comes from feeling so debilitated and dependent increases pride about asking for special favors from family members, who then feel thwarted in their desire to be helpful in a concrete way. A dying patient will, however, often respond with gratitude to a concrete offer of help that he has been unwilling to ask for. The fact that the family member has anticipated his needs makes the sick patient feel all the more given to and recognized.

Here the social worker has two possible roles. The first is that, from her experience with the dying, she can help the family member anticipate the needs of the patient; second, she can educate the member about the difficulty the patient has in asking for help, so that the family member can feel better able to suggest concrete ways of being useful.

SUSTAINING ROLE ACTIVITY

The social worker can be supportive to the family member in helping to encourage active planning with the dying patient. Expectations of the sick role are that the patient should be passive, dependent, and compliant. The family member, out of guilt or his wish to be helpful, often encourages this regression. The social worker needs to educate the members about the patient's need to stay in some control for as long as he is able.

With most dying patients there is planning to be done, if the patient is ready and willing. This can involve anything from funeral planning to settling financial affairs in a rational way, writing letters to different members, and so forth. One dying mother left the hospital to conclude the purchase of a house for her sick son and was thus able to feel that she maintained dignity, competence, and initiative. Most important, she was able to continue her maternal role so that, even after her anticipated death, her son would have a home.

Family members are often confused about whether they have the right to ask anything of a dying person. Lynn Caine (1974), author of *Widow,* was afraid to bring up any discussion of family finance while her husband was dying. Subsequently she became angry at her husband and herself, after his death, because of her inability to initiate this topic.

Naturally, planning around the dying has to be handled in a sensitive way. If a patient is using heavy denial, he is approached in a different way than is the patient who indicates clearly that he wishes to plan for his family after his death. At this juncture the interpreter role and the educator role of the social worker merge as discussion with the family takes place about helping the patient with this issue.

If the more active coping ability of the dying patient is to be encouraged, team planning with nurses and doctors is also essential. In many institutional situations, rules and regulations may have to be modified to accommodate the more active patient stance.

THE ADVOCATE ROLE OF THE FAMILY MEMBER
For some family members, playing the advocate role constructively meets the need to be helpful. There is a sense of accomplishment for the member when, because of his specific efforts, the dying patient receives more efficient service. In order for the family member to be effective in this role, the social worker should be available to impart to the family member her understanding of the hospital's social system. In this instance, rather than an interpreter of the hospital system on behalf of the doctor, she becomes an interpreter of the hospital system on behalf of the family member. The notion is to facilitate the family member's advocacy skills so that he can become more competent in securing patient goals, whether they be comforts, exceptions to rules, or specific medical services.

CONCLUDING THE RELATIONSHIP
With terminal patients the end of the relationship poses for many family members the task of bringing it to a close. The salient issue is what is to be done within the remaining time. Often the family members' desire to use this time to express unfinished business feels contradictory to the needs of the patient. Sometimes even the expression

of positive feelings can feel painful. The family member is in a dilemma that can immobilize him. If the family member had a meaningful relationship with a social worker, clarification might be achieved and action set in motion.

One grown daughter wanted to express her anger toward her mother at what she had missed in their relationship, but she was concerned about overwhelming her mother who was already in physical pain. Because of this conflict she was immobilized in her visits with her dying mother and angry at herself and her mother. In this instance the role of the social worker was the familiar one of helping the family member clarify what she wanted to accomplish with the dying member and guiding her to do this realistically.

It should be understood that in the visitations the family member is facing the end of the relationship and is often grieving the end of hope for what that relationship might have given her. Thus the grown daughter was grieving for her own lost and unrealistic fantasy of a mother she might have had, if only. . . . It is the dying patient who becomes the focus of this fantasy of disappointment, and it is often helpful if the social worker hears out the anger and disappointment. This can lead to developing different satisfying kinds of communication in the terminal period.

Tasks of Survivors and the Role of the Social Worker

This section is devoted to exploring some of the tasks the family member may need to do for his own psychic and physical survival and what the social worker can do to help the efficient performance of these tasks.

Conceptually it is important to separate stress and crisis (Rappaport, 1962; 1967; 1970; Kaplan, 1962). Stress is inherent for the family member during the period of dying. Whether or not the family member is in crisis would be determined by an assessment of his responses, including perceptual distortion, cognitive disorganization, a spread of inability to take action into other areas of the life space, overwhelming helplessness, extensive denial, and so forth. It is our belief that social work intervention applied during this stressful period could contribute to preventing unnecessary crises with their attendant anguish and possible constriction of coping capacities.

Because death is final it signals the end to the best and the worst in any relationship; it also reminds us of our own finite existence and tends to surface terror of our own dying (Becker, 1973). In addition it exposes family members to stresses beyond the loss of the dead person himself. Norris Hansell (1970) has observed that

ordinary life involves stable arrangements of transactions, between the self and the environment, necessary to the self and not incidental. It is a corollary that the self *atrophies* when these attachments are severed. Necessary transactions include (1) food construction materials and information, (2) roles within a family or central circle, (3) interlocking roles with other persons, (4) differential attachments to a small number of persons, (5) status relationships with persons and groups, (6) images of some continuity and sense of solidarity with others, (7) observations and decisions which compose the self-picture, (8) notions of the good life and a comprehensive system of meaning, (9) attachment to the economic systems of the community.

It is axiomatic that, to maintain esteem, one must have a sense of self that is generally related to the perception of one's self in interaction with others. Many of the attachments on which the sense of self appears dependent are most attenuated during periods of death and bereavement. A sense of self in action is enhanced by competent handling of this difficult situation. The social worker can offer support in maintaining the family member's system of attachments, clarifying threats to existing roles, and selecting behaviors consonant with his own psychic needs, and providing anticipatory guidance for management of difficulties resulting from the terminal illness and central to the well-being of the bereaved family.

Social work support in helping the family member cope with his own psychic survival during this period involves certain discrete activities.

STROKING, NOURISHING, AND LISTENING
Positive, regular feedback to the family member about how well he is doing under his burden and grief is a primary task of the social

worker. Despite the obviousness of this role it is one rarely played by the social worker during the dying period. Acknowledgment that his is a difficult and draining job that he is handling competently tends to decrease the oppressiveness of the stress. Relatedness and kindness during the lonely and dreary vigil contribute to increasing the family member's sense of self-worth and to his perceiving that he is not alone in these dread-filled hours.

There is also a need to have one's anger at being saddled with the burden heard and to have one's guilt at the anger listened to. Thoughts that feel ludicrous to family members feel less "crazy" or "bad" when they are listened to in a nonjudgmental way. Thus one brother whose sister was dying from a suicide attempt heard himself saying, "Why did she have to make this attempt this week, just when I had two important papers to write?" This is not a noble thought, but it is a very human one and needs to be acknowledged as such. The anger of family members as they see their financial resources dwindling and wish the patient "to die already"; the desire of a parent whose child will die eventually "to hurry up his dying" because they are tired of their own suffering; the almost universal question, "Why me and why at this time when I can least afford it?" are thoughts that seem more acceptable and less depressive when heard by an understanding social worker.* The social worker needs to be sensitive to the family member's desire for sharing his grief or repressing it and to be open to facilitating the member's choice of dealing with his grief and loss.

Within the family circle the death of a member may have a different meaning to each of the bereaved. To one it may represent the end of a happy marriage and a shared old age; to another, formal ascension to the status of head of the household; to a third, the loss of the only person who truly understood him; to yet another, the confirmation of her own spinsterhood and reinforcement of her middle agedness. These different perceptions may seem to be too conflicting and too intimate to be shared within the circle, and yet they may rep-

---

* Social workers might form impromptu groups that can be used to share common experiences and common sentiments at this time.

resent the core of each individual's grief. The social worker can be helpful both as listener and as the one who helps the family member reconcile all that was, or all that might have been, with the reality and finality of all that is. The social worker can help each person accept his individual as well as his corporate identity.

LIMITING THE BURDEN AND THE RESPONSIBILITY
Social workers have long known that, when a client feels overwhelmingly burdened, he can often do less than when the burden feels more limited and realistic. Regular visits to a dying patient take psychic and physiologic toll. Even if a member feels he is being helpful (and no one can ever feel this all the time), he may experience the responsibility as heavy indeed. The social worker can do a number of things to lighten this burden. The first is to demonstrate to the member that part of the stress is being shared by the worker herself and that she is skilled and knowledgeable in this kind of crisis. Admittedly this can be relieving to some family members and threatening to others. In just the way that caseworkers work with parents who are threatened by their children's seeing a ''good'' therapist in child guidance clinics, the worker needs to be aware of the threat she may represent and to develop appropriate strategies.

Second, the worker can assess with the family member what his realistic capacities are in the helping process. Not everyone does everything equally well; no family member can give everything. The social worker can provide the mechanism whereby family members assess what they can do. Through the mediation of the social worker, assignment of needed services to the dying patient can be made in relation to what family members feel most able to do. In effect rational planning among family members is developed and can result in better service to the patient and make for less guilt among family members.

MAINTAINING ROLE ATTACHMENTS
During the period of dying, family members often tend to focus all their energies in the direction of the sick patient. By so doing they not only cut off sources of personal nourishment, which may come from other members of their role set (Hunt, 1970), but they also

deprive themselves of the sense of competence they have derived from playing other roles. For example the wife visiting her dying mother rarely has the energy or time to talk with her husband. Emotionally depleted in the "daughter" role, she is unable to communicate, get nurturing, or maintain a sense of competence from her marital role.

It has been well understood in family therapy literature that the turn toward the sick member often means that other family members are shortchanged. Our emphasis here is similar, in that we would underline the loss of nurturing and competence that family members experience as all of the energies are focused on the "identified patient."

The social worker's role in this context is to help the family member keep perspective by helping him discuss his functioning in his other key relationships. One member, for example, who was visiting a dying mother regularly in a nursing home, felt she could never fulfill the "daughter" role adequately. She took considerable pride, however, in the way she handled her children during this period and felt a renewed sense of general competence. She had used the nursing home visits to teach her children about human suffering, helped them deal with some of the depressing sights they had seen, and gotten them to bake cakes for the other people. In short she had made the situation into an enhancing experience for herself and her children.

A sense of well-being can come from competently playing roles other than the one being threatened by death. It can also come from playing out the same role with a different family member. One mother of two was focusing all her attention on her visits to her sick son.* Her 5-year-old daughter, feeling ignored and shut out, became increasingly obnoxious, which only added to the mother's frustration. When the mother was able to realize the reason for her daughter's behavior, a plan was made to incorporate her into the visiting routine. The daughter was brought to the hospital with the mother instead of

---

* Although this child was suffering from an extended illness rather than actually dying, the management issues for the sibling were the same.

being cared for by a babysitter at home. While the mother visited her son, her daughter played in a special children's playroom with other visiting children. The whining stopped, the child felt included in the family drama, and what is most important, the mother felt a renewed sense of maternal competence.

Work roles are often neglected or underplayed during this time. Because our society has tended to assign the nurturing, caregiving role to women, they are more apt to relinquish their work role and thus lose some of the support their work identity gives them. Although men are less apt to give up their work role completely, they still have a difficult balancing act to do (Schwartz, 1974). The role of the social worker here is once again to help the family member assess the possibility of maintaining these different roles while still allowing him to meet the dying patient's needs. Easy solutions are rare; the social worker can help the family member through the problem-solving task of choosing imperfect but not self-destructive options.

Lastly, the notion of necessary time away to "recreate" often needs to be discussed with the family member. To satisfy one's pleasure or recreational needs at a time when a loved one is dying may arouse guilt in the family member; not to fulfill these needs may arouse anger and leave him psychologically unreplenished. The social worker can play a parental permission-giving role at this time as she encourages the family member to consider the recreation he needs to engage in, to survive this trying period.

MOBILIZING THE SOCIAL NETWORK
It is a fact of modern living that the nuclear family is the prevalent family structure. Historically American families have felt that they should maintain responsibility for themselves and their own well-being. Modern families may, however, carry within them more traditional family values that impose the injunction to be responsible for, and take care of, their own. This often causes more stress than nuclear families can bear, for they do not have the manpower that the larger extended family supplied to do the job. Commitment to independence may effectively impede their ability to reach out for personal help during this critical period. Learning how to mobilize

others within one's social network becomes a skill to be acquired and valued.

In this context the social worker has a clarifying job with the member. Simply put, the question is, "What are you doing now that is beginning to overwhelm you, that somebody else could do for you, and how do you get that person to do it?" Thus one professor found she could ask a colleague to pick up her mail when she was visiting in the hospital, and she could ask another to step in and take her children for a number of days. Many people who ask to help genuinely do not know what it is they can do. The family member can teach them to be helpful by making concrete requests. On the other hand some offers of help are only pro forma, and the family member may need some assistance if the request is ignored or forgotten.

The social worker can also identify and mobilize formal service networks. Most people simply do not know of the specialized health-related services such as cancer aids, or services to the aged (like meals on wheels), or public health nursing, or special community reach-out programs. In her traditional role the social worker extends the network of the client through her understanding of environmental resources.

PLANNING FOR THE FUTURE

One of the first necessities in planning for the future is some clarity about the medical diagnosis. Because this is such painful information, communication between family members and doctors often becomes distorted. It is crucial, then, for the social worker to have access to the medical information and enough conference time with the doctor so that this information can be clarified. Some family members need to talk, deny, hope; others may require great specificity. Because many prognoses are, in fact, unclear, maintaining some hope may be realistically appropriate, but one cannot judge that unless one is on top of the medical situation. With proper information the social worker can then use her skill in supporting the family members' adaptive capacities.

If the family member has either a positive or negative dependence on the dying patient, it is desirable for him to do some anticipatory planning (Lindemann, 1944; Caplan, 1964; Rappaport et al., 1970). Planning should give the grieving member somewhat more control over his life as he seeks answers to such universal questions as, "How will I survive after the death of my husband, wife, mother, father, child?" The survival fears may focus on a variety of lost supports whether they be affectional, financial, or role definitional. Discussions may range from concrete information about widows' benefits to the expression of terror about life as a single person. Parents may need to know of homemaker service, or they, too, may need some advice about how to help their children through the loss of the other parent. If the family member has channeled all his energy and meaning into taking care of the dying patient, the social worker might want to help the member think about the possibility of felt isolation and real loss. Some discussion about what the member will probably experience at the death might be in order, so that the member has cognitive structures into which to place some of his more disquieting reactions. While planning for the future, the social worker should extend her service to a reasonable period after the death of the patient so that all the supports we have been mentioning are not abruptly removed. In the last phase the social worker serves as a link back to ongoing affectional attachments and to the bereaved's natural social network.

Summary

Family members are confronted with two different sets of tasks: (1) those that they may need to do for the dying patient and (2) those that they need to do to maintain their own psychic and physical well-being. In the emphasis on the dying patient this second set of tasks is often neglected, both in the literature and by the helping professional. This chapter has spelled out both sets of tasks, presenting illustrative case examples and describing the social work role. We believe that, if stresses are reduced during this period, the potential for developing crises as a result of bereavement may be offset.

References

Becker, E. 1973. *The Denial of Death*. New York: Free Press.

Buber, M. 1955. *Between Man and Man*. Translated by R. G. Smith. Boston: Beacon Press.

Caine, L. 1974. *Widow*. New York: William Morrow and Co., Inc.

Caplan, G. 1964. *Principles of Preventative Psychiatry*. New York: Basic Books.

Erikson, E. 1956. *Childhood and Society*, 2nd ed., rev., p. 273. New York: W. W. Norton and Co.

Hansell, N., M. Wodaczyk, and L. Hamilton. 1970. "Decision Counseling Method." *Archives of General Psychiatry* 22, May.

Hill, R. 1965. "Generic Features of Families under Stress," in *Crisis Intervention: Selected Readings,* ed. H. Parad. New York: Family Service Association of America.

Hunt, R. G. 1970. "Role and Role Conflict," in *Current Perspectives in Social Psychology,* 3rd ed., ed. E. P. Hollander and R. G. Hunt.

Kaplan, D. M. 1962. "A Concept of Acute Situational Disorders." *Journal of Social Work* 7, no. 2, April 1.

Kübler-Ross, E. 1969. *On Death and Dying*. New York: Macmillan Company.

Lindemann, E. 1944. "Symptomatology and Management of Acute Grief." *American Journal of Psychiatry* 101, 2, 141–48, September.

Rappaport, L. 1967. "Crisis-Oriented Short-Term Casework." *Social Service Review* 41, March.

—— 1962. "The State of Crisis: Some Theoretical Considerations." *Social Service Review* 36, no. 2.

—— 1970. "Crisis Intervention as a Mode of Brief Treatment," in *Theories of Social Casework,* eds. R. W. Roberts and R. H. Free. Chicago: University of Chicago Press.

Schwartz, M. S. 1974. "Importance of the Sex of Worker and Client," *Social Work* 19, March.

White, R. W. 1963. *Ego and Reality in Psychoanalytic Theory*. New York: International Universities Press, Inc., p. 192.

Part III

Facing Death in Childhood, Adolescence, Middle Age and Old Age

8

Bereavement in Childhood

Erna Furman

The longer I work as a so-called expert on death, the more I come to appreciate that all of us are experts on death. We all share not only the destiny of having to die one day, but also the brief brushes or a more long-term experience with death and bereavement. From these personal experiences we learn as much as we do from working with our clients.

Fortunately, we do not live constantly with thoughts of death. We manage to deny it until suddenly something happens that hits very close and forces us to come to terms. Coming to terms on that narrow line that lies between two extremes is a difficult task. The one extreme is that of feeling so close to the person who is dying or has died and to his family that we cannot extricate ourselves; we have the feeling of being ourselves in their shoes to such an extent that it is impossible for us to step back, to support and help them. With the other extreme we set aside our interest and concern and say "after all this is not me, life has to go on." At that extreme we are in danger of not being able to empathize with people. So we struggle within ourselves between feeling too much and setting aside too much until we reach the middle line that enables us to say "Here, but for the grace of God go I"; we are then aware and able to muster the necessary empathy and sympathy without being trapped in an overwhelming way. All of us who work in this field have had to achieve this point over and over again with each personal experience and with each patient. There is no such thing as steeling oneself for once and always. There is no way out of the anguished struggle, pain, and turmoil that come to all who work with bereaved people and that are essential to empathy.

About 15 years ago a sudden tragedy struck my colleagues and myself. Within the span of a year, two mothers of our young therapeutic nursery school children died quite unexpectedly, and our illusions about how distant we were from death were shattered. The aftermath of these tragedies was a tremendous reassessment, reworking, and rethinking, not to mention the hardship of the feelings as we struggled to cope.

At that time my husband, Dr. Furman (1964), Marian Barnes (1964), and Marjorie McDonald (1964) published some of their related experiences, and we discovered that we already had some other bereaved children in treatment. Over the next few years, by sheer coincidence because we certainly never solicited or sought a bereaved patient, we found that among the 14 of us we had 23 bereaved children in analytic treatment. For many years we had all been consultants in local agencies and hospitals and had encountered these situations, but the opportunity to treat bereaved children analytically by seeing them daily over a long period gave us the unusual opportunity to gain insight into the deeper psychological workings and the extent of the emotional task. Some of these children were bereaved during the treatment, something that had not been anticipated at the beginning of their therapy. Others were being treated for a variety of symptoms, but during treatment it was determined that many of these symptoms could be traced back to an earlier parental bereavement. Some of the children were recently bereaved or were seen actually at the time of the parent's death, whereas others had experienced the loss many years before. Some children had lost a parent when they were as young as in their first year, and the oldest bereaved child among our group was 13 years old when his father died.

They were black and white, rich and poor, and of various religious denominations. They had every variety of symptoms and yet were found to have many things in common. As we worked with them we felt our lack of knowledge and the burden of our feelings, and so we got together to learn together, to share, and to try to work out some ways in which what we learned could be applied prophylactically in other situations. For several years this group met weekly in research evenings. We subsequently published our findings (Furman, 1974).

We learned some things that may appear to be very simple and are indeed very simple. But it is because of this very simplicity that they are so readily overlooked. For example, we learned that death is a unique experience. It is similar to separation, similar to divorce, to rejection, to adoption in some instances, but it is totally different as well, and therefore we certainly learned that it has to be treated as an experience in and unto itself. Its finality brings special fears and hardships but in a strange way also makes it, or can make it, ultimately more manageable because it is a fact. We learned that, among the many forms of bereavement, a parent's death in childhood (and, indeed, at any stage in childhood) is a unique experience because a parent is not only a loved and importantly loved person but also an essential helper in the development of the child's personality. When a parent ceases to be, then progressive personality development is endangered. Another reason childhood bereavement is so special became clear: For a child to conquer his loss and to mourn, he needs his parents' help as he needs their help with many other tasks in daily life. When the parent dies, who can perform this task? The very person being mourned is the person who normally would help the child to mourn, and that presents a special problem. Although, as we learned, bereavement in childhood presents terrible stresses capable of distorting subsequent development and producing deviant behavior, it is also possible to deal with these stresses successfully.

Factors in Dealing with Bereavement

We have had bereaved children as young as under 2 years of age whom we have been able to follow through adolescence and about whom we can say, "Yes, the child has really mastered the stress." Yet, of course, we have so many other children, much older, who are unable to master it. And so we wonder what makes this possible for some and not for others. What are some of the factors that make it possible for a 2-year-old child to mourn successfully, to progress in his development, and to master subsequent developmental tasks? We found that certain factors were crucial, and with many of these the social worker's role was especially helpful.

Perhaps the most basic factor is that a bereavement happens to an individual child whose personality is characterized, not only by his age or development phase, but also by his own strengths and weaknesses. The comprehensive equilibrium and health of his personality at the time of the bereavement will, to a considerable extent, determine how this bereavement will affect him and how it will be coped with. This does not imply that any difficulty is going to become an obstacle to the mourning of a loved one. There are always some personality difficulties that are strangely untouched, but, by and large, we found that a bereavement is such a terrible stress that it bares the weaknesses and conflictual areas in the existing personality. I think there is little that the social worker can do about that at the time of bereavement. For example, Jimmy was 6 years old when his father died of leukemia. In many ways Jimmy was a well-functioning schoolboy, but his own recent appendectomy had been quite a stressful experience that he had not yet mastered bodily or emotionally at the time of the father's death. Moreover, he had to cope with some long-standing troubles—low self-esteem, a tendency to feel disliked· by peers, a symptom of bedwetting, and an intense ambivalence of love and hate feelings that interfered in his relationships and in his ability to enjoy activities. These new and old difficulties, rather than his young age, presented obstacles to his acceptance and mourning of his father's death.

The next factor is the form and circumstance of the death. Parents of young children do not die in a nice way or in a timely way. It is the nature of a childhood bereavement that the parent's death is particularly tragic and untimely. Murders, accidents, the sudden onset of diseases of a peculiar nature, debilitating diseases, or suicides—all the worst forms of death are those that befall a child's parents and, as such, add a significant measure of hardship for the bereaved. The unpredictable suddenness of a parent's death or the debilitatingly painful years that precede it have a tremendous influence on the child's ability or inability to cope with the ensuing stress. Sometimes we have had children whose parents have died in an automobile accident with the child in the vehicle. In other instances, a youngster's care had been neglected for years owing to the parent's increasing disability, or the child had witnessed the parent's bodily or mental deterioration. All such details determine the effect on the child. Indeed, many children have failed to deal with the parental death not because they did not know how to mourn, but because they could never get beyond the acute anxiety of the form of the death to cope with mourning afterward.

Another factor is that of understanding death. In our experience, children become interested in death as toddlers and can, from then on, be helped to understand what death means in concrete and simple terms. When children have experiences with dead flies, ants, or worms, or with dead animals by the roadside, they can be assisted to develop some concept of what death means in realistic terms. For example, when they notice that a dead insect does not move, it helps to confirm their observation, to use the word *dead,* and to add that dead things do not move. With later experiences they may learn some of the other signs of death—that one does not eat, or sleep, or make sounds, that one feels no pain—and gain some understanding of the various causes of death and what happens to the corpse. Those children who had already mastered such basic knowledge, when bereaved, were able to cope better with the loss of the loved one. If the bereavement confronted them with death for the first time and they then had to learn about its concrete aspects, it was very much harder for them; they had to understand death and emotional loss at the same time. It was also much more difficult to grasp the realistic manifestations of death when these had to be related directly to a loved person.

Another aspect that was crucial was the need for personal and psychological safety following the bereavement. Sometimes children of all ages have been portrayed as being selfish after a death, interested only in their mealtimes, in who will buy them the next pair of shoes, or in who will be at home in the evening, while being apparently unable to address themselves to the more grown-up feeling of longing and missing. Our experience shed a different light on this. Every normal adult needs to take care of his own survival first before he can mourn. He does so by planning ahead with insurance policies or family support or getting employment, but his care for himself brings assurance to support his bodily and psychological needs. He has friends and family who survive with him, and it is taken for granted that he will use these relationships to their fullest extent. If he does not take care of himself, he will die. He cannot learn to mourn.

Freud (1915) said many years ago that the pleasure of living has to be greater than the wish to join the deceased, and this is what makes surviving and ultimately mourning possible. The child cannot write insurance policies for himself and cannot summon the community and friends for help. He has to rely on the surviving family to supply his needs. Even more cardinal to the child than to an adult is the threat, and wish, of joining a beloved parent in death. He has to be sure of his survival and of his pleasure in survival before he can address himself to the mourning task, which demands coming to terms with a world that no longer contains the deceased loved one. In some instances surviving parents realize this and elect to reduce their living standards to be able to remain at home, to keep the same house rather than move to a new apartment. One mother said, "You know, we haven't had any meat since my husband died, but we've all been together." It made an enormous difference. In other instances the mother went out to work, the house was sold, the children went to day care centers, and the additional stress, the separations, and upheavals made it quite impossible for the surviving children to begin their mourning. Needless to say, the surviving parent is the one who has the crucial role in so many ways that one is tempted to say it depends on him or her whether the children will be able to mourn. The younger the children are, the more this is so. Older children can sometimes mourn on their own, although it may even be very difficult for them, but the younger the child, the more he needs the parent's "permission," empathy, and understanding to mourn.

I do not mean mourning together in the sense of crying when the mother or the father is crying. The child and the surviving parent had a different relationship to the deceased. They can mourn together in terms of mutual understanding, empathy, and respect for each other's feelings rather than in imitation of each other.

Ways in Which the Social Worker Can Help

The social worker can help most at the time of bereavement in certain specific areas. One is to help a bereaved family maintain the continuity of home, routine, and caregiving that existed before. It is so natural for a bereaved spouse to deal with the initial stress by being highly active and making many changes that it often takes special help to persuade such a parent that the child needs the stability of staying put, that his ability to adjust to the loss of one parent depends on there being as few changes as possible in the rest of his daily world.

The other area is in helping the surviving parent to teach the child about the concrete reality of death in general and of his parent's death in particular. This does not mean overwhelming a child with every gory detail but enabling him to understand the reality and nature of the parent's death, its causes, and the way the body will be disposed of. Sometimes children accept the concrete aspects of death better than parents do. For example, one father, whose wife had died, worked very hard with his young children to help them understand what "dead" meant and what one does with dead people. Some months later their grandfather died, and the father needed to repeat the painful task. When he told his 4-year-old girl that grandfather would be put in a nice comfortable box with soft blankets, she interrupted him and said, "But if he is really dead then it doesn't matter about his being comfortable in the coffin" (Barnes, 1964).

The third area is that of helping parents understand some of the ways in which a child's mourning is revaled; these are not necessarily the same ways as those the adult shows his mourning. Some people feel that open sadness, crying, and raving are proper signs of mourning. This is not our experience. Mourning is an internal, mental piece of work. The affects that go with it may be private and silent in some; for others they may be openly expressed. Parents need to appreciate that mourning takes time and that identification plays an important part in the process; for a child, this can present special difficulties. To identify with a deceased parent may mean, for the child, identifying with the symptoms that led to death. Under these circumstances the parent should sort out with the child which ways are helpful to be like Mommy or Daddy and which are not helpful. If the child's fears of identifying with the parent are so great that they stop his ability to mourn, perhaps he needs help to become like the parent in some ways, but without actually having to die. For example, some months after her mother's sudden death, Laura often played lovingly with her dolls. However, she always pretended to be their auntie or babysitter and became quite irritated when anyone referred to the doll as "her baby." Laura's father understood that she feared being a mother lest she too meet an early death. He told Laura that she was as nice with her doll as her mother had been with her and that he looked forward to the time when Laura would be as nice a real mother as her own had been. He then added that it would be quite safe for Laura to be a mother because most live for a long time and eventually may become grandmothers like her own granny. Laura could therefore have a baby but would not have to die young.

In this brief discussion of parental bereavement in childhood I have attempted to highlight some of the factors that enable children to master this unique extreme stress and to outline some of the areas in which social workers can assist families at the time of such a loss. The limited scope of this chapter unfortunately makes it impossible to do justice to the great intellectual complexity of this topic, as well as to the intense emotional hardship it entails, both for the worker and for the bereaved. I hope, therefore, that it will serve the reader merely as an introduction to further, more detailed study.

References

Barnes, M. 1964. "Reactions to the Death of a Mother." *Psychoanalytic Study of the Child,* Vol. 19, pp. 334–57. New York: International Universities Press.

Freud, S. 1915. *Mourning and Melancholia,* standard edition, Vol. 14, pp. 237–58. London: Hogarth (1957).

Furman, E. 1974. *A Child's Parent Dies.* New Haven and London: Yale University Press.

Furman, R. 1964. "Death and the Young Child: Some Preliminary Considerations." *Psychoanalytic Study of the Child,* Vol. 19, pp. 321–33. New York: International Universities Press.

McDonald, M. 1964. "A Study of the Reaction of Nursery School Children to the Death of a Child's Mother." *Psychoanalytic Study of the Child,* Vol. 19, pp. 358–76. New York: International Universities Press.

9

The Dying Child and His Family

Grace Fields

This discussion examines the role of the social worker with the dying child and his family in a 92-bed rehabilitation hospital. Whereas children are admitted to this facility because of a potential for physical improvement, some are afflicted with lethal diseases; for example, a child with anterior horn cell disease comes for treatment of an orthopedic problem; a child comes for postoperative rehabilitation care following the removal of a malignant brain or spinal tumor. Although these children constitute a small minority within the institution at any particular time, the social service staff has worked with a number of them and their families over the years. By retrospective examination of our work with this population, it was hoped that our collective skill and knowledge base would be strengthened and that our search for improved treatment methods would be provided with a broader focus.

A staff committee was formed to work on this project. Participation was voluntary. The membership * had an experiential perspective on this work; their average length of time on staff was six years. All had worked, or were working, with terminally ill children and their families.

* Staff committee members: Glenn Blake, MSW; Mary Evans, MSW; Betty Flanagan, BA; Allan Zimmerman, MSW; Ellen Sarna, MSW, former staff member.

The approach was to recollect a list of the children with a fatal diagnosis with whom they had worked. A child was defined as fatally ill if he suffered from a disease that, according to medical prognosis, made it unlikely that he would reach adulthood. Although a systematic record retrieval by disease entity would have been possible, we chose the staff recall method, because we believed these to be the children with whom our involvement had been such as to yield the most vital practice information. The clinical charts of 39 children were then reviewed, and the worker involved was interviewed if possible.

Using three constellations of needs—the child's, the family's, and the institution's—as pivotal points, we examined the social worker's responsibility and effort to help.

Helping the Child

The social worker offers the child an honest, open-ended relationship. Though the course, cost, and content of the relationship cannot be plotted in advance, the commitment is that, when a child comes to the institution with a fatal diagnosis, or if such a diagnosis is made while the child is there, his social worker will not terminate contact so long as the child needs him. If the child's transfer to another institution gives him another set of supportive figures, and the withdrawal of our social worker is a constructive action in terms of his using those other helpers, that action will be taken. However, if no case transfer can be made, the obligation is to remain related to the dying child. This is simply the ethic of nonabandonment in departmental policy form.

Played out, it meant that when Jill, aged 16, was undergoing radiation treatment at an acute care facility, her social worker continued to visit her. When Jill's physical condition deteriorated and she could no longer speak, a means of communication was devised through eye blinking. The right eye blinked for "yes," the left eye for "no."

If the child needs to be sad or weak or tired, the social worker does not interfere. A child may or may not discuss his impending death in explicit terms. His concerns may be disguised, but Tom's nervous question, "Where did the boy down the hall go?" or Dan's teasing his social worker by "playing dead" are cues to be responded to with reinforcement of the child's strengths and with tenderness. In an institutional climate, where the norms are optimism and improvement, the specific needs of the dying child and his family may be expressed so subtly that they are sublimated to the pressures of dealing with rehabilitation goals. The social worker's commitment is to offer opportunity for honest acceptance of feelings that may be alien to the milieu of normality, activity, and enthusiasm, while at the same time to help the child draw from that climate a "bank account" of experiences. Those deposits are made up of gains in all areas: physical functioning, intellectual growth, development of skills, nurturing of relationships, and the opportunity for whatever growth the child can make in the time he has.

Helping the Family

The social worker is concerned with and becomes involved in all the needs of the family members. Of the 39 cases we examined there was marital stress or conflict in 12. In another 12 the parents were separated or divorced. In 4 cases a parent was deceased. Eleven families had stable marriages.

Social work intervention was directed toward reducing marital stress and helping spouses to stop battering and blaming each other. In some instances the change in pattern operated only until the death of the child. In others basic problems were resolved within the context of work on inescapable and mutual problems.

Family work involves the balancing of the needs of other siblings against those of the dying child. Tom's sister tired of visiting him in the hospital "to cheer him up," and yet she feared to have him home to visit: "What if he dies here?" Jackie's sister would not wear her dying sister's coat. In various combinations and on separate time schedules, family members are subject to feelings of grief, resentment and fear. They often need help in tolerating and legitimatizing their own and each other's responses.

Parents can be helped to influence the quality of the remaining time the family has together. A father, whose 4-year-old daughter had been diagnosed as having anterior horn cell disease, said, "We don't want her to be a velvet pillow princess." He was seeking a framework of experiences that would use the time well, but the mother could not work on this yet. The social worker had to respond to their separate but interlocked needs.

The social worker serves as advocate as well as helper for the family with the dying child. The physical, financial, and emotional burdens related to prolonged terminal illness are not timebound. Community supports are uneven in quality and availability. When the child is in physical crisis, helpers mobilize; but as the patient's condition reaches a plateau, they fade away, leaving the family and child alone and lonely with the losing battle. Here is an example.

This was a stressful time for the parents. They were overwhelmed by the recommendation that Lora be discharged. They expressed their inability to care for her at home, fearing that she might deteriorate more rapidly. They expressed anxiety about the possibility of her becoming comatose and their inability to procure help for her quickly.

Medically based supports are more effective if the illness is sharply and accurately defined, with the time of death predictable and preferably imminent. If long-term care is needed, if intellectual ability outlasts physical strength, solutions are difficult to find. Community orientation and funding reflect physical rehabilitation as "worthy," but maintenance of the human spirit when the physical battle is a goal with only tenuous roots finds little substantive support in our value system. Results are the lack of such support for families with terminally ill children, the absence of chronic care institutions that are emotionally and intellectually stimulating, and the paucity of educational plans for children whose minds can be more active than their bodies.

At 15 Ernie, suffering from muscular dystrophy since he was 4, was bright but could not read. Mastery of that skill was probably his greatest gain during a three-month hospital stay necessitated by an illness other than his chronic degenerative disease.

Social work cannot change situational reality for any family. What it can do is offer help in searching out the best among undesirable alternatives, respect and empathy for both child and family as their minimal entitlement, and an institutional commitment to comprehensive health care. But all of these are costly enterprises, as the following example shows.

Parents are hesitant about placement in the type of facility available. Counseling has focused on joint exploration about placement or home management, taking into account the needs of each member of the family. Specific concerns about caring for Peggy have been her sister's asthmatic condition and the constant necessity for clinic visits with the possibility of emergency hospitalization, Mrs. K.'s isolation from family and friends who could assist in caring for the children, Mrs. K.'s nervous, compulsive nature that requires supportive medication, Mr. K.'s difficulty in taking time off from work and the threat of losing his job, and Peggy's need for physical care as well as 24-hour supervision and play stimulus. The parents are frightened about Peggy's prognosis and their overwhelming sense of guilt if Peggy should deteriorate suddenly while at home.

Institutional Goals

By clearly articulating the connection between limited or temporary physical gains and the quality of life for the dying patient and his family, the social worker can reinforce the healing nature of the institution for those who cannot be cured. Professional efforts, both physical and emotional, interplay in this record, as illustrated in this example.

Marilyn had a period of several weeks of weakness and discomfort at the acute care hospital but gradually began to benefit from the treatments. On the adult ward in a single room, she had the companionship of elderly patients, with no teenagers and only a couple of young adults. She found the loss of activities and the confinement to bed difficult. She was eager to talk and quickly focused on the realities and problems of planning for her future. As the time of readmission to our rehabilitation hospital approached, Marilyn expressed concern about the loss of her hair as a result of the chemotherapy she had undergone and the reaction of her peers to her appearance. She had a wig that she rarely wore because it was uncomfortable and did not fit properly. The occupational therapist, social worker, and nursing staff became increasingly involved in trying to combat Marilyn's boredom and restlessness. Their interest gave her support and helped her leave her bed and gain some independence in using a wheelchair. Unfortunately, owing to limits in supervision, she was confined to her bed frequently for long periods of near isolation and dependence on television. This was particularly difficult for her since she was able to use physical activities and companionship as ways to keep herself going and to prevent herself from dwelling on multiple problems.

The social worker can help other staff with their involvement with the dying patient. For Ann, who had physical and emotional problems following the removal of acoustic neuroma, this meant collaborating with her teacher, whose feelings of pity for Ann made it difficult for her to make realistic demands on her. Before she had become ill, she had been a bright student and still had the capacity to be productive.

The social worker can help other concerned staff by taking over a post-discharge relationship that they have neither the ability nor the obligation to sustain. The "loving and leaving" problem is thus minimized for the patient.

Within the institution, social service has a responsibility to develop plans that extend beyond episodic institutional treatment for those patients for whom this necessity is predictable. The work is difficult, but when we have been able to effect preplanned linkages, it has made the difference between the patient's having a planned place to belong to and the intolerable insecurity of a frantic search for a place to die. When such plans are well laid, clear spokesmen as well as advocates are needed within the institution.

Robert, who came to us following cancer surgery, was subject to foster home placement if he recovered and to moving back and forth from the rehabilitation hospital to the acute care hospital if the disease progressed and further treatment was indicated. A clearly made commitment on the part of three institutions gave him some protection. Yet the question was raised for Robert, as it has been for other children, "Isn't there some other place where he would be better off?" The social worker must be able to answer a question like this with knowledge and conviction and to parlay that question into consciousness raising and quality-of-life planning.

Unfinished Business

As we reviewed our hospital records, it became clear that the quality-of-life goals were not explicit. Medical, therapy, nursing, social service, and medical staff meeting notes in the clinical chart rarely referred directly to the treatment goals that would be derived despite the terminal nature of the disease process. Although the study group was able to recall ways the institution had set such goals and fulfilled them, department by department, this work was rarely a matter of record. A professional responsibility was felt that had not been institutionalized into that accountability framework of the hospital, the patient's medical chart. We assessed this as a "chart deficit" that we should make efforts to correct, beginning with the social service entries.

These children and their parents offer clues to their needs that can be evaluated only by more mutual and regular examinations of our own efforts. More sharing of what to do with these clues and of what we discover is helpful in specific cases is constantly necessary to refine our skills and provide us with the emotional support needed for difficult, lonely work.

Our reflection on our work with these 39 children has made clear that the knowledge of probable death from a predictable cause within a projectable time period complicates but does not wipe out the setting and realization of certain life goals for the patient and his family. We believe that to understand these goals, even the unachievable ones, is the basis for helping. It is part of the bargaining for time and for something to make that time worthwhile. Such bargaining is the common tie that binds the fatally ill and their helpers together. It is the human condition.

10

Adolescents and Death

Rachel Rustow Aubrey

More than 30 years ago, Lindemann's now historic paper (1944) was published. Many of the subjects in his patient population were adolescents who had survived the Coconut Grove Nightclub fire in Boston. Since that time much research information on death, grief, crisis intervention, and brief therapy has been accumulated (Caplan, 1964; Bellak and Small, 1965; Parad, 1965; Small, 1971), and the effect of a parental death on the young child or on the mature adult has received considerable attention. However, very little is known about the relationship between an earlier parental loss and psychiatric illness that first presents in adolescence, as Seligman et al. (1974) have pointed out. This chapter discusses some of the personal responses to an actual, or anticipated, parental death as reported by adolescents in a clinical and an academic setting.

Documentation of the adolescent's preoccupation with his own death can be found in many sources. Shneidman (1972) presents a moving collection of essays by college students talking with each other about the meaning of contemporary life and death. Typical adolescent thinking about death is revealed in some of the major works of fiction that have fascinated young people for many decades. In the United States of the 1970s, most students from high school age on have been influenced by the existential ideas of Camus and Sartre, the Eastern mythology of Hesse, and the poets of the Beat Generation (Ginsberg, Corso, and Kerouac). Equally important are the life-and-death songs of idols such as Bob Dylan and Janis Joplin.

For present purposes I define adolescence as the years spanning puberty through the early twenties. Although Wittenberg (1968) refers to the late teens as "postadolescence," I have included this group in this study, especially since most of the cases reported here have been drawn from student populations. At present, when economic independence is increasingly difficult to achieve (a situation likely to be aggravated by the current unemployment and depression), a growing proportion of young people in their twenties are still completing their education. For many now in school, academics were interrupted by Vietnam; others dropped out by choice, in search of greater meaning than academic life could provide. Among those who have returned to the campus, some measure of continued dependence on parents, primarily financial but also emotional, is frequently unavoidable. When faced with a crisis such as a death, these young people find it difficult to reject parental coping patterns, even though their adolescent resources might sometimes serve them better.

In selecting the cases presented here I have drawn on several sources. Most of the clinical material derives from the files of a psychiatric office in a large urban university where both undergraduate and graduate students are seen. Additional life history data were volunteered by students in a sociology seminar I have long taught at a city college. Some of my most valuable insights were gained from my own two children, both students away at college, and from their many friends.

The Problem—Some Common Manifestations

Although it has often been said that death is the last taboo in Western society, it would be more accurate to say that the topic remains taboo for most middle-aged and older Western-educated adults; I have not usually found this to be the case with adolescents. In fact the opposite would appear to be true if spontaneous reactions are any valid indication. While doing research for this chapter I tried out the topic on many members of the academic community in which I live. Without exception my young (under 30) friends responded with exclamations of fascination and delight and offers of help. My middle-aged friends (including my professional colleagues) reacted to this project with stony silence and the thinly-veiled implication that I seemed to enjoy morbid preoccupations. I would suggest that in these strikingly opposite responses lies the very core of the problem faced by many adolescents when confronted with a death in the family. Whereas their immediate impulse might readily take them to their peer group for support, deference to, and lack of emotional freedom from, parents may act as a deterrent. The result is often an uneasy assumption of such parental coping mechanisms as denial, despair, guilt, and escape into meaningless activity. Like the adults around them adolescents tend to repress their feelings of anger and rage and thus avoid some of the vital aspects of the grief work that must be done if mental health is to be restored. Clinicians are familiar with the fate of repressed emotions, which are likely to present, often many years later, in very different attire. Four of the cases cited in the present study illustrate this particular phenomenon (Jennifer, Dina, Michael, and Daniel). Three reports demonstrate the importance of immediate psychotherapeutic intervention (Susan) or of spontaneous and creative use of nonclinical interventions and peer-group support (Nicholas and Juanita) in minimizing repression and neurotic symptom formation.

A random perusal of clinical notes on students who presented to a psychiatric service over a 12-month period revealed a very high incidence of cases where there had been an earlier parental loss. A larger number of students reported a family member currently ill with either cancer or major heart disease. With very few exceptions the actual or anticipated loss was not given as the presenting complaint. Instead the students usually presented with the commonly seen syndrome of depression and/or anxiety, concern about academic pressures, loneliness, and existential doubts about the meaning of life. Suicidal thoughts were often but not always elicited. Frequently the recent loss of a significant relationship with a peer (usually a girl or boy friend) had triggered the request for psychiatric help. The degree of distress reported was often excessive in relation to the loss described; only with very careful history-taking would some earlier loss(es) come to light. It then usually became clear to the clinician that the recent loss, however minor, had set off old feelings of abandonment, guilt, and rage in the patient. Once the immediate crisis was dealt with (an exam postponed, a depression brought within limits the student could tolerate), further exploration of the underlying loss was possible, but this was rarely done. Part of the reason is inherent in the mandate of most student psychiatric services, namely, to restore students to their prior level of functioning by appropriate crisis intervention while not usually embarking on intensive treatment. It further seemed, however, that some clinicians actually elected not to probe deeper into the significance of an earlier parental loss, even when continued therapy was undertaken. Although the date of a loss was usually noted, there was often no information on how the student had experienced it; on whether he had grieved then, later, or not at all; on how the loss had changed the family constellation psychosocially; and on what coping mechanisms had developed as a result. In other words the real significance of an earlier parental loss often remained unexplored.

It has been my experience that adolescent patients usually respond with great relief when encouraged to talk about the true meaning of an earlier death. Rapid development of insight, including the etiology of symptom formation and the ability to do reparative work, have often been astounding. Some patients may need to test whether the therapist is really able to deal with death or whether, like most other adults, he needs to be protected. Here a brief allusion to a personal loss may quickly convey the message "It's all right, I have been there," strengthening the therapeutic alliance. Except for the increasingly rare analytic patient with whom complete detachment and objectivity should perhaps prevail, there would seem to be no clinical contraindications to this slightly more personal approach.

In taking a careful history that includes significant data about a death in the family it is important not only to inquire into the cause of death but also to ascertain whether it was sudden or expected. This is especially important when the death—or anticipated death—is caused by cancer. The conspiracy of silence still shrouding the truth about malignant illness is particularly hard to maintain for adolescents used to discussing "heavy" issues with their peers. Family attitudes of denial, frequently encouraged by the family physician, often make it impossible for a young person to deal openly and honestly with the feelings of helplessness and rage so often found in relatives who are "survivors." Fears about heredity, or at least a predisposition to developing cancer, are rarely verbalized unless the clinician specifically elicits them. In my random review of cases, cited above, I found a very high proportion of students who had lost a parent through cancer; in several instances the other parent, or a sibling, was also ill with a malignant disease.

Recent research points to the importance of psychogenic factors in the etiology of cancer. LeShan and Worthington (1956) have shown a statistically significant relationship between object loss and cancer morbidity. In a study of 152 female cancer patients and 125 healthy controls they advance a three-stage pattern of development that they observed in 72 percent of the former. The early years of the cancer patient were characterized by a sense of loneliness resulting from a trauma, usually occurring before the age of seven. This was resolved in young adulthood by a meaningful relationship. When the latter terminated (through separation or death), the patients developed cancer within six months to eight years. Although they continued to carry on normal activities without overt symptom formation, they received little libidinal satisfaction and depleted themselves by continually giving to others more than they were able to receive.

Bahnson and Bahnson (1969) located the impact of loss in an etiologic psychic chain. In clinical life-history studies of 80 patients who developed cancer the authors found that a personal loss, such as a death, appeared to have been extremely traumatic and crucial to their future adjustment. Although the complex etiology of cancer has yet to yield its secrets, these findings should be of relevance to clinicians interested in cancer prevention. In their work with adolescents they may want to be particularly alert when case histories detail a recent loss, earlier losses, or a history of malignancy in the family. By continuing therapy with such patients beyond the immediate crisis it may be possible to help them do delayed mourning and grief work and thus lessen the tendency to regress somatically rather than behaviorally (Sohl, 1975).

Some Possible Interventions

The sending of professional crisis teams to the scene of a fire, tornado, or other disaster has slowly gained momentum. This technique for intervention is based on the gradual acceptance (in the Western hemisphere) of the concept that immediate ventilation of pain, grief, and rage, though hard on the bystander, is more likely to ensure full emotional recovery than is the traditional stiff-upper-lip approach on which so many clinicians were raised. I would suggest that there is an equally urgent need for outreach intervention when an adolescent death has occurred, especially if it was a suicide. College administrators and clinicians alike still nurse the fantasy that death should be a private affair, but it very rarely is—least of all when it is a sudden death in a college community. Almost invariably one or several peers of the suicide, or one-car-accident victim, had long known that he had been seriously depressed or playing Russian roulette with drugs, alcohol, and pills. These peers, acquaintances, or fellow residents will respond most readily to the student personnel worker or medical office clinician who drops by for a chat or makes it known his office door is always open. Such outreach interventions allow us to deal promptly with the inevitable guilt and "if onlys" that those left behind after a death almost invariably experience; further, they give us a unique chance to teach and demonstrate in action some of the most basic principles of crisis intervention.

For many years I have used several periods of a small undergraduate sociology seminar to teach crisis theory, with special reference to suicide prevention. Students in these seminars range from freshman to senior; they come from many different academic fields; a majority are poor and nonwhite. Few know the concept of crisis intervention, but a great many have already had to cope with very serious life crises, often alone. Using a very informal discussion format, I can invariably build on case illustrations volunteered by seminar members. Often one or several students will approach me later for some individual counseling and referral. A few years ago, invited by the senior class of a private high school to do a series of "rap sessions," I used the same approach with positive results.

It is my contention from these experiences that some discussion of death and basic crisis theory should be incorporated into high-school and college courses, much as sex and contraception have increasingly become part of academic curricula. A team network—including faculty, peer-group counselors, guidance and student personnel staff working in close liaison with mental health clinicians—might be most effective. Telephone hot lines, if properly staffed and supervised, can and already do render invaluable help to adolescents, and to an increasing number of their parents as well. Outreach programs at the school, college, and community levels could help greatly in alerting adolescents to some of the normal life crises they are likely to encounter and serve as a focal point for quick and more effective referrals for professional help when this is indicated.

As alternatives, or adjuncts, to psychotherapeutic interventions, I would like to stress the very vital role of art, music, and drama. When sad or depressed, many adolescents almost automatically put on a record or tune in their favorite station. Deference to parental feelings about such "escapism" may make some adolescents refrain from activities that could be highly cathartic (see case of Nicholas). If it is true that, given the freedom to use their own coping devices, many adolescents will do so instinctively, then parents and clinicians alike may need to be more flexible and creative in helping young people deal with a death in the family.

Case Illustrations *

Jennifer, the older daughter of a white middle-class family, was 15 when her father died suddenly of his first heart attack. Three days earlier Jennifer had left home to attend boarding school in another city, over her father's objections. She came home for the funeral, offered to stay, but was relieved when her mother encouraged her to go back to school and kept her younger sister at home. For the next 10 years Jennifer led a very stormy existence in her search to become the artist her father had not wanted her to be. She had several close brushes with death through heavy involvement in the drug scene and by taking an overdose when rejected by a lover. At 25, on the

* All names and certain identifying data have been changed.

verge of marriage to an illiterate farmer in another country, she was persuaded by friends to see a therapist.

Jennifer presented as a highly attractive but seriously depressed young
woman, with a partial paralysis of her right arm that prevented her from
preparing for her first art show. For years she had been able to draw only
when she was on stimulants acquired on the black market. She suffered
frequent short periods of depersonalization and was very promiscuous.
Crisis intervention included substituting an antidepressant medication for the
stimulants and discussing her fear of success as an artist. Her initial response
was dramatic; she regained full use of her arm, took a part-time job, and
embarked on twice-a-week therapy. She and her therapist soon learned that
whenever Jennifer was about to go into "one of my states" (depersonalize),
they would have to probe for rage: at the father who deserted her, having
never really loved her, and at the mother who let it all happen and kept the
younger sister home while Jennifer was encouraged to make it on her own.
Considerable delayed grieving was done in the sessions, and much more
reparative work lies ahead. Jennifer is beginning to learn that adult life,
including her lovers, cannot make up for the love she missed as a child,
even before her father's death. Support from significant others of the parental generation has been a crucial adjunct to psychotherapy, as has Jennifer's
ability to write out her feelings, diary fashion, even when she is unable to
verbalize them.

Susan, the younger child of white professional parents, was 15 when her
stepfather died of recurrent cancer. Susan's mother and father had been
divorced when she was 5, and she had had a year of biweekly psychotherapy
at age 9, at the time of her mother's remarriage, to help her work out her
conflicting loyalties to her two fathers. Stepfather's primary cancer was
diagnosed shortly after the new marriage, but Susan's mother elected not to
tell the children, since, following his surgery, he was pronounced cured. After
about 2 years Susan switched all of her loyalty to her stepfather, and a relationship of deep love and trust developed. When the cancer did recur in incurable form some 5 years after the initial surgery, the parents told both
children and let them help in caring for stepfather at home, where he died
some six months later. Recognizing that this new loss might reopen many
old scars, Susan agreed that she should reenter therapy, this time with a
young male therapist; her first therapist had been a woman. She stayed in
therapy for 2 years until she went away to college.

Now 20 years old and in her junior year abroad, Susan offered the following comments:

"I guess the immediate effect of a death depends a lot on what the relationship was like—whether the child is a son or daughter—I know more

sons than daughters who have lost a parent (why do fathers have to die more often?).

"Maybe it leaves you sort of scared of your own future—especially in relationships—I always wonder: will I be left alone? As a result, I am either afraid of reaching out, or of letting go of friends. I have many fantasies that important people may die, especially my grandparents—this fear is especially bad when that anniversary date (of stepfather's death) comes around again.

"I think it (stepfather's death) has given me a greater sense of responsibility, not only toward my mother and brother, but also toward my studies and future plans—maybe because I know I have to break my own ground and create my own image that much more.

"For a long time I was mad at my mother for telling me about the impending death two months after she told my brother. I know she felt I was so very young and might get through Christmas a bit easier not knowing—but I knew anyhow. . . ."

Susan's mother reports that, though Susan went through some stormy adolescent periods, her overall adjustment has been very good. As a measure of her emotional independence Susan decided to go abroad for her junior year—her first long separation from her mother and brother, to whom she is very close. It has been a positive experience for her. Undoubtedly the two periods of psychotherapy, plus the open sharing in the knowledge of impending death and being allowed to help, made this young woman's adjustment much easier than that of Jennifer.

Dina, age 23, presented to a college counseling service with a mild mood depression and some vocational questions that she used as rationalization for seeking help. The oldest of three children of a poor black family, Dina had never known her father. Her mother died when Dina was six, after a long illness described as hepatitis but sounding to her therapist like a form of malignant disease. Dina vividly recalls when the ambulance came to take mother away for the last time, leaving Dina in charge of the family that night. The children were then separated and raised by different relatives. Dina resented all of her relatives and was soon going it alone, on her excellent intelligence and pleasant manner. She maintained little contact with her siblings and made but a passing reference to the "mysterious" death of a sister next younger in age (probably of an overdose) when Dina was 20.

After considerable testing out in the therapeutic situation Dina established a strong relationship to her therapist and began to reveal what is clearly a lifelong depression, most successfully masked by numerous activities to help others and specifically those of her race. Increasingly Dina became aware that others would "dump" on her and that she resented it.

Dina never allowed her therapist to dwell on the meaning of her early losses (father and mother before the age of 6; sister at age 20). Intellectually she could connect these traumas with her fear of closeness to men; though a very attractive young woman, she allowed herself to stay only in brief relationships. Concurrently with seeing her therapist Dina wrote beautiful and often very angry poetry that she sometimes brought to the sessions.

She terminated therapy when she felt "much better" and had become totally involved in her graduate studies. The therapist shared with her the fact that much more work needed to be done some day if she was to have an emotionally gratifying personal life. Since Dina never truly grieved her early losses and had never sustained a genuinely close relationship as an adolescent, one might predict that the loss of a significant relationship in the future may precipitate a serious crisis.

Michael, age 23, sought psychiatric help in a university clinic ten days after arriving in New York for graduate study. The youngest of four children of a very religious family, Michael had spent four years in an all-male sectarian college, where he was looked up to as a leader and could hide from himself his lack of interest in girls.

Presenting symptoms were typical of those frequently seen in out-of-town first-year graduate students: vague depression and anxiety about more rigorous academic standards, loneliness, and many existential doubts about the future. Less typical was Michael's painful confession that he was still virgin and terrified of being impotent with a woman. He presented as a highly defensive and intellectualized young man who willingly reported facts but rarely revealed any related feeling.

Michael's early years were studded with losses. The only child of his mother's second marriage, he had a half-brother who was 3 years old when his father was killed in a car accident. Mother then married Michael's father, who left the family when Michael was 3, the divorce becoming final when he was 5. Michael was exceedingly close to his mother and slept in her bed until, when he was 12, she was married a third time, to a widower with four children. He disliked his stepfather and stepsiblings and was glad to get away to school, even though this required embracing stepfather's very devout religion.

It took considerable probing before Michael "remembered" that mother had had a serious cancer operation the previous year and was making a rather slow comeback. He had never discussed this with her, nor, as he suddenly remembered, the fact that mother herself had almost died in the car accident that killed her first husband. She was pregnant at the time and told Michael the doctors opted to save her and let the baby die.

It was decided that Michael would benefit from combined individual and group therapy. Though most skeptical at first, he slowly opened himself to feelings. He has had his first heterosexual experience, which was just that and no more, since Michael continues to fear involvement and closeness. His academic work has improved and with it his commitment to staying in therapy. Much work remains to be done.

Daniel, also age 23, was brought in a state of acute crisis to a university psychiatric office by his roommates. Presenting symptoms included inability to take impending exams or to concentrate on any academic work, insomnia, anxiety, a fear of losing control and breaking things, and a lifelong history of depression. The oldest of three children of a middle-class, white, Catholic family, Daniel led a lonely and anxious existence punctuated by somatic complaints as he went through parochial school and college. Now in his first year of graduate study Daniel had many doubts about his abilities. Precipitating the acute crisis, in addition to the exams, was the fact that father was slowly recovering from his second heart attack, had had a plastic aorta replacement, and could no longer work. A hard-driving, self-made immigrant who had been brutalized in his childhood, the father repeatedly suggested that Daniel drop out and earn a decent living as a mechanic, even though he had maintained a superior academic record since grade school.

Crisis intervention included excusing Daniel from the midterms, prescribing a mild tranquilizer, and giving weekly therapy sessions. Daniel responded by quickly returning to his prior level of functioning. He then requested continued therapy, confessing to a preoccupation with sex but a fear of losing his virginity. He recognized that his sexual conflict was more serious than that of his many Catholic peers and that "something" was urging him to find a girl and marry her quickly.

Daniel was readily able to accept that his sense of panic was at least in part related to knowing his father would probably not survive another heart attack. His fear (wish?) that father might die and leave him responsible for the family was explored and worked through. After a few weeks of therapy Daniel had his first heterosexual experience, after which he tortured himself trying to decide whether the girl was worthy of his love. At this point he felt he was taking on the entire Catholic Church. The therapist suggested they enlist the help of a liberal Catholic priest. After a few sessions with him Daniel began to make very great strides in therapy. Three months after he first presented for help he has taken several exams and is determined to finish his graduate degree. He is finding it difficult to give up his current girl friend, though he knows he does not want to marry her and would really like to "play the field" for a while. It is hoped that enough therapeutic work can be done to ensure that Daniel will go on living his own life when the father does die.

Nicholas, age 18, the older of two children of white professional parents, had left home for his freshman year at college when his father's illness of some months was diagnosed as an incurable malignancy. In a long phone call, his mother explained the full truth to Nicholas and suggested he talk it out with his best friend before coming home to visit. When he did come down for the first of many weekend visits, the father had asked and been told the exact details of his condition; he knew that he would have at most only a few months to live. He rejected hospitalization and with it the option of experimental therapies that might have added a little time to his life. Instead he decided to use his time in the most creative way possible, insisting that everyone go about their usual business while he continued work on a writing project and also put the family affairs in order. On his weekend visits Nicholas had many long talks with his father about his future and about life and death. He promised to help look after his younger brother and his mother. Often the family grieved together quietly; sometimes the boys would sit in the kitchen trying to imagine how life would be without father. A small kitten joined the family and was a great comfort to all. Each week Nicholas returned to college, where he received vital support from his roommates and also from two professors in whom he confided.

When the father died four months later, Nicholas stayed home for one week to help out. He offered to transfer to a city college but was relieved when encouraged to stay on at his chosen school. The day before returning to college he was cast in the lead of a college dramatic production. In deference to what he assumed his mother would wish, he was about to turn down the offer when she insisted he take the lead. Six weeks later, Nicholas gave a strong and moving performance in *The Marriage* by Witold Gombrowicz. The play explores the shifting relationship between reality and imagination; Nicholas's role was a multiple one portraying both father and son. As he tore about the stage shouting out his pain and rage at life and death, few in the audience knew how vitally cathartic this role was at this critical time in his life.

Nicholas has had no therapy and does not feel the need for it. He has done very well academically, and, five years after his father's death, is in the graduate school of his choice. He lives in an excellent relationship with his girl friend and has maintained meaningful contact with his mother and younger brother.

Juanita was just 17 and a high school graduate when she married her 20-year-old husband. Both were first-generation New Yorkers of Latin American immigrant families. Seven years after their marriage her husband died of a sudden heart attack, leaving her with two young children, a girl aged 5 and a baby boy of 10 months. Three years later she enrolled as a freshman at college. An unusually attractive and sensitive young woman, she has greatly enriched the seminar mentioned above with insights gained from her personal experiences as she gradually recovered from the death. She offered the following comments:

"After the first hard grief, I was totally scared; in all my married life I had been protected; I had never worked. Though everyone was very supportive, what they said seemed incoherent to me.

"Rather than turn to my family, who wanted to baby me, I turned to a few close friends who did not try to suffocate me with their love; they alone recognized that I had to get my own head. They sat around with me in endless rap sessions and I talked and talked. I felt I should do everything at once. Being suddenly single again means many different things: it means some of your couple friends drop you because you have now become a threat to their marriages; it means that good male friends who used to respect you as a married woman suddenly desire you just because you are now available. It also meant that some of my married girl friends took another close look at their marriages, realizing it might just happen to them; two went out to find themselves jobs.

"My most difficult problem was my children: they had been so very close to their father. When I sat down with my daughter to tell her Daddy was dead, she began to cry, like a whimper, and then she never referred to him again for a whole six months. Only then did she open up because she had had a dream about her Daddy. Then she began to cry and talk of her fear that I might die, too. I tried to comfort her and keep the memory of Daddy alive by having pictures around. I also told the children that while we had sometimes quarreled (which they had seen), we always loved both of them very much.

"My baby boy at first did not seem to miss his Daddy very much, but suddenly he began to cling to whatever male might be visiting. I noticed that the little boy had no structure to his life; I felt terrible for having neglected him! Again my friends (two young couples and two single people) came to my aid and said: 'All right, so you were not fully with it for a while, but that's only natural, and now you will shape up and stop being so self-centered!' Then I knew I have to start living positively again and make it up to the children. . . .

"I now have a close relationship with a man who is divorced and has three children. It's as if we were drawn together by default. At first my children totally rejected him, but now they sense his love for me and for them, and it is getting easier. . . .

"Coming back to school has been hard for all of us. I am often scared, but deep inside I know I will make it."

Summary and Conclusions

This chapter discusses the personal response of adolescents to an earlier parental death, as reported by some students seen in a psychiatric setting and by others who volunteered life history material. Although sudden death of a parent or anticipated death following a long illness is a common event among high school and college populations, apparently few adolescents seek professional help when the loss actually occurs. Instead they either turn to the peer group for support or attempt to cope alone. A later and relatively minor loss, such as the breakup of a romantic involvement, may set off considerable distress, and the student, often in a state of acute crisis, is then referred to a clinician.

Analysis of relevant case material suggests strongly that clinicians may need to go beyond the usual brief interventions if the adolescent is to be restored to mental health. The importance of careful, in-depth history-taking is stressed, with the goal of better understanding the psychodynamic and sociocultural meaning of an earlier parental death. Given an opportunity to make conscious and work through related feelings, some adolescents may recover with almost dramatic speed. Others, especially isolated young people without the support of significant others, may need long-term psychotherapy.

It is suggested that, whereas the topic of death still remains taboo for many adults, including clinicians, adolescents may be much more open to an honest discussion of it. A possible reason may be inherent in their very youth; to a healthy young person personal death seems remote unless he has already experienced a personal loss. Furthermore, as one-time members of the student drug scene and avid consumers of existential literature and songs focusing on death, adolescents may be better prepared to accept death as a fact of life. However, unresolved parent–child conflicts may inhibit them from dealing with a personal death in their own way. Such feelings may be readily transferred to a clinician and thus block therapeutic work, unless the adolescent senses that the therapist has truly come to terms with his own feelings about death.

I believe that the basic concepts of crisis theory, grief, and mourning can, and should be, included in college and even high school cur-

ricula. More meaningful peer-group support and more effective referrals for professional help would result; it would also add to what is as
yet a very small body of knowledge on death and the adolescent.

References

Bahnson, C. B. and M. B. Bahnson. 1969. "Ego Defenses in Cancer Patients." *Annals of the New York Academy of Sciences*, pp. 164–72.

Bellak, L. and L. Small. 1965. *Emergency Psychotherapy and Brief Psychotherapy*. New York: Grune and Stratton.

Caplan, G. 1964. *Principles of Preventive Psychiatry*. New York: Basic
Books.

LeShan, L. and R. E. Worthington. 1956. "Personality as a Factor in the
Pathology of Cancer: A Review of the Literature." *British Journal of Medical Psychology* 29.

―― 1956. "Some Recurrent Life History Patterns Observed in Patients
with Malignant Disease." *Journal of Nervous and Medical Diseases* 124.

Lindemann, E. 1944. "Symptomatology and Management of Acute Grief."
American Journal of Psychiatry 101, no. 2 (September): 141–48.

Parad, H. J. 1965. *Crisis Intervention*. New York: Family Service Association of America.

Seligman, R. et al. 1974. "Effect of Earlier Parental Loss in Adolescence."
Archives of General Psychiatry 31.

Shneidman, E. S. 1972. *Death and the College Student*. New York: Behavioral Publications.

Small, L. 1971. *The Briefer Psychotherapies*. New York: Brunner/Mazel.

Sohl, P. A. 1975. "Psychogenic Factors in the Etiology of Cancer." *Smith
College Studies in Social Work* 45, February.

Wittenberg, R. 1968. *Postadolescence*. New York: Grune and Stratton.

11

The Losses of Middle Age and Related Developmental Tasks

Mary K. Parent

In the lifetime of the generation of Americans who are now between the ages of 44 and 65, certain population trends have emerged that promise great opportunity for this and future generations of mature Americans. Longer life, earlier child launching, better health for all, greater affluence, and higher general levels of education have converged as trends to produce a whole generation of individuals who can live a third of a lifetime in relative leisure. Yet, even as these trends have developed, it has become increasingly evident that the mature generation is beseiged with loss experiences affecting every area of life. Known as "omniconvergence" this phenomenon can be so devastating as to lead to profound states of depletion (Cath, 1965, pp. 40–44). Thus the "new years," as Simon (1968) called the period of relative freedom between child launching and retirement, may be a time of opportunity for life enrichment on the one hand or a time of profound grief and anguish on the other.

I have elsewhere suggested that certain developmental tasks are associated with the stresses of middle age and that the successful performance of these tasks is a necessary prerequisite to the mastery of the last of Erikson's developmental crises, "integrity versus despair," (Erikson, 1959, pp. 98–99). The tasks I have suggested are: (1) completion of life's goals, (2) evaluation of life's performance with resolution of conflict about life's failures and disappointments, and (3) preparation for decline (Parent, 1976, p. 16).

The position taken here is that the losses of middle age erode the self-esteem based on the role-bound identity of youth and that the aforementioned tasks lead one toward a self-affirmation that is more nearly role free. It is further suggested that this self-appraisal serves as an underpinning to the integrity of old age. Basic assumptions are that the functional roles of life are gradually given up during late maturity and that each such role loss may be perceived as a threat to one's very identity. Thus the loss of a role partner, such as a spouse, is perceived in much the same way as a mutilating experience such as loss of a body part (Parkes, 1972, pp. 343–49).

The fact that such losses are now occurring earlier in the lives of a significant number of people—people who are better able to cope with the resulting stress—has implications for social planning and for preventive intervention by all helping professions. The potential for new roles not restricted to survival and reproductive functions is an exciting prospect.

Completing Life's Goals

Climacteric is a word taken from the Greek work *klimakterikos,* meaning top rung of a ladder, and is thus fittingly symbolic of maximum attainment prior to decline, whether that be in the sexual area, as the term popularly suggests, or in any other area of life.

When people enter middle age they are likely to be climaxing careers, winding up child rearing, and participating in civic and religious affairs in ways appropriate to their capacity and attained status. In short they are coming near the end of the stage of life that Erikson spoke of as "generativity," a stage in which people are concerned primarily with establishing and guiding the next generation, though not necessarily their own offspring. Indeed, the term *genera-*

tivity may be used synonymously with terms such as *productivity*. During the stage of generativity the ego of the individual grows and expands through what Erikson poetically describes as "losing oneself in the meeting of minds and bodies" and results in "libidinal investment in that which is being generated" (Erikson, 1959, p. 97).

In the past many tasks of the generative stage continued well into old age. Families were larger and children were spaced throughout the child-bearing period, and so child launching occurred much later in life. Now, most couples have fewer children, spaced close together in the early years of marriage. Most prefer to have their children during their twenties. During the late forties and early fifties they launch their children and relinquish their child-rearing roles, a fact that may be more threatening to ego identity than loss of child-bearing potential, which was perhaps voluntarily abdicated at 30, or object loss, which modern research suggests is more a myth than a reality (Troll, 1971, pp. 188–192). Those women who regard themselves first as mothers are likely to feel threatened when this role is no longer appropriate. Loss of parental roles is a major loss of the middle years for all parents, but for those who have taken seriously those social expectations concerning "women's place," the loss may be devastating. Loss of parental role, then, becomes one of the first of a series of identity-threatening losses suffered by people during middle age.

Men, who in modern times enter the labor market later than before and leave it earlier (Neugarten and Moore, 1968, pp. 5–28), are vulnerable to identity-threatening losses in work roles. Rapid technological changes and the knowledge explosion make obsolete the knowledge and skills of older workers, forcing them perhaps first into subordinate positions and later into premature removal from work roles. The gradual transition of responsibility to hand-picked and personally trained successors in work roles is increasingly a phenomenon of the past. While retirement continues to be associated with the 65 and older age group, more middle-aged people are voluntarily or involuntarily slowing down in work roles, and some are taking early retirement.

Females, on the other hand, turn to the labor market in middle age. The modern trend is for women to enter the labor market earlier than men, retire from it during child rearing, and return during middle age. More women choose to work after children are grown, perhaps seeking satisfying roles to replace those lost. Widows and other female heads of households may work out of necessity. Fourteen percent of American women are widows, and half of these are under 65. Furthermore women are less likely than men to remarry after losing a spouse (Simon, 1968, pp. 3–88). To the extent that career women derive part of their identity from work roles, they are subject to the same threats as men regarding the loss of these roles. The woman who has chosen a career in lieu of marriage and children may be particularly distressed when these roles are threatened.

Object losses occur with increasing frequency throughout middle age. It is typically during this period that people lose their aged parents. Mixed emotions may accompany this loss, which may follow a prolonged period of anticipatory grief, a role reversal with diminishing reciprocity as senile parents fail increasingly to provide positive feedback, a sense of failure at caretaking (which is a major function of the stage of generativity), ambivalence, and guilt. In addition conflict may arise between siblings concerning the care of parents, which may result in loss of a source of support as an aid to coping with stress. One study indicates, however, that there is a strengthening of relationships between sisters during the middle years (Cumming and Schneider, 1961, pp. 498–507).

Many women and some men lose spouses during middle age. Much of the literature on bereavement deals with the nature of this most devastating loss. Identity is so tied to union with spouse that loss of the spouse is perceived as a loss of a major part of self. Repercussions are felt throughout the role network as the bereaved adapts to the status of single survivor and withdraws from couple-related positions. Disruptions in steady states of all relevant systems—social, psychological, and physiological—may be expected.

Other object losses occur in middle age. Friends and relatives, who themselves are growing older, die. Others may be lost as a result of those life-style changes that modify the composition of social networks. Not all such changes are traumatic losses, but any change involves some readjustment, and those that involve loss of partners in role functioning are always stressful.

Finally the biological changes of middle age may be perceived as loss. Primary and secondary aging processes produce modifications in feeling and appearance. Body image may suffer a narcissistic blow. As youth, beauty, and virility diminish, the middle-aged person may question his desirability in sex roles and his capacity to perform them adequately.

Although this constitutes only a partial list of the multiple losses of omniconvergence, it may be sufficient to demonstrate the extent of such losses and the way they are threatening to a role-bound identity. In our society men and women do tend to value themselves in relation to their accomplishments. They thrive on feedback from others about such accomplishments and are crushed when they feel they have failed to accomplish.

The middle aged person who, like others, needs affirmation of personal worth based on accomplishments in role performance, is highly vulnerable at this point, for the accomplishments of generativity are not personal accomplishments. To claim success as parents or employers, based on the accomplishments of grown children or employees, is to deny the children and the employees their own sense of accomplishment. Furthermore roles of the stage of generativity are by their very nature time limited. As the functions of such roles are fulfilled, the roles come to an end. This is, at first, threatening, and the middle aged person may call upon his repertoire of ego defenses to combat anxiety. Sublimations do help in the sense that they give time for the person to strengthen self for the deeper stages of life assessment yet to come.

Evaluating Life's Performances

Cath (1965) quoted an anonymous source as having said, "It is man's vanity to presume to matter." In the years of generativity the average individual had enough immediate feedback and hope regarding the future results of his work to cause him to believe that he mattered. In completing life's goals, as described above, with its resulting, and/or coincidental, role losses, he may begin to have rather serious doubts that he mattered. As he begins to assess his life's performance he may realize that indeed he mattered very little. This humbling and frightening experience would seem to be a necessary condition for the exploration of one's authenticity, which is part of the process by which integrity is to be acquired. As one looks back, he may recognize that it was vain of him to presume to matter so much.

This life evaluation process is likely to begin with an effort to see life in perspective. This is likely to dovetail with the relinquishing of role performance as a measure of personal worth, for, as he recognizes that he cannot credit himself for accomplishments of role partners, he seeks some other value base on which to judge himself. He may turn to religion or philosophy or he may involve himself in civic and philanthropic works or creative ventures.

This represents an effort to perceive himself as he exists, quite apart from what he may have meant to others. At first this is a belittling and frightening experience, for one's whole perception of self-worth is at stake. There is danger of regression, and indeed Cath (1968, pp. 40–44) warns of the danger of depletion when stressful experiences are too prolonged or too severe. Cath's description of states of depletion corresponds to Hans Selye's "stage of exhaustion," the last of three stages of the general adaptation syndrome by which the body adapts to stress. Selye described the stage of exhaustion as "a premature aging, a second childhood" (Selye, 1956, p. 14).

On the other hand, the life review process is in part an attempt at restitution. Restitution is another of Cath's concepts. In one sense this refers to nature's attempts to restore what has been damaged by such processes as producing new cells to replace those that die or through emotional renewal of affect by means of sublimation or other ego maneuvers. In a broader sense restitution is seen as an opportunity to make amends for past failures, mistakes, and inadequacies. In this sense it represents a rebirth of opportunity, a second chance to make life meaningful (Cath, 1965, pp. 40–44).

Life review is essentially a lonely process, for, stripped of role significance and hope of satisfaction from role performance and positive feedback from role partners, the person stands nude in his own sight.

At this point he is likely to see his own defenses for what they were. Supportive friends may be appreciated, but the individual must decide for himself if he had worth independent of the roles of generativity. Perhaps those who can help are those who share his memories. These are his contemporaries, people whose life experiences were comparable to his own or overlapped his. By reminiscing with them in his life review, he may be able to see past indiscretions and failures in their long-range perspective and be able to cope with them. More significant now in the "new years" is the opportunity to develop new roles that are less restricted to functions of survival and reproduction and more open to creative experiences and life enrichment.

Preparing for Decline

There is, I believe, a third task to be accomplished in late middle age, and that is preparing for decline. I refer to something more than the practical preparations for old age, such as simplifying life-style, preparing for financial security and physical care during decline, and, with some, the effort to win brownie points in spiritual areas. All of these are parts of the process, but it is the appraisal of the road ahead that gives the older person a totally new perspective, for it is at this point that he gains an emotional awareness of the fact that he will die. Emotional awareness lies somewhere between intellectual knowledge of a fact and emotional reaction to imminent threat. It is a quality of awareness that permits reflective consideration of what it means to die and thus what it means to have lived.

The reflection on death as an outcome of life may require some relief from the emotional upheavals and grief work of the losses of middle age. This may be the function of disengagement, an idea that demands further study.

At this point perception of his place in world history, as described by Erikson (1959 pp. 98–99), begins to both humble and glorify the individual. It includes a realization of the insignificance of one's life in relation to all time and all space, and yet it involves some awe that one so humble might have lived at all. Thus life itself is seen as having value, and one's own life becomes precious. When life is seen as transient, each moment is regarded as an opportunity to live more meaningfully. Order, beauty, truth, love, and other virtues are sought because they enhance life. I believe it is out of this type of reflection that integrity evolves.

Grotjahn (1955, pp. 419–27), commenting on the integrative task of the aging person, said the mature person is rare, but wisdom (the outcome of integrity according to Erikson, 1959, p. 98) is even more difficult to achieve. "Man is mature," he said, "when he has learned how to deal with the problems of living; he may be called wise when he has found his way of dealing with death."

Summary

In recent years population trends have converged to produce a generation of mature Americans who have the means, the education, and the freedom from socially defined, functional roles to embark on new life-enriching tasks. Yet the loss of functional roles has a devastating effect on the personality, for identity has been intimately bound to these roles from youth. The multiple losses during middle age subject the individual to repeated severe stress reactions that can lead to premature aging, depletion, and exhaustion.

It was suggested that there are certain developmental tasks that, when accomplished sequentially, aid the person in relinquishing his role-bound identity and affirming a self-worth that is more independent of the roles he has played in life. This process makes it possible for the individual to acquire integrity and to live a more meaningful life.

References

Cath, S. 1965. "Some Dynamics of Middle and Later Years: A Study in Depletion and Restitution." In *Geriatric Psychiatry: Grief, Loss and Emotional Disorders in the Aging Process,* eds. M. A. Berezin and S. H. Cath, pp. 21–72. New York: International Universities Press.

Cumming, E. and D. M. Schneider. 1961. "Sibling Solidarity: A Property of American Kinship." *American Anthropologist* 63 (1961):498–507.

Erikson, E. 1959. "Growth and Crisis in the Healthy Personality." In *Psychological Issues,* pp. 50–100. New York: International Universities Press, Inc.

Grotjahn, M. 1955. "Analytic Psychiatry in the Elderly." *Psychological Review* 42 (1955):419–27.

Neugarten, B. L. and J. W. Moore. 1968. "The Changing Age–Status System." In *Middle Age and Aging,* ed. B. Neugarten, pp. 5–21. Chicago: University of Chicago Press.

Parent, M. K. 1976. "Stress, Coping and Growth in Middle Age." Doctoral dissertation, School of Social Work, Columbia University.

Parkes, C. M. 1972. "Components of a Reaction to Loss of a Limb, Spouse, or Home." *Journal of Psychosomatic Research* 16 (1972):343–49.

Selye, H. 1956. *The Stress of Life.* New York: McGraw-Hill Book Co.

Simon, A. W. 1968. *The New Years: A New Middle Age.* New York: Alfred A. Knopf.

Troll, L. E. 1971. "The Family of Later Life: A Decade Review," *Journal of Marriage and the Family.* (May 1971):363–90.

12

Social Work with Geriatric Patients and Their Families: Past Neglect and Present Responsibilities

Jordan I. Kosberg

Death and the reality of the dying client have been ignored by the profession of social work. The profession is dedicated to the rehabilitation, positive change, restoration, or otherwise improvement of clients; death and dying are thus viewed as the antithesis of social work. Yet death and dying are omnipresent, and social workers do deal with death and dying in their professional capacities and their private lives.

As with death and dying, social work has had little involvement with geriatric patients within institutional settings. Indeed, the combination of "slowly dying," ill, and elderly patients within institutional settings further removes professional social workers. Social work assistance is seldom provided to the families of these residents; as a result, the elderly, in varying stages of dying, with fatal illnesses, and in fear of death are deprived of much needed social work assistance. Where and when families or elderly spouses grieve, there may be no social-work involvement to help with such reactions and responses to death of the loved one.

Social work and death have been discussed in relationship to working with the families of dying children, the loss of the wage earner, suicide prevention, terminal cancer, catastrophic events (e.g., earthquakes, hurricanes, train crashes), or crises to a nuclear family. Little has been written specifically about social work with the dying geriatric patient, and this is especially true for such patients within institutional settings.

This chapter focuses on reasons for the lack of social-work involvement with dying geriatric patients within institutional settings and with their families. Roles and responsibilities for the profession of social work and the professional social workers are discussed. This chapter does not discuss treatment modalities and intervention methods; rather it presents an overview of issues and problems that permeate society in general, and the profession of social work in particular, as related to death and dying in geriatric institutions.

Social Work Within Geriatric Institutions

Institutions and institutional care have been widely discussed and criticized (whether prisons, mental hospitals, nursing homes, general hospitals, or others). Critics have assailed the characteristics of such facilities as being incongruent with the basic needs of the institutionalized populations, leading to such conditions as disculturation, psychological damage, isolation, stimulus deprivation, mortification, psychological stripping, and stigmatization (Sommer and Osmond, 1967; Goffman, 1961).

The institutionalization of the ill aged has been used as a panacea. As Glaser and Strauss state (1968): "In many countries, special institutional provision is made for people who are expected to live for some time while dying slowly." They refer to nursing homes, mental hospitals, and geriatric wards found in Veterans Administration and city and county hospitals. However, we know that the ill health of aged residents exacerbates adverse reactions to institutionalization. Findings of high mortality rates, deterioration, and other adverse effects are too consistent to be refuted. Further, institutions for the aged, whether nursing homes, homes for the aged, or mental or general hospitals, are generally the final setting for the residents. This fact has led social scientists and practitioners to describe institutions for the aged as "hiding places to die" (Markson, 1971), "the last refuge" (P. Townsend, 1964), and "the last segregation" (C. Townsend, 1971). Gustofson (1972) has written, "Dying: The Career of the Nursing Home Patient." The great majority of nursing homes in our country are proprietary, which further complicates the situation. There are many who doubt the possibility of providing both adequate care for ill and elderly residents and profit for owners.

Who would deny the potential importance of social workers within institutional settings for the aged? The roles for social workers are prodigious in assisting the institutionalized aged who are "the most powerless, voiceless, invisible, and uncared-for group in this country" (Kosberg, 1973). Whether at intake, giving casework to residents, relieving the guilt of family members, working with groups, making referrals, organizing volunteers, training staff, caring for the dying patients and their bereaved families, or dealing with the anxieties and fears of patients nearing death, the roles are numerous and important.

Yet the involvement of social workers has been limited and their presence within institutional settings for the aged infrequent. In my study of 214 nursing homes in Chicago I found only two nursing homes having full-time social workers, 21 having part-time social workers, and 180 having no social work involvement at all (Kosberg, 1971). From a study of a sample of Florida nursing homes, Austin and I (1976) learned that 45 percent of the respondents indicated they had social services at least once a week. It was further learned that those responsible for social services ranged from social workers to secretaries and that social services were seen to be synonymous with recreation. Further, even when social workers are employed in such institutions as mental hospitals, homes for the aged, or general hospitals, their involvement is most often limited to the intake process and discharge planning.

In an earlier article (1973) I addressed the question of why the lack of social work involvement in one type of institution for the aged, nursing homes. This lack was based upon negative attitudes of social workers to four distinct issues. First, social work involvement within nursing homes has been primarily provided by consultants in private practice, and social workers have viewed such colleagues with a sense of disdain, as profiteers. Second, more than 80 percent of all nursing homes are proprietary, and such settings are viewed as inappropriate for social workers. Third, institutions and institutional care are negatively viewed by social workers (as is true of society, in general) and are avoided. Fourth, social workers prefer to work with client groups that can demonstrate improvements or change. The potential for rapid and marked improvement of ill, aged populations is generally small. Therefore, few social workers are found within these settings.

The fact that death and dying are commonplace within institutions for the aged adds to this avoidance by social workers. Death and dying remind us of our own mortality. The death of an elderly client may cause conflict or guilt to the professional. It is quite possible that working with dying geriatric patients and their families is viewed by the profession as lying outside the realm of social work. Such involvement may be seen as appropriate for the physician, nurse, psychiatrist, or clergyman, but not for the social worker.

The Death of a Geriatric Patient

The death of an elderly person within an institutional setting and the impact on the family can be viewed in a unique and distinct manner. Social work involvement may be precluded and not seen as necessary, owing to commonly held notions regarding the death of geriatric patients.

It may be thought that the death of a geriatric patient may not be disruptive to the family. In many cases this is true; indeed the death may be somewhat of a relief. Financial obligations for institutional care will no longer be necessary. Guilt from placing the elderly relative may be resolved with the death of the aged person. The trouble caused by periodic visits to the institutionalized relative and the ensuing guilt from not visiting, will no longer be an issue. Therefore, "post-mortem 'scenes' with grieving families, so characteristic of other kinds of death, are here almost lacking. Families may not appear at all" (Glaser and Strauss, 1968, p. 56).

It is often thought that the institutionalized aged may look forward to death. Researchers and practitioners involved with aged in institutions have been aware of the fatalism, the futureless orientation, and the morbidity of the elderly. Suicides are not uncommon. The reasons for this apparent desire for death are understandable and can be related to the loss of role and status by the elderly, their dependent position, and their possible stigma and shame in being placed within an institution by their grown children. Severe pain, diminishing capabilities, loss of functioning, and loss of spouse can further the potential for welcoming death.

In institutions for the aged, death can be perceived to be a normative event. " 'It is natural for old people to die.' This theme and its variations are frequently voiced by laymen, by professionals in the health and human sciences, and by personnel who work directly with geriatric patients" (Kastenbaum, 1972). Institutions for the aged are viewed as places to die, and expectations by society and staff within these facilities are that death will occur. Accordingly the care to be given the aged is seen to be medical and nursing, and many believe that the best to be done for the elderly is to keep them clean, fed, and out of pain until they expire. From such a perspective the roles for social workers are minimal. Some would argue that other client groups are more in need of social work than are old, ill, and dying individuals.

In our society death in old age is considered the ideal; it is viewed to be a blessing, timely, and preferable. While the death of those not old is always called "untimely," when an elderly person dies one often hears: "He lived a full life." "He was blessed with longevity." "He died peacefully in his sleep of old age." "God willing, we will all be senior citizens some day." Viewing death in old age as desirable can gloss over the anxieties and problems to the dying person and his family. Social workers may thus fail to focus on existing problems related to the death of an elderly person.

Because the death of an elderly person is neither disruptive nor unwelcome from the point of view of some families and some elderly persons, social workers need to guard against accepting stereotypes and clichés about old age, death and dying, and geriatric institutions. Such overgeneralizations preclude viewing the individuality of dying geriatric clients, as well as the unique responses of their families. Although death in old age can be viewed as the ideal (we would all probably wish to live long and full lives, rather than to die at younger ages), social workers should be aware that geriatric patients have the same tensions, fears, and despair as any other age group facing death.

Impetus for Change

It has been my observation that, although social workers find themselves in positions where they are in contact with dying persons and their families, skills are developed from experience rather than from training. This is especially true for social workers employed within institutions for the aged. If social workers are to become more fully involved with and better prepared for assisting elderly patients within institutional settings, the impetus for change can come from at least three different directions: social work education, the social work profession, and social policy. Each will be briefly discussed.

In preparing students for future practice, social work education has an important role to play in creating an awareness of the needs of dying geriatric patients. As best as can be determined, there is no school of social work that offers preparation and training for working with the dying patient and his family. This is especially true for the dying geriatric patient. When universities do offer courses on death and dying, they are primarily introductory courses that are general and interdisciplinary. Although such courses are popular and sensitizing, they do not develop practice skills for social workers, and there is no opportunity to apply knowledge gained from the classroom. Berengarten emphasizes the need to bridge the classroom and practice: "That there can be no dichotomy between conceptualization and performance is a major premise of the social work profession. The student, as a developing social worker, must have the opportunity to apply progressively in practice the concepts and principles learned in class'' (Berengarten, 1968). One exception to this general trend was the course offered at the University of Chicago by Dr. Kübler-Ross. Her graduate course on death and dying was for the future practitioner, whether a physician, psychologist, nurse, social worker, or clergyman. The actual interaction between terminal patients and Dr. Kübler-Ross provided students with an experience unavailable to those taking more elementary courses. It is believed that the Council on Social Work Education has a role to play in seeking to inculcate curricula with content on death and dying. This is related not only to developing skills and preparation for practice but also to changing attitudes toward death and the dying geriatric patient.

As professionals, social workers can be guided and encouraged by their professional organizations and associations. Social workers who are employed in settings where there are geriatric populations are in host agencies, not social work agencies. Hospitals, nursing homes, and convalescence centers are primarily medical facilities. This has implications for the opportunities that social workers have for assisting the dying geriatric patient and his family. Whether as a part of an interdisciplinary team of professionals working with dying patients or in more hierarchical relationships, we know that social workers often find themselves beneath the formal and informal authority and leadership of physicians. Kahn (1974) has pointed out that obstacles to interprofessional activities within organizations can be based on differences in status, orientations, value systems, and social class. Yet, given these problems related to working with and for members from other professions, social workers must become advocates for the clients being cared for within institutional settings; they must make every effort to ensure the existence of professional staff trained in and committed to working with the dying geriatric patient and his family. This social work advocacy necessitates an awareness of the needs of dying patients. The National Association of Social Workers must take the initiative in making social workers aware of the needs of dying clients and reaffirming social work's responsibility to dependent persons, including dying geriatric patients. This could be accomplished, in part, through editorials and articles in NASW publications and through guidelines and workshops for practitioners.

It is somewhat naive to discuss the importance of the social worker to institutional care, and the roles for social workers with dying patients within such settings, if social workers do not exist and are not required to exist in such settings. If the need for social work with dying patients and their families can be stipulated, such involvement can be mandated by social policies. It has been mentioned that social workers should be advocates for dying clients in host agencies, seeing that appropriate social and psychological care is provided along with nursing and medical care. It has also been mentioned that social workers are infrequently employed within institutions for the aged. Accordingly, there is a need for social legislation to ensure the inclusion of social workers in institutions for the aged, so that they may be a part of interdisciplinary teams and advocates for the aged and their families. For example Medicare requirements no longer necessitate social workers within extended-care facilities. Medicaid requirements for social services are minimal. Hospitals have social service staffs that may be involved, not with the dying patients, but with the relocation of discharged patients; yet, "the hospital social worker, in addition to being a caseworker, needs to be a group therapist, family therapist, social systems intervenor, educator, consultant, and perhaps most important, a change agent" (Hollowitz, 1972). Social policies can mandate a role for social workers by requiring their employment within institutions. But such policies for change require two important preconditions: an awareness of the needs of dying geriatric patients within institutional settings and a realization that it can be professional social workers who can perform this important function.

Activities for Social Workers

Reasons for the lack of social work involvement within institutions for the aged have been discussed, as have three areas that can bring about changes. Stipulated is the importance of social work. The potential activities for social workers involved with geriatric patients within institutional settings are many. Because this chapter proposes to present an overview of topics, these activities are only briefly mentioned. The following activities and topics are presented mainly for discussion purposes.

Casework is the traditional social work role and form of intervention. The use of such an individualistic approach is related to working with the dying geriatric patient and his family. The theoretical framework of such intervention and assistance can and does vary, depending on the orientation of the social worker. It is imperative that social workers trained and educated to work with death and dying be available within geriatric institutions. They can establish relationships with dying patients, grieving or depressed patients, their families, as well as with staff members having difficulties in caring for these patients. Social workers need to be able to interpret the psychosocial needs and behavior of dying patients to family and staff. As Abrams (1972) states this: "there are times when the social worker reaches out to the professional personnel, the family, friends, clergy, and community both to deepen her understanding of the patient and his needs and to translate these findings to his caregivers."

Staff development is another activity for social workers. The most effective use of limited time by a social worker employed (perhaps only part time) in a geriatric institution is to train and sensitize staff. Reaching staff members in an institution for the aged and alerting them to the needs of dying patients, concerns of family members, and reactions of other residents might be a most profitable way of inculcating an institution with an enlightened orientation. Although staff may respond to situations (such as the dying and death of a patient) emotionally (that is, with "gut-level" reactions), most often such responses are inappropriate and incorrect. For example, attempting to cheer a dying person or telling him not to feel sad may better serve the needs of the staff member than of the dying person. Staff often believe that discussing suicide with a distraught elderly person may precipitate a suicide. However, "patients are often relieved to be able to talk about their suicidal preoccupation with a supportive and willing listener," (Broden, 1970). There is no substitute for knowledge about the needs of the dying and reactions to death, and social workers can play an important role in educating staff.

Some of the effects of institutional care have been discussed, and there is the need for organizational change. There are roles for social workers to attempt to make institutions congruent to the needs of elderly residents and the needs of dying patients. While we are still on the threshold of knowledge about methods of deinstitutionalizing facilities for the aged, it is believed incumbent upon social workers to seek greater individuation of care and treatment. This necessitates a reduction of rules and regulations, standardization, and impersonalization. The methods involved and tactics to influence institutional decision-makers pose a challenge to social workers.

Community planning determines which resources exist in the near and distant future. It has been pointed out that institutional care may be detrimental to the needs of ill and elderly persons and may result in high mortality rates. Further, it is known that institutional care is used because of a lack of alternate resources in the community. Social workers refer to the self-determination of clients, and yet lack of alternatives makes a mockery of this notion. There is a great need for social workers to create alternatives for ill, elderly persons through their involvement in community planning. The focus should be on independence and community-based living, preferably in one's customary dwelling. This necessitates the creation of outreach programs and services for the ill and the dying elderly person. Frequently the response of society to the ill is institutionalization in a nursing home or mental hospital, and for the dying person it is hospitalization.

The manner in which we care for dying geriatric patients is a reflection of societal attitudes. Accordingly social workers should attempt to enlighten citizens and seek attitudinal changes. There is a need to reaffirm the fact that dying geriatric patients have human needs and fears. Our society tends to equate human worth with capabilities, and this is wrong. Social workers possess the professional and humanistic values and principles that mitigate against such a point of view. That a person is dying does not mean, ipso facto, that the person is any less a human being. Furthermore, there is a self-fulfilling prophecy that exists in the institutional care of elderly persons. This is the belief that by the time an aged person is institutionalized, his life is over, he cannot be returned to the community, he cannot be rehabilitated. Accordingly little is provided in way of care or therapy, and the person's physical, social, and psychological condition does worsen and capabilities atrophy. Yet research tells us that the ill, elderly person can often be rehabilitated to function at a higher level, if only attempts were made to help the person (Hefferin, 1968). Social workers can play a significant role in changing expectations and attitudes, if only by pointing out what is possible and what is humanly decent.

It is expected that little research is done on death and dying in schools of social work or in social work agencies. However, social workers are increasingly concerned with ensuring that services provided clients are congruent with needs, as well as that these social services are effective. I see several areas for social work research related to death and dying that are needed to better assess the effectiveness and benefit of present types and forms of care for the geriatric patient. The following are but a few questions in need of answers: What are the advantages and disadvantages of institutions only for the dying (hospices), as opposed to facilities for both dying and nondying patients? Should institutions for the aged be segregated by age (only for older people) or age integrated (for all age groups)? How can institutional care be made congruent with the needs of the dying geriatric patient? How can home-based care be provided to dying patients? What is the difference in the dying process between a geriatric patient with family as opposed to one without family? What are the differences between social classes in care of dying patients? What is the effect of race or ethnicity on the dying process, if any? What supports can be provided an aged person to relieve the impact of the loss of a spouse? What are the ramifications and impact on an aged parent, living in an institution, who has lost a grown child?

Conclusion

This chapter has presented a brief overview of some issues regarding the institutionalization of the aged and institutions for the aged. The point has been made that social workers have been little involved in these facilities. Accordingly they have been unavailable to care for dying geriatric patients and their families. Several reasons were given to explain this: Social workers have tended to avoid private practice, proprietary facilities, institutions, and working with elderly clients. Social workers have also avoided dying clients. Further, social work has not been involved with dying geriatric patients, because there is perceived to be no family crisis; death may be welcomed by the aged and expected by staff and can be viewed as an ideal.

Social work education, the social work profession, and social policy can all play a role in changing the present situation, a change that can result in a growing role for social workers within geriatric institutions. Several roles for social workers were noted: casework, staff training, organizational change, community planning, changing attitudes, and research. In addition, social workers must be advocates for geriatric patients within institutions.

It seems inevitable that the profession of social work will be more deeply involved with the care of ill, elderly populations. First, the number of elderly persons is increasing, and the proportion of our population who are old will probably grow as well. Second, the greatest growth for social work manpower in the future is estimated to be in the health care field (Stamm, 1969). This is to suggest that the future will find a growing number of social workers employed in agencies, programs, and institutions within community health care systems. And these systems will, in turn, be caring for a client group increasingly composed of the elderly.

Beyond such trends and future projections is the role and responsibility of social work for meeting the unmet needs of ill, old, and dependent institutionalized populations. I believe the needs of dying patients within institutions, and the needs of their relatives, are not being adequately met, if, indeed, even acknowledged. This is caused by social attitudes, institutional rigidities, professional biases, and lack of knowledge and preparation on the part of institutional staff. That the dying geriatric patient can die alone and without needed professional support is neglectful. That the families of these patients cannot and do not receive assistance or comfort is unfortunate. We must begin to change this situation; social work can and should play a major role in this effort.

References

Abrams, R. D. 1972. "The Responsibility of Social Work in Terminal Cancer." In *Psychosocial Aspects of Terminal Care,* eds. B. Schoenberg et al., p. 180. New York: Columbia University Press.

Austin, M. J. and J. I. Kosberg. 1976. "Nursing Home Decision Makers and the Social Service Needs of Residents." *Social Work in Health Care* 1(Summer):447–55.

Berengarten, S. 1968. Quoted in *Teaching Psychological Aspects of Patient Care,* eds. B. Schoenberg, H. F. Pettit, and A. C. Carr, pp. 162–163. New York: Columbia University Press.

Broden, A. R. 1970. "Reaction to Loss in the Aged." In *Loss and Grief: Psychological Aspects in Medical Practice,* eds. B. Schoenberg et al., p. 211. New York: Columbia University Press.

Glaser, B. G. and A. L. Strauss. 1968. *Time for Dying.* Chicago: Aldine.

Goffman, E. 1961. *Asylums.* Garden City, N.Y.: Anchor Books.

Gustofson, E. 1972. "Dying: The Career of the Nursing Home Patient." *Journal of Health and Social Behavior* 13(September):226–35.

Hefferin, E. A. 1968. "Rehabilitation in Nursing Home Situations: A Survey of the Literature."*Journal of the American Geriatrics Society* 16(March):296–313.

Hollowitz, E. 1972. "Innovations in Hospital Social Work." *Social Work* 17, no. 4 (July):97.

Kahn, A. J. 1974. "Institutional Constraints to Interprofessional Practice." In *Medicine and Social Work: An Exploration in Intraprofessionalism,* ed. H. Rehr, pp. 14–25. New York: PRODIST.

Kastenbaum, R. 1972. "While the Old Man Dies: Our Conflicting Attitudes Toward the Elderly." In *Psychosocial Aspects of Terminal Care,* eds. B. Schoenberg et al., p. 116. New York: Columbia University Press.

Kosberg, J. I. 1971. *The Comparative Analysis of Nursing Homes in the Chicago Area.* Chicago: Welfare Council of Metropolitan Chicago.

Koberg, J. I. 1973. "Nursing Homes: The Social Work Paradox." *Social Work* 18, no. 2 (March):104–10.

Markson, E. 1971. "A Hiding Place to Die." *Transaction* 9(Nov.–Dec.):48–54.

Sommer, R. and H. Osmond. 1967. Quoted in *Institution and Outcome,* ed. L. Ullman. New York: Pergamon Press.

Stamm, A. 1969. "NASW Membership: Characteristics, Deployment, and Salaries." *National Association of Social Workers Personnel Information* 12, no. 3. (It is estimated that of all NASW members, 12 percent are in health services and 21.6 percent are in mental health services.)

Townsend, C. 1971. *Old Age: The Last Segregation.* New York: Grossman Publishers.

Townsend, P. 1964. *The Last Refuge.* London: Routledge and Kegan Paul.

Part IV

*Interdisciplinary
Resources
in the Community*

13

Home Care for the Terminal Patient and His Family

Barbara McNulty

During the past five years I have been working in the Home Care Service at St. Christopher's Hospice (London), and my concern has been the dying cancer patient and his family at home. I lead a team of three nurses, a health visitor, and a social worker. We have available the advice of a physician and the services of a physiotherapist and an occupational therapist. But perhaps most important of all, we have the special-care beds of the Hospice behind us should the home situation deteriorate unexpectedly. It is the knowledge that these beds are available that gives us and our families the confidence to try to hold a difficult situation at home, for our aim is to support the dying patient and his family in their own home for as long as they wish and to the end if possible. Since we are a hospital-based team working in the community, we form a bridge—a liaison between the hospital consultant and the family doctor, between the hospital and the home. We ensure a continuity of care for the patient who is able to go home and a guarantee that he will be readmitted when he needs it.

The longer I do this work the more I am convinced that the essence of good care is a united team. This requires that each member be a responsible, mature person with some vision of the total pattern and some understanding of the individual threads by which it will be achieved. It must be a team whose members do not feel threatened by one another, where there are no hard and fast boundaries between the work of one member and that of another. Although much of the work I do could be called social work, I am, in fact, a nurse—a nurse in a unique position. The team I lead is a bridge between different disciplines and services. Each team member relates warmly to the family, identifies their needs, knows how to mobilize every available appropriate resource to help them and provides support of all kinds during this period of stress and crisis.

A family caring for a dying member at home is faced with several well-defined problems. Even in England, where the National Health Service provides a home nursing service and where the welfare state makes a token effort to meet the needs of the patient, there are glaring deficiencies and gaps. These observations are based on five years' work with 1,500 terminal patients and their families.

The Patient

The adjective "terminal" is often used loosely with any incurable illness, however long the expectation of life may be. For my purposes terminal means the last weeks of a person's life, when there is a marked, irreversible downward trend. The period may vary from a week or so to as much as two or three months. Generally such patients will have had many months or even years of hospital experience involving surgery, chemotherapy, radiotherapy, and endless tests and examinations. They react in two different ways, which, although apparently contradictory, can coexist. They express a horror of any further hospitalization or any further treatment, but also voice a fear of going home, of leaving the protective and supportive environment of the hospital. They want to go home but are afraid to do so.

Often conflicting reasons may have brought about a patient's discharge from the hospital: a remission or temporary improvement in health or a sudden panic on his part as he realizes that he is getting worse (and going home may be an unconscious effort to escape "doom"). One sees these reactions also in the patient who may feel a desperate need to see home once more, to put his affairs in order, or to be present at a special family occasion, such as an anniversary or wedding. Regardless of how poorly he feels, he may insist on going home. Some patients do recognize that they are coming to the end of their lives and elect to go home to die.

Another category of patient, the young mother with small children, needs to be at home; for her every precious minute counts. This is not always easy to organize, but every effort must be made to overcome the difficulties so that the home is run as smoothly as possible throughout the illness and death. Often the husband must be assisted in making foresighted preparations for the future care of his children. This is difficult to do, for few husbands can bear to plan for a future that will not include their wives. Whatever the reasons for the home care of the terminally ill, there is nearly always considerable anxiety, if not in the patient himself, then in his relatives. "What will happen? Will I be able to cope?" In these situations the Home Care Team plays a vital part.

The Problems of Home Care

Problems encountered in providing home care for terminal patients fall into the following categories: medical and nursing, social and financial, emotional and psychological. Because so wide a range of problems cannot be dealt with by any one person, there is the need for a closely integrated team with constant two-way communication. Each member must be able to contribute his insight into the situation and draw upon the expertise of his colleagues.

PRACTICAL PROBLEMS
In each instance the home conditions and the social and financial situation must be evaluated. There are no absolutes to help us decide whether or not a dying patient can remain at home; each case is individual. For instance a single person living alone may well be able to

manage if his financial resources are adequate or if he has attentive friends and neighbors. One not so well endowed cannot. Poor home conditions do not always preclude home care. Even when the home may fall far short of the ideal and the care given not come up to our standards, the home may still be the best place for a particular patient to die in, despite inconvenience and discomfort. His need for familiar surroundings outweighs anything the hospital may have to offer. When assessing the suitability of a home for terminal care, one must look closely at who will be giving the care, who will bear the brunt of it, and how it will be given—whether with love or with resentment. The whole decision turns not only on the material circumstances but also on the quality of the human relationships within the home.

Every family suffers financially when a sick member is nursed at home. Bills of all kinds, from heat and light to food and laundry, increase. Financial help will almost certainly be needed.

The nature of the illness and the degree of incapacity sometimes put home care out of the question. Yet I believe, and experience has proved it to be true, that far more people could be cared for at home if medical and nursing resources were better mobilized. Perhaps in the United States, even more than in England, people are hospital oriented, but both caregiving systems are guilty of thinking in terms of the need for high-powered technical care that is often inappropriate for the dying patient. I would like to see more home nurses, more social workers, more family doctors willing to take on the burden of the dying patient in his own home, for this kind of teamwork is, I believe, the pattern for the future.

EMOTIONAL AND PSYCHOLOGICAL PROBLEMS

The emotional and psychological problems encountered both in the patient and in his family are considerable. Any worker in this field must be familiar with the anger, bitterness, and resentment, the denial, grief, and fear so traumatic in patients facing death. It is not enough to note these responses; one must know how to meet them and how to lead both patient and family through the anger of "Why should this happen to me?'' to the calmer waters of ''I know I am going to die. I'm not afraid now.''

For the family the dawning realization of the impending loss clouds life with sadness. If you add to this the anxiety of wondering whether they will be able to cope and the weariness of giving constant care, you get some idea of the emotional burden carried by these families. Yet this burden can be lightened just by sharing. A sympathetic listener who can also give practical help and assurance is invaluable, and it is in this situation, with these problems, that my team is working. Three case reports of people we have helped illustrate these problems.

Case Report 1. The home is very inadequate, a small prefabricated structure erected during World War II as emergency housing for those who had been bombed out. Although it has been under a demolition order, it is still being lived in. Built of asbestos sheets on a wooden frame, with a flat tarred-felt roof, the whole is raised off the ground on bricks. There is no insulation to keep out cold or dampness. The building is the property of the Local Authority and is rented to the inhabitant. There is a gas hot-air system that more often than not is out of order. There is town water supply and drains, but no hot water. In this tiny two-bedroom chalet lived an old lady of 78, her dying daughter of 34, and her granddaughter of 12, a child with spina bifida and a transplant of ureters to an ileostomy. The child's father had deserted at her birth. This household's financial assets included the grandmother's old age pension and her daughter's unemployment benefit, sufficient to pay the rent with a few pounds left over for everything else. At the time I met this family, the sick daughter, Ivy, was earning a little pin money by doing piecework at home for a button factory, but this had to be concealed from the authorities, for it would have meant a reduction in her unemployment benefit.

Ivy was deeply attached to her old mother and obsessively devoted to her handicapped daughter. She knew that she was dying and could not bear the thought of leaving them both. Her need was to remain at home for as long as she could. We knew her for a period of 14 months, during which time she had to be admitted briefly to the Hospice on ten occasions. A great deal of help and support was required for this family, and the problem became one of coordinating the many agencies involved.

The granddaughter, Susan, was supervised by a social worker from the pediatric hospital she had attended since infancy and where she was still being seen regularly. Although this social worker was in touch with the head mistress of the special school attended by Susan, neither knew about the child's mother and her approaching death. The mother had minimized her own illness, for obvious reasons.

The old lady was known to the health visitor in her area as one of the hundreds of inadequately housed geriatric patients for whom she was responsible. She was also known to the welfare authorities who paid her old age pension and to the housing authorities who received her frequent requests for urgent repairs to the crumbling fabric of the house. None of these knew about her daughter's illness or her granddaughter's handicap. Why should they? It did not concern them.

The family doctor knew only about the young mother, for the child was treated by the pediatric consultant, and the old lady had refused all medical attendance. The total situation was known to the home nurses who cared for Ivy, and the home maker, both of whom came in daily. However, these two worked in a circumscribed area and had no power to alter anything. St. Christopher's became involved on the medical side to assess and control Ivy's considerable pain, which, it soon became obvious, was closely related to her anguish for her family and was not to be relieved by drugs alone.

The basis of our work with this family was a loving, trusting relationship that took time to build up and required an unjudgmental attitude to a situation that, on the surface, was totally inadequate. Once we had gained the confidence of each member of the family and had seen the situation from each of their points of view, we were in a better position to offer help.

The first step was to contact all the other agencies involved and arrange a meeting with each worker to pool our knowledge. We then agreed upon what steps should be taken to improve things and who should be responsible. Throughout Ivy's illness St. Christopher's remained the coordinating and centralizing agent. Though pain control was our main reason for becoming involved, our next most important role was that of listener. Each member of this family needed a friend, someone to confide in who would understand her needs. Ivy above all needed someone with whom to share her fears.

Secondly we looked into every possible way of obtaining nonstatutory help. A local convent made regular gifts of food packages; there were volunteers to do shopping or to escort the child to hospital; private charities made small grants and gifts; the local Boy Scouts redecorated the living room; and a holiday (the first in her life) was arranged for Susan. This was social work in its broadest sense. But the support given did not end there. In time Ivy died, and her mother grieved deeply and was inconsolable. With little strength left over to give anything to her orphaned grandchild, she felt resentful of the child and yet was fearful for her and overprotective. Susan withdrew into herself and refused to speak of her mother. She resented her grandmother's protectiveness and became insolent and uncooperative, often staying out late and refusing to account for her movements. A state of bitter, silent warfare rapidly developed in which both participants grew increasingly unhappy. Not surprisingly Susan looked elsewhere for companionship and love, and a friendship developed between her and a 17-year-old boy. It fell to the St. Christopher's visitor to listen to the grandmother's constant complaints against Susan and to give her someone on whom to vent her anger and distress.

Susan's needs were even more urgent. She was growing up a precocious miss, physically handicapped and not very bright. She had known us and trusted us for a long time; we had known and loved her mother and had been part of her past life. She accepted our further intervention in her life almost with relief. She was now 16 and going steady with the boy friend. It seemed a natural extension of our relationship with this child to advise her about the problems of her friendship with the boy, both of them under the legal age of consent, and also to give her contraceptive advice and instruction. Later we widened this help to include the discussion of plans for her marriage and help with finding living accommodations and suitable employment.

The role of the social worker in terminal care is not likely to be brief, nor is it cut short by death. On the contrary it is ongoing and continues with those left behind. In this case we had an old lady, who needed help in adjusting to her bereavement, and a young girl, who was starting out in life with considerable disadvantages. Our association with them continues still, though it has been more than four years since Ivy's death.

Case Report 2. This report illustrates a very different problem. Mrs. B. was a widow living in the basement of an old house that had been converted into apartments. She and her husband had moved there 40 years earlier at the time of their marriage. The house was now semiderelict, uninhabited except for herself, and under a demolition order. Her flat was damp and dark, with mold growing on the walls and mice under the floorboards. Yet she resisted being rehoused, for the place was home to her. Since she had cancer and her life was limited, it was decided to do everything possible to allow her to remain at home for as long as she could.

The first problem was to gain access to the house, for Mrs. B. was a recluse and, as the result of many years of solitude, feared visitors and strangers. She also feared compulsory eviction and was thus doubly suspicious of any callers. Early conversations were carried on through the letterbox. It is not easy to get on intimate terms with anyone through a letterbox, still less if the conversation has to be carried on in a tone only slightly below a shout. Nevertheless, we finally met face to face in her squalid hallway.

In a way I suppose this was a social worker's dream, or possible nightmare, for there was so much to be done; the problem was where to begin. We started with creature comforts—food, warmth, and bedding. A small grant was obtained from the Marie Curie Foundation and another from the National Society for Cancer Relief to buy blankets and warm clothes. The local authority was asked to repair the broken gas fire and to replace the defunct water heater. The welfare department supplied hot meals four days a week to ensure at least some nourishing food.

Mrs. B.'s medical condition had been grossly neglected, for she had refused to see a doctor, and her cancer was well advanced. As a nurse my role was to get her seen by a doctor and to make sure that she continued to take her medications properly. My other, less definable role required that I help her face her predicament more realistically and support her through the phases of fear, anger, and depression so that she might reach some degree of acceptance of her illness and coming death.

If one is really going to be able to help the dying and support the family through the crisis of bereavement, two things are essential. The first is that one should be able to face the reality of death oneself, and the other is that one should be prepared to stand firmly beside the patient and the family as they come to terms with the truth. This may sound obvious or even simple, and yet how few of us handle it well.

As Mrs. B. learned to trust us, she became able to talk more and more freely about her fears. One was tempted sometimes to evade her searching questions. We had to learn to give just as much of the truth as she really wanted and could stand while never telling her an outright lie. Gradually she came to accept that she could not remain alone in the house, that she needed proper care, and, finally, that her life was coming to an end. At this point she asked of her own accord to see a lawyer and to put her affairs in order. After her death there were no relatives to claim her small estate or to wind it up. It fell to us to arrange her funeral and to hand over the house to the demolition squad.

Case Report 3. A slightly different emphasis marks this illustration. The patient, a young mother in her midtwenties, had bravely faced major surgery for cancer of the stomach and then several courses of radiotherapy in the vain hope that the malignant growth would be destroyed. She passionately wanted to live, for only 18 months earlier she had given birth to twins. But as the weeks went by, she grew thinner and thinner, and her pain increased out of all endurance. Her anxious young husband absolutely refused to contemplate the thought that she was not going to get better. As she grew weaker, it became increasingly urgent to consider the future care of the infants, and yet neither parent could be brought to the point of looking at the future. There were no relatives living near and no one who could be asked to help. Because we were able to control her so well (pain became almost negligible and vomiting ceased), it was even more difficult for this couple to believe in the steady downward progression of the illness. Finally we were reduced to a certain amount of subterfuge and guile. We obtained the address of the mother, who lived in the north of England, and took it upon ourselves to inform her of her daughter's condition. Immediately she closed her own home and came to stay with her daughter and son-in-law. Although she arrived only a few weeks before her daughter's death, there was time enough for her to get to know the children and for them to transfer some of their love to her. When their mother died, their loss was softened, their sense of abandonment eased by the presence of a grandmother who represented love, safety, and security. These infants were fortunate, for their grandmother has continued to care for them, and they have made a satisfactory adjustment to bereavement.

Conclusion

The satisfactory care and support of the dying patient and his family require a multidisciplinary team working closely together. The boundaries of each discipline must be blurred, not rigid, each team member overlapping and complementing the work of the others. The problems encountered in families of dying patients are threefold—medical, social, emotional—and attention must be given to all these areas. Work with the family should start as early as possible in the illness to help patient and family come to terms with the truth, and it should continue after the death to enable the survivors to make a good recovery. The social worker has a definite role to play, but her usefulness will be limited unless she has, to some extent, come to terms with death herself.

14

The Social Worker and Terminal Illness

Jean Markham and Sylvia Lack

Social work skills aim to maximize the social functioning of the individual, with a special focus on interpersonal relationships and social roles, which in turn profoundly influence the manner in which people meet and deal with the various crises in the life cycle: birth, school entrance, adolescence, career entry, courtship, marriage, parenthood, and so forth. Dying is another major life crisis and is equally deserving of social work's attention (Goldberg, 1973; Goldstein, 1973). The experiences of the interdisciplinary Home Care Team at Hospice (New Haven, Conn.), a center for the care and treatment of patients and their families during this final phase of life, exemplify social work's contribution in regard to this major event in the life cycle. The interactions between the patient and family, as well as those between the family members themselves, are bound to undergo at least subtle, and often dramatic changes, adding to the complexities to be considered by members of the helping professions as they serve during this stressful time. The manner in which social work intervention can take place as part of the multidisciplinary team approach is illustrated in the following case summaries of families served by the Home Care Program of Hospice.

Nellie N., an 85-year-old widow, was referred to the Home Care Team by her physician with a diagnosis of terminal cancer of the uterus and a prognosis of four months to live. The staff nurses who visited Nellie found her living alone in a rundown house, in conditions wretched in terms of cleanliness, nutrition, and sanitation. Nellie's diagnosis of terminal cancer seemed almost incidental to the general neglect of her person, her social isolation, and mental deterioration. Her personal hygiene was deplorable, complicated by incontinence of her bladder and bowels and by mental confusion. Her diet was grossly inadequate, consisting of what little food she could prepare, and she was under constant danger of setting herself on fire at the gas stove. Housekeeping routine was nonexistent. Her marginal finances were limited to monthly Social Security checks and partial Medicare coverage of medical expenses. She had no children or close relatives. A nephew living in another part of the state had some family concern but no closeness to his aging aunt or willingness to participate in direct care.

The other occupant of Nellie's house lived in the upstairs apartment. He was a single man in his sixties whose own hold on reality was at time tenuous and interrupted periodically by his drinking. Nevertheless he "handled" Nellie's monthly Social Security checks for her, paying her share of the rent to the absentee landlord, and supposedly returning the rest to her. Nellie was very dependent on the help and services of a neighbor who, although solicitous, was burdened by her own family responsibilities and worried about her children's safety in Nellie's unhygienic vicinity. She could assume only a limited amount of responsibility for Nellie's care at home, especially because she was due to move away.

Nellie lived in a world where past and present were blurred and confused, a world that often frightened her and from which her only retreat was sleep. Her greatest strength was a strong inner drive, manifested at first by irritability at having the Hospice nurse take over aspects of her personal care that she felt she should be able to manage independently. She also became increasingly anxious and unwilling to participate in planning for her own care as she correctly perceived that the possibility of being placed in a nursing home was being considered. Her negativism and refusal to hear about any possible change in her life situation were defenses against being overwhelmed by those forces over which she had no control: failing health and existence in an uncaring world.

The social worker on the Home Care Team saw Nellie as an individual with an inner core of strength but urgently needing supportive services. This evaluation led to the social worker's direct involvement in the team treatment of Nellie through the mobilization of various other community resources. Intervention included participation in team visits to Nellie and conferences with the man upstairs, with the neighbor, and with the nephew to determine the extent and limitations of their accessibility to Nellie. Exploration of available nursing homes resulted, not surprisingly, in Nellie's reaching her own decision that she would prefer to stay at home and also in her own recognition that she needed more help to do so. The role of the social worker in this process included consultation with the Hospice team members involved and, in particular, encouragement and conscious use of the meaningful relationship that had developed between Nellie and one of the Hospice nurses. The team was thus able to help Nellie work through her feelings of discomfort about applying for assistance so that she could receive the Title XIX benefits for which she was eligible and which she needed to pay for home health aide services beyond the amount covered by Medicare.

The happy result, one year later, is that Nellie is a contented, well-cared-for person, living in her own home, with some renewal of interest (mild, but meaningful to her) by her nephew, and with a sense of dignity. Gone are the mental confusion that had been apparent and the negativism that caused her to order nurses away. Long gone is the four months' prognosis; and with physical symptoms under medical control Nellie's terminal cancer has receded in importance compared to her greatly improved total life situation, although objectively the tumor continues to grow. Nellie does not fear death, but neither does she long for its escape as she did when first known to Hospice.

Mario X., a 20-year-old man (also among the first patients served by the Home Care Team of Hospice) was referred with a diagnosis of terminal cancer, with a prognosis of only a few months to live. His own mother had died several years earlier, and his father was not close to Mario, either geographically or emotionally. Since his mother's death Mario had lived with his older sister and her three children (the sister having been divorced for several years). These were Mario's closest relationships, and he was very dear to his sister and her children, holding an important leadership position in relation to his younger nephews. His sister had come to center much of her life around Mario since his illness, and so had her eldest son, two years younger than Mario. She wondered, as did the Hospice Home Care Team, how she and her children, the oldest especially, could cope with the loss of Mario.

Mario himself was very much in touch with his own feelings about dying and, with help, was able to express them and handle himself very well. Team assessment indicated the necessity to focus also on the emotions of his sister and her children to help them meet their own needs, both before and after Mario's death. (The Hospice approach to care of the dying patient includes bereavement counseling with the family after the patient's death.)

One of the Hospice nurses had a relationship with Mario's sister that was especially meaningful and potentially therapeutic for the sister. This relationship was consciously used to provide much-needed support for the sister and, with social work consultation, also to help her examine and question some of her own reactive tendencies. For example, and perhaps most importantly, after Mario's death the sister was encouraged to consider and plan for several months before rushing precipitously into marriage with her boy friend. She did eventually marry him, and the benefits of her waiting included her not needing to use the boy friend to "replace" Mario, not needing immediately to have a baby to "replace" Mario, and not expecting her boy friend suddenly to become capable of meeting all her emotional needs.

Mario's oldest nephew was much moved by Mario's illness, and it was anticipated that he would feel Mario's loss keenly. The social worker was able to mobilize personnel in the nephew's school to be supportive of him during the latter stage of Mario's illness (when the nephew's absences, to be with Mario, needed to be explained to school staff) and also after Mario's death. There were many sensitive, caring people in the school, and the support given to the nephew there, especially from his hockey coach, was most meaningful. The social worker in the school where his younger brother and sister were students was also alerted and was able to provide them support.

Help to Mario thus included much aid to his family in addition to encouragement and acceptance of Mario's expression of his own feelings and especially of his angry feelings. The eventual outcome for him and his family was a more peaceful acceptance of the inevitability of his death.

These case histories illustrating the social worker's role on the Hospice Home Care Team were selected at random. It is significant, however, that the patients described here include the very oldest and very youngest served by the team in its first several months of existence. The implication, with respect to the stages of man as discussed by Erikson (1963), and their significance in relation to social functioning, interpersonal relationships, and enduring ego qualities, are manifold. One outcome of the Hospice Home Care Team's first year of experience is an increased conviction of the value of a social worker's contribution as an integral member of the team giving care to the patients and families during the phases of life that precede and follow the end.

References

Erikson, E. H. 1963. *Childhood and Society,* 2nd ed. New York: W. W. Norton and Co.

Goldberg, S. B. 1973. "Family Tasks and Reactions in the Crisis of Death." *Social Casework* 54, no. 7 (July):398–405.

Goldstein, E. G. 1973. "Social Casework and the Dying Person." *Social Casework* 54, no. 10 (December):601–8.

15

Effective Nursing Home Placement for the Elderly Dying Patient

Lee H. Suszycki

Social service workers and the attending physician have the responsibility for helping the elderly dying patient and the family cope with death and adapt to a nursing home transfer. There are reactions to this type of transfer that must be considered carefully, and there is a sensitive process that involves the careful selection of a nursing home. The social worker's task is to recognize and deal promptly with the complex emotional and practical aspects that permeate this level of care and placement for the "dying" or preterminal patient who no longer requires the care given in a hospital setting.

Since most patients and their families are wary of nursing home care today, they prefer a hospital setting and resist nursing home placement. The patient prefers to die in the hospital or in his own home. However, at times, neither of these more desirable settings presents a realistic or possible option. Whenever it is medically and socially feasible, the attending physician will request a social service consultation for home care as opposed to nursing home placement, or he will keep the patient in the hospital when death seems imminent, recommending supportive counseling measures for the patient and/or his family.

Mary Adelaide Mendelson (1974, p. 240), the principal investigator of more than 200 nursing homes, has presented these interesting figures:

The New York City Bureau of the Budget calculated, for example, that in 1971–1972 the city spent an average of $592 per month for people in nursing homes, compared to $110 per month for people it was helping to keep at home. And yet, even if everything possible is done to keep people out, there will still be hundreds of thousands of people who cannot be anywhere but in a nursing home.

The medical and nursing needs of the patient may require abundant or skilled care that cannot be sufficiently monitored at home. The services of a registered nurse or licensed practical nurse at home, around the clock, are costly when the patient is not insured for this type of service; and very few are.

Social and emotional aspects can influence a transfer to a nursing home. The spouse of the patient may be physically or emotionally debilitated and may not be able to withstand the emotional and physical strain of caring for the patient even when a supportive service is obtained. Children of the patient may be emotionally or geographically removed from their parent, and may be involved with their own family problems, and therefore may be unable to care for the patient in their own homes.

A patient may have only one or two dear friends in the picture, more than likely his "healthier" peers, who also cannot give him proper care, and thus the patient himself may wish to be in a setting that offers medical care and some emotional and social gratification.

In arranging continuing care plans for the dying patient, the social worker is faced with a complex and challenging task. Skillful handling is especially required when, upon having fully assessed the patient's medical needs and his or the family's emotional, social, and financial status, as well as their coping patterns and levels of stress, it becomes obvious to both physician and social worker that a nursing home placement should be the continuing plan of care.

The social worker is the supportive guiding light, the sensitive counselor, and the core of resource material for a nursing home referral. Since the social worker's special province lies in her adaptive counseling skills, she examines carefully, by the casework process, the total needs of the patient. This evaluation encompasses the emotional, social, financial, spiritual, and cultural arenas of his life, all or most of which are bound to be affected by the process of dying and some of which through her assessment can be used as positive adaptive and strengthening sources in preparation for and adjustment to a nursing home setting. Because the family's feelings, reactions, and attitudes strongly intersect or interweave with those of the patient, these, too, warrant equal exploration and support.

The social worker maintains close ties with the patient's referring physician and holds his counsel in high regard, since it is to him that the patient initially entrusts all of self: his life, health, and hopes for defeat of death. The patient and his family turn to him also for any suitable posthospitalization recommendations when medical intervention has exhausted its resources.

Attending physicians possess an excellent knowledge of a patient's medical needs and are generally aware of the family's emotional, social, and financial capabilities. As a rule the physician himself initially suggests to his patient and family that a nursing home may offer the most suitable plan for continuing care. He will state that he will seek the expertise and guidance of a social worker in collaboratively assisting him in further assessing and planning the course of post-hospital care.

In most instances he will apprise the patient and family when he decides the patient should leave the hospital (barring medical complications), since "active treatment" will no longer be required. They are assured that the nursing home plan has their physician's sanction and approval, and they have been exposed to the fact that the patient cannot stay on indefinitely in the hospital.

This is a frustrating task for the physician to handle, especially when he has known the patient and his family for many years and is genuinely fond of them. We have all encountered the patient who will implore his physician not to let him go, neither from his care nor from the hospital. In anger and desperation he will say that he is being "thrown out" when he "most needs care" and that his doctor is interested in him only as a "disease that is not responding," and not as a "human being with feelings," and so on. The family will say that they are still able to pay the "doctor's fee as well as the hospital bills" and will continue to "cooperate in every way as long as patient can stay in the hospital just a little while longer"—and then a while longer after that.

The author has observed that the physician's concern for what happens to his dying patient from that point on keeps him strongly and deeply involved in the terminal stages of the patient's illness. He participates in the casework process that will help prepare the patient for a carefully selected nursing home facility. The physician remains available to both patient and family—in terms of keeping his patient comfortable and carrying out any necessary medical regimens, and also in interpreting and clarifying medical needs as often as is warranted. Most important of all he remains available emotionally as a giver of his support.

The social worker must be aware of what the physician has shared in terms of diagnosis and prognosis with the patient and his family. The degree to which these are shared with the patient is based upon the physician's evaluation of the patient's readiness to know or to deny his dying. The diagnosis and prognosis shared with the patient will almost always offer a glimmer of hope and encouragement.

Most of the alert terminally ill, when confronted with a nursing home transfer, are aware that their condition might be fatal and that death might be near, but the majority still hope for a better tomorrow.

"There's one thing you can count on when you're as old and as sick as I am—death and nursing homes. But, still, maybe there's some small hope of pulling through," some will comment. Such patients will peacefully submit to the nursing home transfer to preserve a peaceful status quo for their already burdened families and professional caregivers. This type of dying patient will feel that only through compliance can he maintain everyone's good will and efforts.

Those who have led a very independent, active, and healthy life before illness may be irascible and hostile and begrudgingly accept a nursing home placement in the hope of regaining strength: "I've pulled through successfully in many things in my life and this is not going to drag me down,'' a patient will remark with all the assurance he can muster. Denial is of tremendous emotional sustenance to this patient, who has dominated his environment through pursuit of challenging activities.

Patients who have been in constant pain and suffering ask for death to free them from emotional and physical anguish. A patient who wishes to die will in most instances directly share this wish with the physician or social worker. ''I want to die. I'm old, I don't want to be a burden to anyone, especially to myself. If only God could take me now—I wouldn't have to think about a nursing home.''

Those who have reconciled themselves to the inescapability of death will want to know their medical status so that the precious remnants of their lives may be imbued with a special meaning for them and their families. Most of these patients have coped with strength and stamina with past crises in their lives and have wished to be aware of the pros and cons of any given situation.

In dealing with the emotionally charged discussion of death many have a need to have this simplified and ''the wish is for a cookbook answer for treating everyone the same way; for telling every patient everything or every patient nothing'' (Schowalter, 1976). The task is hardly that simple. It must be based on a clinical assessment of the patient's ego needs, his defense structures, and his coping mechanisms that have been obtained through the steady and warm relationship.

One of the more frustrating, but nonetheless reality-based, elements for the social worker to be aware of and work with is the patient's discharge date from the hospital as determined by his physician. An early referral allows ample time whereby the patient and family are offered prompt and relevant help through crisis intervention with their most immediate and pressing concerns and thus hospital discharge is not delayed. If the patient is mentally alert and physically strong enough to participate in the planning process, all efforts must be made to engage him in the decision making. After all, he is the one who' is dying, who is in need of nursing home care, and who will have to adjust to a new, unfamiliar setting. To treat the patient as if he were already dead, someone to be disposed of and reckoned with through indirect and clandestine methods of communication, negates the ethos of the social work profession and demeans the dignity and sacredness of the individual human being.

Field (1954, p. 267) emphasizes that "it is the social worker's role to help the patient feel that in spite of twin handicaps of sickness and age, he still maintains his identity as a person." Acceptance and adjustment to a nursing home setting pose significant and threatening alterations in the life of the patient. Long years of life have inured him to many adaptive processes and losses; however, now these differ quantitatively and qualitatively. Painstaking efforts have to be taken to treat this loss and finality with a special kind of sensitivity and regard to maintain life in dignity for the dying and help sustain it for the living.

The social worker encourages a sharing and discussion of the patient's psychological state of being to his illness, explores his resources in terms of emotional support from family or friends, and assesses his comprehension of and attitude toward a nursing home placement. She creates an atmosphere of freedom and comfort that allows the patient to discuss whatever is of importance to him and respects those areas he wishes to hold in reserve.

Many patients have been exposed through the mass media to the poor quality of certain nursing homes, and as a result they are anxious, depressed, and angry that they have to go to one. An honest discussion of nursing homes should ensue, emphasizing that every effort will be made to choose his home with special attention to his needs and with his participation and involvement. This reinforces the patient's self-esteem and helps him prepare for transfer with more confidence and less panic.

The social worker does not dictate a nursing home placement to the patient. She strives to engage him in ascertaining for himself some of the reasons why he should be transferred to such a setting. According to Routh (1968, p. 45), "If patients are going to follow through on any type of planning, they must do so on their own motivations." A sharing relationship with the patient, whenever possible, maintains his dignity and pride.

Preparation of the patient for nursing home transfer is carried out in recognition and understanding of the patient's feelings (especially in the area of death and dying) by the physician, social worker, or key family member—individually or as a unit. Consistent communication must prevail between the social worker and physician in planning care. A patient may develop a medical complication that bars him from nursing home entry completely or postpones it indefinitely. The social worker, being aware of this, promptly shifts therapeutic gears, not only with the patient, but also with his family and thus helps the patient die in the hospital and gives his family maximum support in coping with a death that may be much more imminent than was initially anticipated.

One cannot focus on the patient, his attitudes, and needs without fully addressing himself to his caregivers, who are equally in need of comfort and assistance. They are beleaguered with considerable guilt, anxiety, resistance, and/or helplessness, since, despite their roles, they are powerless in granting the patient an emotionally acceptable alternate plan of care. As well intentioned as they might be, they can quite unconsciously impede the patient's disengagement from the hospital and his adjustment to the nursing home setting. The family's human dalliance and/or umbrage with the fact that the patient has to leave the hospital is silently conveyed to the patient, who, through his dependency needs, exacerbates the conspiracy of resistance. The social worker encourages the family to expose and shed some of the pain and guilt evoked by this situation. Additional clarification may be needed about why the patient requires nursing home placement, and reassurance may have to be given about why this care cannot adequately be given at home.

The social worker engages the support of related disciplines to whose care the patient is also entrusted (the nurse, clergyman, and others) in further sustaining the nursing home plan of care with the patient and family and thus offers them a wide range of emotional support and sanctions. The patient and family, in preparing for a nursing home transfer, are aware that this is the prologue to the patient's death, and grief is evident. Whether the patient and family withdraw from each other or come closer during this period depends on past and present relationships and on their ability to handle their feelings in regard to the nursing home transfer. However, premature pulling away will not only isolate them from each other but also will detract seriously from the effectiveness of planning for nursing home placement. In addition this may greatly diminish the returns of any positive adjustment to the home.

In this regard it becomes imperative for nursing home administrators to participate in courses that deal with death and dying. According to Noreen M. Clark (1974), "there are very few metropolitan institutions [in New York] which offer such courses for nursing home administrators. Plans are being made to include death and dying in every course or give separate continuing education courses on the subject. In the Columbia University School of Public Health, this subject is regularly a part of the curriculum for the basic course for licensure offered to nursing home administrators."

The National Association of Social Workers (NASW) is committed to establishing various reforms in the care of the aging. In addition to their other recommendations, NASW (1975, p. 1) states that "in-service training and staff development programs in all facilities for the aged need to be strengthened and assurances provided that this requirement be carried out."

The social worker gives the patient and family a choice of those homes she had selected on a discriminating basis on their ability to meet the patient's needs. It must be stated that there are some excellent nursing homes (mostly voluntary) that provide good medical and nursing care and a humane and caring aura that helps immensely to meet the needs of the dying patients and their families.

She is knowledgeable about standards of care in the various homes most likely to be situated in her immediate geographic frame of reference where she and her colleagues have visited. This is helpful in yielding a certain amount of knowledge and understanding about what type of diagnoses these homes accept and how they are handled medically and in regard to nursing, staffing patterns (How many RNs, LPNs, aides, are available? How many physicians are affiliated with the home? Is a social worker on staff?), the staff's level of sensitivity to the needs of the dying patient and/or his family, the cleanliness of the home, and so forth.

The patient and family may inquire about homes in areas with which the social worker is not familiar. In these instances the author has often turned to the social service department of local community hospitals or public health departments of the particular areas in question for referral to homes to which they themselves have transferred patients and have been pleased with the care given.

With the social worker's help a compromise is achieved between the patient and family on the homes to be visited, their location, and the costs involved. If a patient requires "skilled" nursing care, homes that participate in the Medicare program must be discussed and selected for visit. Homes that participate in the Medicaid program must be chosen for those patients who qualify for this assistance.

Patient and family should be told the rough median cost of homes if this will be paid for out of pocket. The majority of patients, their spouses, and families discover that paying for nursing home care can be very costly; thus they may fear financial destitution. Medicare and Medicaid programs and their relationship to nursing home payment must be fully explained to dispel any erroneous beliefs the patient or family might have about the programs. For example, many think that Medicare will contribute toward a placement only if the physician prescribes it and only if transfer is effected from the hospital. They should know that Medicare recognizes only "skilled" nursing care as opposed to "custodial" care. These concepts of care are to be fully discussed, for not all dying patients are in need of "skilled" care as defined and reimbursed by Medicare standards.

Aware of needs, preferences, and financial status, the social worker insists that as many family members as possible visit those homes either she or they have selected, those that, apart from giving the necessary medical and nursing care, embody the criteria that hold the most meaning for the patient and his family. She advises the family to visit two or three homes, since the family's first choice may not be able to accommodate the patient on or around the time of his discharge from the hospital.

The family may learn that the patient's total needs may not all be met under the same roof. At best they need to select a home on the basis of practical aspects that in the long run are of the most value to the patient's adequate care and emotional well-being.

Priorities must be quickly established. If nursing homes that offer the desired Christian atmosphere, a Kosher diet, or a luxurious setting have long waiting lists or are difficult to get to, a home that offers good nursing care, meets the patient's or family's financial criteria, and is accessibly located for frequent visiting should be selected instead. This home becomes highly attractive and emotionally appealing to the family in terms of meeting the patient's basic needs. Visiting the dying patient as often as possible is insisted upon, for it is imperative to his emotional survival. At the same time the family can check on how well or poorly his physical needs are being met.

When a specific nursing home is decided on, all information about it and the reasons for selecting it are promptly shared with the patient. A discharge summary giving pertinent and thorough medical, nursing, and social data is forwarded to the home. This report is the initial representative and image of the patient and depicts the variety of his needs for the nursing home staff. It is also helpful if the social worker contacts the home and speaks with either the admitting department, director of nursing, or the social worker. By doing so she can describe the patient's needs and emotional status at time of discharge and answer any other questions they might have. It is even more imperative to follow up closely and be in touch with the home in regard to what approximate date a bed will be available for the patient and to relay this information to the patient and family, his physician, and the nursing staff.

When the social worker learns the exact transfer date, she promptly apprises the patient's physician, the patient, and his family and helps with any other last-minute arrangements that have to be made. She informs the nursing staff and the other disciplines involved in the care of the patient of the name and location of the home in case they might wish to visit. The social worker should, whenever possible, maintain sporadic ties with the nursing home in regard to the patient's status, keep in supportive touch with the family, and thereby demonstrate to them and to the nursing home the hospital's continuing interest in the patient's welfare.

The social worker's intervention on a guiding, supportive, and environmental level helps effect a more positive self-image for the elderly, terminal patient, giving respect and acknowledgment to the many inner strengths present. Keeping the patient fully involved in the decision-making process enables him to structure his life more meaningfully and prepare for death in a manner that has most value to him and his loved ones. Encouraging the family to care genuinely and the patient to allow himself to be cared for meets and fulfills many of their needs. A suitable nursing home that provides good nursing care and gratifies the patient's spiritual needs can make it possible for an elderly, terminal patient to die in peace.

The fear, resistance, and grief associated with a nursing home referral can be mitigated through the guiding, sensitive, and supportive approach of the social worker and physician handling it and be abetted by the coordinated efforts of others on the interdisciplinary team.

References

Clark, N. M. 1974. Personal correspondence with Ms. Clark, Assistant Professor, Health Administration, and Director, Continuing Education, School of Public Health of the Faculty of Medicine, Columbia University.

Clark, R. E. 1974. *News,* no. 74 (November 12):8. Albany, New York.

Dormin, K. B. 1975. Personal correspondence with Ms. Dormin, Director, Bureau of Hospital Nursing Services, New York State Department of Health (Division of Hospital Affairs), Albany, New York.

Field, M. 1954. *Medical Social Work with the Aged.* Chicago: University of Chicago Press.

McNulty, B. 1972. "Care of the Dying." *Nursing Times* (November 30).

Mendelson, M. A. 1974. *Tender Loving Greed.* New York: Alfred A. Knopf.

National Association of Social Workers (New York Chapter). *Policy and Platform on Aging and the Nursing Home Crisis.* Approved by the Board of Directors, January 22, 1975.

Routh, T. A. 1968. *Nursing Homes: A Blessing or a Curse?* Springfield, Ill.: C. C. Thomas.

Schowalter, J. E. 1976. "Death Comes to the Communications Media." In *Communicating Issues in Thanatology,* eds. T. P. Fleming et al. New York: MSS Information Corporation.

Additional Bibliography

Broden, A. R. 1970. "Reaction to Loss in the Aged." In *Loss and Grief: Psychological Management in Medical Practice,* eds. B. Schoenberg et al. New York: Columbia University Press.

Blacher, R. S. 1970. "Reaction to Chronic Illness." In *Loss and Grief: Psychological Management in Medical Practice,* eds. B. Schoenberg et al. New York: Columbia University Press.

Cockerill, E. 1954. "The Social Worker Looks at Cancer." In *Readings in the Theory and Practice of Medical Social Work.* Chicago: University of Chicago Press.

Field, M. 1954. "Medical Social Work with the Aged." In *Readings in the Theory and Practice of Medical Social Work.* Chicago: University of Chicago Press.

Gavey, C. J. 1952. *The Management of the "Hopeless Case."* London: H. K. Lewis and Co., Ltd.

Gordon, E. 1954. "Treatment of Problems of Dependency and Illness." In *Readings in the Theory and Practice of Medical Social Work.* Chicago: University of Chicago Press.

Kaplan, D. M. 1968. "Observations on Crisis Theory and Practice." *Social Casework* 44 (March).

Prichard, E. R. 1970. "Planning for the Terminally Ill Patient." *Archives of the Foundation of Thanatology* 2 (Fall).

Rappaport, L. 1967. "Crisis-Oriented Short-Term Casework." *Social Service Review* 41 (March).

Rosenblum, C. 1973. "Nursing Home Care—A Painful Decision." *The Sunday Record* 79 (August 12).

Slater, P. E. 1964. "Prologomena to a Psychoanalytic Theory of Aging and Death." In *New Thoughts on Old Age*. New York: Springer Publishing Company, Inc.

Toffler, A. 1970. *Future Shock*. New York: Random House.

U.S. Department of Health, Education and Welfare, Public Health Service. *A Guide for Social Services in Nursing Homes and Related Facilities*. Developed by a Committee of Selected Social Workers.

Weisman, A. D. 1972. *On Dying and Denying*. New York: Behavioral Publications.

Yuncker, B. 1975. "Nursing Homes: The 12 Kinds and What They Do." *New York Post*, February 18.

16

Program Development for Problems Associated with Death

Sharol Cannon

Social Work and Thanatology

Social work is one of the most versatile of the professions; it addresses itself to a great variety of problems in a variety of ways and with a variety of people. This versatility, together with ideals such as viewing the total person in his environment, makes social work particularly well suited for dealing with the multiple problems associated with death. These problems may be physical, psychosocial, economic, philosophical, legal, educational, or vocational. Problem resolution may mean referral of a single bereaved individual during an office visit, or it may require intervention with a terminally ill patient and with his family and other social systems both before and after the death. In either case, social work offers one the breadth of knowledge and skills to approach these problems in any social environment. Some problems, such as physical pain or legal matters, cannot, of course, be directly resolved by social workers, but our special training in assessing needs and in finding or creating resources could provide the only link to a client's receiving the necessary services.

In spite of the suitability of social work for meeting needs associated with death, at least two factors have greatly reduced social work's impact on the problems. The first is avoidance of the whole area of death. Credit is due, of course, to those medical social workers and others who have dealt directly with death, but in general social workers, together with other providers of human service, and indeed with our whole society, have given little specific attention to the needs of the dying and the bereaved. Although this avoidance is well documented by writers such as Kübler-Ross (1969) and Rolfe-Silverman (1967), one need only scan the textbooks and journals to see the small amount of attention given to death compared with other problem areas.

This avoidance of death is apparently the result of the personal fear and denial that is widespread throughout our society. It seems that our own discomfort with the thought of death prevents our studying the subject or developing adequate services in this area. There is evidence of growing interest, however, manifested by the record-breaking response of 30,000 readers to a *Psychology Today* research questionnaire on death (Shneidman, 1971) and by a general expansion of the field of thanatology. As social workers, we need to cope with our own discomforts and become leaders in this emerging interest.

The second factor that has reduced the impact of social work on death is a tendency for those social workers who do concern themselves with this field to provide direct services rather than to become key administrators in program planning and implementation. This is particularly true in medical settings in which the physician–nurse hierarchy traditionally has the major decision-making responsibility. Studt (1971) comments on a similar phenomenon in the correctional system, telling how social workers initially involved themselves in diagnosis and treatment rather than management of prisons, so that now they have relatively little impact on the overall programs of the many large correctional institutions.

In addition to working through our own discomforts with death, therefore, we social workers must use our administrative skills to build the comprehensive programs needed to approach the multiple problems of death. If we fail to take a lead in this manner, there is danger that specialized but isolated and uncoordinated services will develop, resulting in lack of continuity and gaps for the client.

The Life Service Center: One Program Model

One example of a comprehensive agency is the Life Service Center, currently being developed in Phoenix, Arizona. The purpose of this Center is to provide crisis intervention and referral services, education, and research in the areas of death, dying, and bereavement. The agency was organized by this writer, who is a nurse–social worker, together with Ms. Peggy Allaire, an educator who spent 18 months providing followup services for a Phoenix mortuary. Although this Center is still in the developmental phase, a description of the plan and its implementation is provided here as one of several possible program models.

HISTORICAL DEVELOPMENT

As indicated earlier, the initial step for working in the area of death is confrontation with one's personal feelings about death. This confrontation first took place with my co-founder, Ms. Allaire, when at age 15, she went on a tour of a mortuary with her service club. One month later, on Christmas day, her father died suddenly at home from a heart attack. In spite of her own grief Ms. Allaire was able to be of great service to the other members of her family in this crisis, owing in part to the knowledge she had gained during her previous visit to the mortuary. From that time on she was interested in helping the bereaved, and she became a pioneer in the Phoenix area when she was hired by a mortuary to develop a widow-to-widow program. She eventually developed a followup service, available (without cost) to all families who wished to use it, and a program of education, in the hope that others would benefit from knowledge before a death as she had.

This writer has also experienced personal losses through death and as a nurse worked with dying patients and their families. She became involved in the Life Service Center when one, and later several, funeral directors sought social work consultation for the development of a nonprofit corporation that would provide services to their bereaved clients and would be jointly funded by several mortuaries. Drawing upon social work knowledge, this writer, together with another social worker (Ms. Sarajo Esch) suggested expansion to a more nearly comprehensive program model. Since there were no other programs in this geographical area in which the primary focus was on death, it was suggested that problems such as the psychosocial aspects of dying be included within the scope of the proposed corporation. In this way there could be more continuity in services for a family before and after a loss. It was also suggested that research and education be included as part of the program. A target population would be readily available for research, and further hard data would be added to the existing body of knowledge. The research component could also serve as a means of providing public accountability in the form of program evaluation. Education could serve as a vehicle for disseminating information obtained from research, as well as knowledge already in existence. The public could be helped to cope better with a variety of problems associated with death, and consultation could be offered to providers of human services.

When this program was outlined for the funeral directors, they expressed interest and encouraged further exploration of the possibilities. Since Ms. Allaire's employer was one of those interested, we joined forces and, again using a social work approach, informally explored the extent of need for services to the dying, their families, and the bereaved. It was found that not only do the dying patients and their families need services but also many physically healthy persons need help in preparing for their own deaths. Both public and professionals were found to need (and in some instances were requesting) more knowledge about death. Proposals for a Center on death, dying, and bereavement were prepared and sent to some 50 health, education, and social organizations. Some did not respond, but the majority of those who did indicated a need for such a center. No one opposed the idea, though a few suggestions were made and most were adopted. Several funding organizations invited us to apply formally for funds.

This detailed description of the early development is given to encourage social workers to plan and present programs to potentially interested parties, even though those social workers may not already be in top administrative positions. In the area of death the need appears to be rather universal, and so if one can demonstrate it is not already being met in a specific geographical area, and the program proposal is sound, there will be influential individuals or organizations who want to be associated with it for one reason or another.

ORGANIZATION AND PERSONNEL
The Life Service Center has been incorporated as a private, nonprofit organization under the direction of a citizens' policy board. A Citizen's Advisory Committee has also been formed to broaden community participation. This writer is serving as Administrator and Acting Director of Research, and Ms. Allaire is Director of Education and Services. Outside consultants, including a psychiatric consultant, will be used as needed. It is anticipated that, eventually, there will be a director and staff for each of the service, research, and education divisions. Full- and part-time volunteers will be used throughout the program.

SERVICES
Problem areas with which the Center will be concerned will include the psychosocial, economic, philosophical, legal, educational, and vocational aspects of death, dying, and bereavement. Target populations (as well as staff and volunteers) will include persons of both sexes, and various ages, ethnic origins, religions, and socioeconomic groups. The majority of client contacts will be in the form of hospital, nursing home, and home visits, since it is anticipated the majority of clients will be physically or psychologically unable to make office visits. The number of visits will vary but will seldom exceed six, so that clients will be encouraged to use other community resources for their continuing needs. Since problems with mourning frequently develop after family and friends withdraw their added support, followup phone calls will be made, or letters sent, three, six, and twelve months after the initial contact with a family. These contacts will

serve as means of offering support and assessing progress with the mourning process.

A large proportion of the services will be provided by trained volunteers. A corps of previously bereaved volunteers will serve as resource persons to the newly bereaved. These volunteers will make home visits, will assist in leading discussion groups, and may form social or recreational groups to assist in resocializing widows and widowers. The volunteer program will in itself assist in the resocialization of persons who serve as volunteers.

RESEARCH AND EDUCATION
Research activities will include baseline assessments involving the public, clients, human-service agencies, and members of the helping professions. Followup studies will also be done, as will special studies on such factors as client functioning, methods of intervention, public and agency policy, and professional education. Consultation and education will be provided through seminars and symposia, speaking engagements, mass media, professional articles and reports, professional consultation, field placements, internships and traineeships, college courses, and a local clearinghouse for information on death, dying, and bereavement.

FUNDING
The initial annual budget for the Center totals approximately $60,000. About half that amount has been verbally committed to date. Seed money and continuing funding are being sought from private and public funding organizations and from business and individual contributors. Every effort will be made to avoid charging fees for service, since many of the clientele will already be burdened with financial concerns, and fee charging in the midst of their crises could result in refusal of a needed service.

OBSTACLES
The main obstacles to the Center's formation were time and money. Time devoted to this effort has had to be spare time. It has taken approximately one year to progress from initial exploration of need to

beginning operation. Available funds have been markedly reduced, of course, by the current state of the economy. Just as industry tends to reduce hiring before reducing its current work force, many agencies are turning down new programs instead of reducing funding for established ones. No organization has totally refused funding, but several have delayed it, inviting us to apply or reapply anywhere from three months to a year later.

In spite of the obstacles, we have already begun some educational activities in the form of speaking engagements and radio and television interviews, and other services will be offered when more funds are raised.

Other Program Models

The Life Service Center is only one of several types of programs that could be developed by social workers. Comprehensive programs could be developed within medical facilities, community agencies, schools of social work, and research institutes or as independent agencies. In a medical facility social workers could design an interdisciplinary program to meet the psychosocial needs of the dying and their families, with an outpatient followup service for the families after each death. Social workers in a community agency such as a mental health clinic or a multiservice center could develop a specialized counseling service for all experiencing problems associated with death. Clients with such problems might include the terminally ill and their families, the bereaved, those flirting with or seeking death, those instrumental in the death of others, those whose anxiety about death interferes with functional living, and those providing services to these groups. Specific techniques could be studied for appropriateness and effectiveness with each type of problem.

Schools of social work could establish programs centering on death, either as a special institute or as a component of a gerontology program. (In Maricopa County, Arizona, in 1973, 57 percent of the deaths occurred among persons aged 65 or older.) Such a program could provide a variety of educational experiences for students, including crisis intervention and referral; individual, family, and group therapy; family network intervention; environmental intervention, including some community organization; supervision; administration; research; and social work consultation and education.

Research institutes could develop comprehensive programs around the problems of death as demonstration projects and as a means of attracting a population for the study of death and its effects. Such a project would need to be long term, however, to allow sufficient time for full program development. Some provision should also be made for continuation of the services upon completion of the project to avoid the appearance of exploiting pain just for the sake of knowledge and to provide a vehicle for continuing community benefit from the knowledge obtained.

There are at least two possible forms of an independent agency providing comprehensive services related to death. One is that used by the Life Service Center, in which services are restricted to crisis intervention and referral and to creation of a network involving multiple agencies. Another form might be an agency that provides its own followup services, such as legal assistance, financial counseling, transportation, and long-term psychiatric treatment. Because of the multiple needs of some clients involved with death, these auxiliary services should be available in any program serving the dying or bereaved. If few services exist in a community, the program may need to provide its own, but in most cases, a close working relationship with agencies to be used for referral will be enough.

The advantages and disadvantages of using one type of setting over another for creating a program will vary with the circumstances of time and locality, but there are some general considerations. An advantage to planning a program as part of an existing institution such as hospital or community agency is the availability of space, utilities, and administrative support services. The cost of items such as clerical help, accounting, telephones, and data processing can often be absorbed in the costs of operating the larger institution, so that the actual program budget is reduced. (This can, of course, operate in the reverse, where an institution charges a higher percentage for administrative costs than would be required in a self-operated program.) An advantage of establishing an independent agency, on the other hand, is that one can avoid limiting factors such as geographical service area boundaries; agency restrictions regarding intakes and home visits; or an agency image that could turn away some populations. An agency might, for example, be perceived as serving only the white middle class, or only those with psychiatric problems, and so those seeing themselves as not fitting these categories would not use the service. Establishment of an independent agency, then, can provide a specialized service to a specific population over a broad geographical area, with the opportunity to create its own image.

Conclusion

Thanatology is in its infancy. In spite of the fact that we are all touched by death (or maybe because we are), very few programs exist that address themselves specifically to the problems associated with death. Even fewer programs are comprehensive. The needs are, however, beginning to receive recognition. Services could grow in a patchwork manner like many other services in this country, or they could be systematically shaped into comprehensive, high-quality networks by social work that offers the breadth of knowledge and skills to accomplish the task. If we social workers really believe we can benefit society, the opportunity is at hand. We must face our own discomforts regarding death, apply our administrative knowledge, and demonstrate our worth.

References

Kübler-Ross, E. 1969. *On Death and Dying*. New York: Macmillan Company.

Rolfe-Silverman, P. 1967. "Services to the Widowed: First Steps in a Program of Preventive Intervention." *Community Mental Health Journal* 3, no. 1: 37–44.

Shneidman, E. 1970. "You and Death." *Psychology Today* 2, no. 8: 67–71.

Studt, E. 1971. "Crime and Delinquency: Institutions." In National Association of Social Workers, eds. *Encyclopedia of Social Work*. New York: NASW.

When Should the Clergyman Be Called?

John Freund

At an interdisciplinary discussion group a psychiatric social worker posed this question to me: "When do you as a clergyman feel you should be called in the case of a terminal patient?" Working from a concept of ministry as service and concern for a person, rather than for some disembodied spirit, and sensing that my questioner conceived of ministry to the dying in a way that was similar to mine, I quickly responded, "The earlier the better."

What I had in mind was certainly not the limited conception of ministry as the routine utterance of a few pious platitudes or, in the case of someone of my own tradition, quickly "going through" a ritual anointing that would magically prepare this person for death in 30 seconds. More on my mind was the fact that here would be a fellow human being who must now face the ultimate mystery—death, with its finality and uncertainties, both as to time and meaning, and its many sacred and secular concerns. Perhaps this person would need only an understanding individual to talk with about his fears for himself or his loved ones. Perhaps he would be someone who, aware of a personal rift with some significant person in his life, would like to come to some sort of reconciliation with the other or, if that were not possible, at least with himself. Perhaps it would be someone who would find comfort in sharing similar, even if not identical, concepts of God.

My "the earlier the better" was met with a truly pained response, "Why, that is terrible. Do you mean to say that you really believe that?" I said "yes" and was about to explain why, when someone else asked whether clergymen today were being given a different kind of training that made them more sensitive to the dynamics of grief. As I was trying to respond to both questions, I noticed the first questioner gather her things, say she would be back, and then leave. I never did learn what were the roots of her reluctance to call in a clergyman early in the process, but apparently she was certain she knew where I was coming from and had ruled out the possibility that we could have anything in common or learn from each other. I suspect she was also unaware of some major shifts in trends in pastoral care.

The discussion then moved on to some nursing concerns. After a few minutes a physician in the group stood up, murmured something about the concerns of the group not being broad enough for him, and left. Apparently he had concluded there was nothing he could learn or share in a group of nurses or clergymen concerning work with the terminally ill. It was interesting to hear these nurses later talk about the insensitivity of physicians to some patient concerns that they as nurses were acutely aware of.

I mention these two incidents from an interdisciplinary discussion group without any intention of singling out either physicians or social workers. I have been in other groups where it has been the clergyman or the nurse who has been closed to dialogue. I mention these incidents only to suggest that the title of an article that appeared in the *Journal of Religion and Health* (Bruder, 1962) entitled "The Myth of the Healing Team" may still be apropos today.

As I say this I also do not intend to deny that much progress has been made. I am personally aware of many instances where a true healing team exists and the patient is the ultimate, but by no means the only, benefiter. I am merely raising an issue of unfinished business that can and does sometimes interfere with meeting the needs of the patient, the person who is our mutual concern. The unfinished business I am referring to is a lingering reluctance to bring in an "outsider." The outsider I am referring to is the clergyman, but I suspect that in some hospitals it is the social worker or other professional.

Some Stereotypes

It is my conviction that such reluctance is rooted at least partly in prejudicial stereotypes about what outsiders can bring to the process of caring for the whole person. It is also my conviction that, when these limiting stereotypes cannot be broken, it is the patient or client who suffers.

My purpose in the remainder of this chapter is to reflect briefly on some of the stereotypes prejudicial to clergymen, their possible roots, what is happening today in the formation of clergymen that would be of interest to other professionals working in grief situations, and finally some areas of contribution and cooperation. The more common stereotypical expectations seem to run the gamut from harsh judge, through naive fool, to court of last resort when all else has failed. For some, when the clergymen enters the picture, it is expected that one of his primary concerns will be to convict a person of sin and guilt. No matter how subtly, he will heap up condemnation of the ways of the world and add guilt and fear to a person who already has enough problems to deal with. No matter what other problems the person is facing, the clergyman, out of his concern for the immortal soul, will single out man's fear of the unknown and play upon it to extract some form of confession and conversion. In this perspective it is easy to see why the clergyman is someone from whom the client or patient should be protected.

For others his advent represents the coming of an irrelevant meddler who speaks of things that have no practical meaning for the client or patient. It is expected that he will read or quote scriptures at the person, utter some platitudes, rattle some prayers, or subject the person to some empty and magical ritual. All this can do little good. But then, neither does it seem to do much harm in most cases, and so toleration is called for.

For still others his coming is the sign of defeat. All else has been tried without success. Perhaps the holy man, or misguided magician, depending on one's own prejudgments, can do something that no one else can. Thus his coming is a sign and license for retreat on the part of the staff and for fear on the part of the patient. Putting aside for a moment what might be a more positive view of the role of the clergyman in a terminal situation, I would like to reflect briefly on a few possible roots of these expectations.

Possible Roots of Reluctance to Call in Clergyman

One possible source may well be one's previous poor experience of clergymen in caring situations. Since these negative expectations are based on fact, they say more about the clergyman than about the social worker or other professional. Unfortunately it is true that each of us has had negative experiences with clergymen who unnecessarily and inappropriately upset people by their insensitivity to human suffering. In some instances this has been manifested through a mechanical and ritualistic approach to people. In other instances this insensitivity has been manifested through a compulsion to feel they must cheer a person up or answer unanswerable questions. In yet other instances it has been their own distortion of the implications of their faith's traditions that has led them to excess. These situations may have been multiplied by the tendency in the past, in some traditions, to assign men to chaplaincies either because they were too old to do anything else or had been creating too many problems elsewhere.

While not excusing some of these negative experiences I would hope that just as, for example, social workers would wish not to be judged poorly as a group because some in their profession have failed to keep up with sound developments and attitudes in their field, so also others would not judge all clergymen on the basis of one or even many negative experiences. It would strike me as unfair as stereotyping all social workers as people who dehumanize their clients by harassing visits to see if the father of a welfare family lives at home.

A second source of the reluctance to call in a clergyman could be the extension or projection of a professional's own feelings and beliefs. A professional whose personal beliefs (even atheism involves the belief that there is no God) do not include a need for the sacred or transcendent may never explore the possibility that the person he is dealing with believes otherwise. The patient may welcome the opportunity to speak with someone who represents these concerns.

Not to explore such possibilities would seem to me to be similar to a doctor's saying "I have no need of salt in my diet and therefore neither should you" or to his implying that his tranquilizers by themselves will get at the roots of an emotional problem. It certainly does not represent an attempt to see the meaning of the situation from the patient's point of view.

It may be that after exploration the person prefers not to speak with a clergyman. But it may be that, just as medical staffs have been known to project to patients their own inability to discuss impending death, so also professionals may have projected their own view of the values of religious beliefs. It may be surprising to them how often terminal patients are not so reluctant to discuss religious questions.

A third possible source of reluctance to call in the clergyman might be a lack of awareness of the shifting and broadening concepts of ministry being communicated, especially to younger ministers, in seminaries today.

A Shift in Emphasis in Ministerial Training

I have already referred to the question of whether clergymen are being given a different kind of training today that allows them to be more sensitive to the dynamics of grief and to personality dynamics in general. This has been one of the more significant shifts in emphasis in ministerial training in relatively recent years.

In the past a candidate for the ministry might well have found himself in an academic atmosphere virtually devoid of any input from the suspect behavioral sciences. What mattered was the grasp he could acquire of a body of theological knowledge that included a knowledge of scripture, the systematic and in various degrees dogmatic reflection on the scriptures as interpreted in his tradition through history, and some understanding of the ethical implications. Instruction in preaching and the rubrical details of worship as practiced in his tradition would constitute his practical training.

Since the 1920s and the birth of the clinical pastoral training movement there has been a slow but steady growth of input from the behavioral sciences. Tody it is virtually impossible to find any seminary that does not offer and indeed require its students to take a variety of courses that draw heavily upon developments in psychology and sociology. Most require their students to engage in more or less extended units of field education where they engage in ministry under the supervision of persons well versed in the behavioral sciences. It is not unusual today to find a course on pastoral care of the grieving in a seminary curriculum. Nor is it unusual for the seminarian to have had the opportunity during his formative years to sit in on interdisciplinary case conferences.

As a result many younger ministers have a much deeper appreciation of what other professionals are trying to do. They are also much more acutely aware of the psychological dimensions of their own theological stance and ministrations.

Contributions a Clergyman Can Make

With this in mind, perhaps we can return to the original question about when it is generally appropriate to consider calling in a clergyman in a terminal situation. It seems to me that there are many areas where he can make a unique contribution, especially in light of his symbolic role. These run the gamut from freeing a person from some imprisoning distortions of God and religious belief, to providing a vehicle for peace and reconciliation with God and neighbor, and to representing the caring concern for a person of his faith.

For some people it will be the clergyman who can bring them through the stage of denial to the initial coming to grips with the knowledge that one will die sooner than anticipated. The clergyman can gently but effectively reinforce the medical diagnosis and prevent prolonged denial, especially when such denial is tied into religious symbols.

A clergyman can facilitate healthy emotional expression. On the one hand he may encourage the person to express his anger at God for his impending death rather than keep it in and feel guilty at a deeper level for the unconscious stirrings of anger. When a clergyman says it is all right to feel anger toward God and that God is bigger than our anger, it seems to carry more weight than when someone else says the same thing. On the other hand he may have the opportunity to counteract negative attitudes about self rooted in the belief that the sickness is certainly punishment by God for some unrecognized sin. When a clergyman points out that Job, the suffering Servant in Isaiah, and Christ were not being punished for their sins, it can carry much weight.

One of the more frequent forms of the bargaining stage is that of pacts with God. The clergyman can be helpful in preventing fixation here. Kübler-Ross (1969) has indicated that the bargains are often psychologically associated with quiet guilt and that it is a sensitive chaplain who is the first, and in some cases the only one, to hear these concerns.

In the stage of depression the minister can also be effective in a variety of ways. Especially in the case of reactive depression caused by unrealistic guilt or shame, the person may be more readily able to recognize the unrealistic aspects when these are pointed out by someone who clearly represents a religious tradition. In the case of grounded guilt the clergyman can be a very effective instrument in aiding a person to come to a sense of forgiveness and self-acceptance.

Finally, at a time in a person's life when meanings that had been taken for granted are being called into question by the stark fact of impending death, the minister has much to offer a person struggling to find peace. Frankl (1963) is fond of quoting Nietzsche, "He who has a Why can bear with any How." As one whose whole life has been dedicated to searching out meanings (and whose primary ministry has been described by some as a "ministry of meanings" [Clinebell, 1966]), the minister should be more attuned than most to the struggle and process of arriving at meanings. This does not mean that he rigidly imposes his system of meanings on others. To the degree he has struggled in his own search for meanings, he serves as a resource to help a person arrive at his own meanings. When he is dealing with someone who shares his own system of meanings, the minister can be a strengthening comfort in providing the opportunity to speak of these meanings. Whatever the meaning arrived at, it is important.

In conclusion I suggest that, just as it should be kept in mind that not every clergyman called into a terminal situation will be a help to a person, nor will every person have a need to respond to even the best of clergymen, so also it should be kept in mind that perhaps far more people than this apparently secular age might suspect would profit from contact with a sensitive clergyman during terminal illness.

References

Bruder, E. 1962. "The Myth of the Healing Team." *Journal of Religion and Health* 2, no. 1:61–73.

Clinebell, H. 1966. *Basic Types of Pastoral Counseling*. Nashville: Abingdon Press.

Kübler-Ross, E. 1969. *On Death and Dying*. New York: Macmillan Company.

Frankl, V. 1963. *Man's Search for Meaning*. New York: Washington Square Press.

18

Cultural Perspectives on Death as Viewed from within a Skilled Nursing Facility

Larry Lister

The range of social service activities in a skilled nursing facility includes attention to the needs of residents and their families during the resident's terminal stage of illness. Although skilled nursing facilities are not terminal care hospitals, many patients die in such facilities—sometimes soon after admission and often after many years of residence. For example, in the 135-bed facility in which the data and observations for the present discussion were gathered, 26 patients died during the 1973–74 year. What occurs for residents, families, and staff during this sometimes lengthy, sometimes brief period of terminal care is the subject matter of this chapter—with special consideration given to possible cultural variations among the participants. The intent of this chapter is to provide social workers with a further heightened awareness—as the recent years of social work thinking and practice have already done with regard to cultural influences in so many life areas—of the part that people's cultural orientation might contribute to their experiences with death.

In the mixed culture of the United States there is no one attitude regarding death, dying, and survival. In Joseph Heller's recent novel, *Something Happened,* he has his main character state:

I never make hospital visits if I can avoid them, because there's always the risk I might open the door of the private or semiprivate room and come upon some awful sight for which I could not have prepared myself. . . . When friends, relatives and business acquaintances are stricken with heart attacks now, I never call the hospital or hospital room to find out how they are, because there's always the danger I might find out they are dead (Heller, 1974, p. 6).

On the other hand Hochschild, in a book based on his experiences living in a small San Francisco apartment building of older people, reports:

It was a fact of life in Merrill Court and there was no taboo against talk about it. . . . Customs gave those left a chance to cry, to express sorrow, to comfort, and to be comforted without fear of embarrassment; and it gave them a chance to do something—call people, buy flowers, bake pies (Hochschild, 1973, pp. 80–81).

These two examples show only two ways in which members of our society approach or avoid death. The concept of culture can in small measure help account for why a business executive might avoid all contact with the dying, while a group of aging widows actively respond to this more immediately relevant fact of life. Consequently the information of this chapter must be seen within the context of how the data were gathered, the setting for the study, and the community in which the nursing facility is located—a community comprising a rich blend of peoples of Caucasian, Polynesian, and Oriental backgrounds.

Data-Gathering Method

The staff of Leahi Hospital in Honolulu, Hawaii, were asked to fill out a questionnaire related to certain issues concerning death; 86

questionnaires were returned, these representing responses from physicians, nurses, aides, occupational and physical therapists, social workers, and dietitians—and representing the various ethnic groups that constitute the staff population. To supplement these questionnaire responses, the author used both personal experiences and discussions with staff, as well as a review of a series of medical records of patients who died during the 1973–74 year.

The questionnaire data were gathered simply to explore whether any major variations in patient, staff, and family experiences with terminal illness occurred when patients (and also staff) were considered in terms of their ethnic backgrounds. Some staff found it impossible to respond because, in their judgment, too many factors other than ethnic background accounted for variations in responses to terminal illness. Most of those staff who did respond placed multiple check marks after each question, since in their experience either several responses were characteristic of any one ethnic group or the responses applied equally to more than one ethnic group. Consequently the findings from the survey are presented with the objective of seeing what are *common* patterns of behavior regarding final illness and what may be variations from these patterns among ethnic groups. Also analyzed were data showing whether the persons reporting had different responses based on their own ethnic backgrounds. The ethnic groups selected for presentation here are also the five groups with whom staff have had the most extensive experience.

The following tables present the questions asked of staff and the number and percentages of check marks placed by them under the various ethnic groups, the percentages based on the total number of check marks. Along with the tables are presented general remarks related to the subject matter that formed the basis for the question.

Presentation of Findings and Discussion

The first question presented in Table 18.1 is derived from Kübler-Ross's (1969) description of the reactions that dying people experience. While it is recognized that many of these stages are transitory

**TABLE 18.1. IF THEY KNOW THEY ARE TERMINALLY ILL,
THESE PATIENTS TEND MOST TO BE:**

| | Patient Ethnic Background | | | | | | | | |
| | Caucasian | | Chinese | | Filipino | | Hawaiian | | Japanese | |
Responses	n	%	n	%	n	%	n	%	n	%
Angry	44	32	8	8	8	8	19	19	7	5
Depressed	35	26	33	35	33	32	25	25	40	30
Accepting	7	5	13	14	13	12	13	13	29	22
Hopeful	16	12	9	9	11	11	25	25	15	11
Quiet	6	4	29	30	28	27	8	8	35	26
Protesting	31	22	3	3	10	10	11	11	7	5

and that staff respondents may not interpret their meaning in the same
way Kübler-Ross has formulated them, it is nonetheless interesting to
note that the most frequently observed reaction appears to be depression.

Caucasians tend to protest and to be angry, whereas the other
groups tend more to be quiet. There was a tendency for more Japanese staff to see Japanese patients as depressed while more Caucasian
staff saw them as quiet, indicating there may be some cultural barrier
to a full appreciation of the inner experience of the paient who,
though responding quietly, is not doing so out of a sense of serenity.

What may be of most importance here is that workers with the terminally ill must be attuned to the depression that, for many patients,
is an affective state accompanying the whole process of dying. Rather
than view depression as a phase that passes, it may be important to
recognize it as a recurring affect within a continuing process. There
will be times of hope, of some acceptance, of bargaining, and of
other reactions, but the recognition of pending loss will recur, and the
depressed state will again emerge as the dominant affect. With the
support, availability, and acceptance of caring people, however, the
depression of patients may be borne and, at times, modified, if staff
and family do not abandon them and if their depression is not interpreted as only anger and protest or as quiet serenity.

The fear of pain connected with terminal illness is one of the factors contributing to the avoidance of death in our society, this avoidance expressed both through the difficulty many people have in visiting the dying and through the common preference that healthy people express for dying quietly in their sleep. That painful deaths are not the norm is borne out by such reports as Hinton's. He states that a "proportion of about one chance in eight of experiencing pain in the terminal illness seems to be a fair generalization from the various sources," but goes on to say that "it seems to be more common than it should be" (Hinton, 1972). The antidote for pain can often be found in the relationship between the patient and the attending staff, wherein an easy, confident communication seems to be correlated with fewer complaints of pain requiring relief (Hinton, 1972, p. 71).

That responses to pain can be culturally determined has been reported in at least one classic study (Zborowski, 1952, pp. 16–30). Therefore, one question in the present survey was designed to explore whether any characteristic responses to pain were seen among the various groups studied.

As can be seen in Table 18.2, the Caucasians and Hawaiians tend most to active responses to their pain, through requesting medication, making demands on staff, or crying. The other groups tend to respond more quietly, but the data show that a frequent response for all groups is to seek relief through medication.

The discomfort, the progressing debility, and the alterations of consciousness of dying people all contribute to their reactions to other people. A question was posed, however, about reactions that might characterize the various groups in their interaction with staff. As

TABLE 18.2. IF THEY ARE IN PAIN, THESE PATIENTS TEND MOST TO:

	Patient Ethnic Background									
	Caucasian		Chinese		Filipino		Hawaiian		Japanese	
Responses	n	%	n	%	n	%	n	%	n	%
Cry	31	25	8	11	18	26	22	26	8	8
Remain quiet	4	3	23	32	21	30	13	15	51	50
Make demands on staff	45	37	17	23	6	9	23	27	13	13
Want medication	42	34	24	33	24	35	26	31	30	28

TABLE 18.3. THE REACTIONS TO STAFF BY THESE PATIENTS IS MOST TYPICALLY:

	Patient Ethnic Background									
	Caucasian		Chinese		Filipino		Hawaiian		Japanese	
Responses	n	%	n	%	n	%	n	%	n	%
Withdrawn	7	7	12	22	16	22	9	14	25	28
Accepting of whatever is done	12	12	24	44	34	48	29	40	48	54
Wanting much contact	32	34	13	24	12	17	17	23	8	9
Overly in need of attention	43	46	5	9	9	13	17	23	8	9

shown in Table 18.3, the majority of patients are accepting of whatever is done for them, except that Caucasians appear to seek much contact. This response was given by Caucasian as well as non-Caucasian staff and so appears not to be the result of any culturally based difference on the part of the respondents.

Withdrawal is not, moreover, the most frequent behavior for any group. In reading the medical charts on the sample of patients who died during the year of the study, it becomes clear what an active period of help-giving the final days and hours of life require of the nursing staff. Nurses are involved with intensive, frequent contact; much of it, of course, is devoted to physical procedures, but all of it is accompanied by an intense awareness of the affective and interpersonal responses of the patient.

As has been pointed out, attitudes toward death in our society cannot be considered in either–or terms, since "individual Americans seem to possess contradictory attitudes toward their own deaths, and the culture of the Unied States appears to embody equally paradoxical attitudes toward death in general" (Dumont and Foss, 1972, p. 96). The paradox has been explained in terms of the rational awareness that comes to every person that everyone else eventually dies, combined with the unconscious conviction of the impossibility of personal mortality—"man cannot have an inner awareness of a world in which he himself would not be the central point of reference" (Dumont and Foss, 1972, p. 104).

With appreciation of this paradox, a question was nonetheless posed about "general attitudes toward death," as perceived by staff, of the many patients and families with whom they have contact. The data in Table 18.4 show that a majority of all groups, with the exception of the Caucasians and, to an extent, the Hawaiians, accept death more than they protest it.

TABLE 18.4. THE GENERAL ATTITUDES TOWARD DEATH OF PATIENTS AND FAMILIES FROM THESE ETHNIC GROUPS SEEM TO BE:

	Patient Ethnic Backgrounds									
	Caucasian		Chinese		Filipino		Hawaiian		Japanese	
Responses	n	%	n	%	n	%	n	%	n	%
Very accepting	16	25	28	62	26	54	21	38	41	62
Protesting (e.g., "why us," "why now")	32	51	9	20	15	31	21	38	15	23
Nonaccepting	15	24	8	18	7	15	13	24	10	15

The acceptance of death is, however, an impossible concept to tap through a single question. For the patient in the final stages of illness there is usually a struggle—which occurs beyond any level of conscious intention—simply to continue to resist inertia. This struggle almost goes beyond ego and into the realm of pure biology.

For the family, on the other hand, the acceptance of the actual death of one of their members has often to do with the degree to which they have completed their obligations to the patient and to their perception that the patient's struggle is final. Families are particularly attuned to staff during this period, and their acceptance is often fostered when they perceive that a fully caring staff is clearly involved with the patient up to the time when the patient can no longer respond. This does not mean that heroic measures need to be taken, but rather that the patient is not abandoned and that the family have easy access to staff for physical assistance to the patient and psychological assistance to themselves.

The next question touches on the interaction between the patient and his family (Table 18.5). The data indicate that the greater number

TABLE 18.5. TERMINALLY ILL PATIENTS FROM THESE GROUPS SEEM TO WANT THEIR FAMILY:

| | Patient Ethnic Backgrounds | | | | | | | | | |
| | Caucasian | | Chinese | | Filipino | | Hawaiian | | Japanese | |
Responses	n	%	n	%	n	%	n	%	n	%
To stay away	4	6	2	5	1	2	0	–	7	9
To visit at the families' convenience	10	15	14	37	13	24	13	19	27	36
To come often	37	54	17	45	27	50	34	50	25	34
To stay long	7	10	3	8	12	22	18	26	12	16
To do more than the family can humanly do	10	15	2	5	1	2	3	4	3	4

of patients from all ethnic groups want their family members to visit often. The Japanese tend to defer to what is convenient for their families, whereas the Hawaiians tend most to want their families to spend much time. Hawaiians are traditionally family oriented, and it is not unusual for many relatives to gather at the bedside of a patient, regardless of the seriousness of the patient's condition.

The data produced by this question support our general knowledge that fear of abandonment is great on the part of dying people and that the presence of familiar people is a protection against the often awesome sense of aloneness. Since, however, many patients have lived in the skilled nursing facility for years before they enter any active stage of terminal illness (for example, the average length of stay of residents in the study facility during 1973–74 was nearly 3 years), some families have often long since discontinued anything but "holiday" contacts, and some patients have even outlived their families. Thus staff often become the substitute family and help provide to the patient the needed sense of contact with caring people.

With the data showing a need for frequent contact by the patients with family members, a question follows about the content of conversation between them. As shown in Table 18.6, for all groups there is talk that circumvents the central issue of the patient's pending death.

Conversation tends to be directed toward bringing outside news of the family to the patient or to remarks that tend to deny the reality of

TABLE 18.6. THE CONTENT OF PATIENT AND FAMILY CONVERSATION TENDS TO BE:

| | Patient Ethnic Backgrounds | | | | | | | | | |
| | Caucasian | | Chinese | | Filipino | | Hawaiian | | Japanese | |
Responses	n	%	n	%	n	%	n	%	n	%
Small talk (e.g., "the weather")	21	24	7	15	10	18	10	14	13	14
About family events	20	23	16	34	17	30	24	34	27	30
Mainly about the patient "looking good," "getting better," etc.	28	33	12	25	18	32	21	30	35	39
About how the patient and they are really feeling	14	16	5	11	8	14	13	18	9	10
About plans for after the patient dies	3	3	7	15	3	6	3	4	6	7

the patient's approaching death. There are many logical reasons for communication to be directed to family news or more superficial aspects of the patient's condition. It is usually painful for patients and families to talk about their real feelings of depression, pending loss, or future plans. Some of this significant conversation has already taken place over the months or years during which the patient has been in the nursing facility; this content is often facilitated by the social worker in pursuing long-range-care plans.

Another factor contributing to the type of communication among the patients and family members relates clearly to the patient's condition. Often in the terminal stages of illness the concern of everyone is focused on basic biological processes of respiration, eating, discharge of wastes, and the like. With these vital functions at the center of concern family members often spend time helping the patient eat, or wait while nursing care is given, or simply sit in attendance as the patient drifts in and out of sleep. Such a situation does not allow for much conversation among the participants. In fact what often matters most to the patient is that someone important is there.

In actual "deathbed" conversations a brief statement or a gesture may be all that is communicated about the true situation being faced, and all participants read much into the communication. For example, one woman who was asked to visit her dying friend made one remark about how—when the friend was feeling better—they could visit again in the friend's home. The patient responded simply, "Oh, I'll never be back there again." Nothing more was said about the issue, but both friends knew that the truth had been spoken, and it was then possible for them to proceed to write a few farewell letters to other friends and relatives and thus complete the real business that the patient had in mind when asking the friend to visit.

It is important that social workers—in a desire to bring practice continually in line with the real needs of people—do not become overzealous in pursuing the currently heightened focus on the needs of the dying person. There may even be a need to protect the patient from other people who might be intruding on the patient's desire not to discuss his state, as in the case of the patient who told his social worker that one reason for his great fatigue following visiting was that "everybody who comes in here wants to talk about death and dying. Can't anybody talk about anything else? I wish they would stay off the subject because I don't want to talk about it."

The data presented so far have focused on the patient and the patient–family interaction. The final three questions deal with the family and the family–staff interaction.

TABLE 18.7. CLOSE FAMILY MEMBERS TEND TO:

| | Patient Ethnic Backgrounds | | | | | | | | | |
| | Caucasian | | Chinese | | Filipino | | Hawaiian | | Japanese | |
Responses	n	%	n	%	n	%	n	%	n	%
Stay away from the patient	5	8	2	4	2	4	3	5	1	1
Visit occasionally	17	25	6	12	9	17	10	18	10	13
Work mainly through the staff	15	22	7	14	8	15	5	9	9	12
Visit often	25	37	25	52	23	43	27	46	37	49
Want to be around all the time	5	8	9	18	12	22	13	22	18	24

As shown in Table 18.7, close family tend to visit often among all ethnic groups. Frequent visiting is, of course, facilitated both by hospital policies and by staff attitudes that permit flexibility of hours, the bringing of food from home, lengthy bedside visits, and the like. There are, however, factors that do not facilitate frequent visiting, such as the reality that many homemakers also work full time (Honolulu has the highest proportion of women working outside the home of any city in the country.) and are therefore unable to visit during the day.* Consequently visiting tends to be concentrated on evenings and weekends, though when the family are aware the patient is rapidly approaching the end, greater flexibility in visiting occurs.

These data tend to refute the criticism sometimes heard that older people are being abandoned to die in isolation in impersonal nursing homes. Of course, being "visited often" is not the same thing as living full time within the bosom of the family, and aged patients often continue to feel alone and families feel guilty, in spite of great efforts that families make to visit frequently. Thus, again, the vital role of staff as substitute families cannot be overstressed.

Physical expressiveness often differs among ethnic groups, and so a question was asked about the type of physical contact that occurs among the patients and families. This question was asked, not only to tap differences among ethnic groups, but also to learn how the quiet presence or tactile contact from others brings an important sense of security to the dying person. It is sometimes difficult for family members to provide tactile closeness, since both the medical equipment and the patient's fraility often make visitors fearful of approaching closely.

The data presented in Table 18.8 tend to indicate that touching follows ethnic lines, with more physical contact among the Caucasians, Hawaiians, and Filipinos. These data would thus suggest that physical contact follows more from the life-styles of the participants than from a reaction to the condition of the patient. The older generations of Orientals are often less physically demonstrative, and so solace is experienced by them as much through the presence of fam-

* This is said with a full awareness that our society continues to view the visiting of the sick as more the obligation of women.

TABLE 18.8. WITH A TERMINALLY ILL PATIENT, FAMILY MEMBERS TEND TO:

| | Patient Ethnic Backgrounds | | | | | | | | | |
| | Caucasian | | Chinese | | Filipino | | Hawaiian | | Japanese | |
Responses	n	%	n	%	n	%	n	%	n	%
Keep a physical distance when visiting	8	14	9	22	3	6	1	2	7	12
Get close but not touch	6	10	19	46	20	43	3	6	32	56
Touch some (e.g., kiss hello, shake hands)	28	49	12	29	19	40	29	52	14	25
Touch a great deal	15	26	1	3	5	11	23	41	4	7

ily as through the physical contact that may be more characteristic of the other groups.

The final question is directed to the type of interaction that specifically occurs between the staff and family members. Table 18.9 shows that, in the facility of the study sample, the interaction is mainly casual and friendly, or somewhat confiding. Extremes of aloofness or intense contact seem not to be present.

TABLE 18.9. FAMILY MEMBER'S RELATIONS WITH STAFF TEND TO BE:

| | Patient Ethnic Backgrounds | | | | | | | | | |
| | Caucasian | | Chinese | | Filipino | | Hawaiian | | Japanese | |
Responses	n	%	n	%	n	%	n	%	n	%
Aloof	6	8	3	6	4	7	–	–	4	5
Casual, friendly	21	29	23	47	20	36	31	45	28	38
Confiding, ask questions	26	36	13	27	22	39	16	23	25	34
Know staff names	12	16	6	12	7	13	14	20	10	13
Intense, much contact	8	11	4	8	3	6	8	12	7	9

When these data were examined in terms of the ethnic status of the staff respondents, there was no indication of different intensities of interaction among family and staff members from different ethnic backgrounds.

At times, because of years of residence of some patients, families become attached to various staff members in the same way that staff form strong bonds with patients and families. Consequently, along with the grieving over the death of the patient, there can sometimes be a form of grief over the lost attachment to the facility. The social worker, in followup contacts with the survivors, is in a particularly good position to help with the process of emancipation from the deceased relative and with the separation of family from staff. As a broker of information between staff and families during this followup period, the social worker can often help both groups to loosen the threads of an often lengthy association and thereby help facilitate the process of mourning.

Conclusion

The skilled nursing facility referred to in this presentation has a staff and patient population representing the diverse mixture of cultures found in its surrounding community. Generalizations about these cultures are difficult, however, since each apparent cultural fact is repeatedly disproved by the reactions of the next individual patient. But it is in the nature of social work to attempt to understand both the common—as well as the idiosyncratic—features of the people whom it serves.

A host of intracultural variables would need to be accounted for to refine the generally global findings of the present study. As it stands, the information supplied by staff in this survey would indicate there are more culturally related common elements than differences among patients and families during the terminal phase of life. To have both the similarities and the differences understood and respected is to continue to offer the individualizing services that nurture—until the very end—the uniqueness of each individual being.

References

Dumont, R. G. and D. C. Foss. 1972. *The American View of Death: Acceptance or Denial.* Cambridge, Mass.: Schenkman Publishing Co., Inc.

Heller, J. 1974. *Something Happened.* New York: Alfred A. Knopf.

Hinton, J. 1972. *Dying,* 2nd ed. Middlesex, England: Penguin Books.

Hochschild, A. R. 1973. *The Unexpected Community.* Englewood Cliffs, N.J.: Prentice-Hall, Inc.

Kübler-Ross, E. 1969. *On Death and Dying.* New York: Macmillan Company.

Zborowski, M. 1952. "Cultural Components in Responses to Pain." *Journal of Social Issues,* no. 4.

Part V

Therapeutic Approaches and Concepts

19

Talking about the Unmentionable: A Group Approach for Cancer Patients

Phyllis Mervis

Within at least the last 10 years death and dying has received a great deal of attention. Much material has been published, while college courses and workshops, television documentaries, and popular magazines now address themselves to this topic. Such core issues as anticipatory grief, mourning, isolation, alienation, patterns of communication, and dignified or meaningful death, as well as suggested models of treatment, have all been greatly illuminated in print and lecture. But little has yet been said of the group process as a therapeutic approach to aiding cancer patients. This chapter is an attempt to describe such a method as it has been practiced at Mount Sinai Hospital in its Chemotherapy Clinic, where a weekly outpatient group met for two years.

The recognition of existing, informal patient groupings in the Clinic combined with a professional awareness of cancer patients' needs provided the impetus for the group that began in January 1972.

The Chemotherapy Clinic, in which patients with metastatic disease are treated, has a procedure requiring that patients arrive at the clinic by 12:30 P.M. to have their blood drawn. They must then wait until at least 2:00 P.M. before all the "counts" are ready and they can be seen and treated by their doctors.

Patients were found to spend this waiting period engaged in animated conversational groupings. Casual at times, the conversations ultimately always focused on such things as illness and current symptoms, medications, side effects and pain, frustrating experiences, and feelings of despair. Moreover, even when these discussions were casual—and certainly when they moved to more serious considerations—I was aware of underlying anger, fear, depression, and anxiety, unresolved because these feelings were left unacknowledged and unexpressed.

These informal conversations clearly and concretely conveyed the reality of life-threatening illness and the patients' struggle to cope with the experience and with their multiple feelings and reactions. The aim of a group program was to encourage patients to share and express these fears, concerns, anger, guilt, and depression within a therapeutic setting. A group would provide the opportunity to discuss openly a subject and feelings generally considered taboo but with which patients have to live. Put simply, the group contract offered was, "It can be said here. Whatever it is, we can talk about it because in the end the truth is a relief."

A group approach would also provide a beneficial way of confronting and coping with, as well as offsetting, feelings of loss of control and the sense of impending catastrophe as identified by Kübler-Ross (1971). The group would help patients prepare by helping them realize that such feelings are shared and that they can be dealt with openly and rationally. Also, opportunity for successfully dealing with and closing up real problems and unfinished work would enable and enhance coping and resolution.

To have the group viewed as an integral part of the medical service, I needed the support of the Chief of Oncology, as well as of the physicians and nurses who staffed the clinic. I presented them with the purposes and goals of the group, as well as information about its structure and meeting time (during the long waiting period for blood counts), so as to indicate how it would not interfere with any medical activities. Initially, some of the clinic physicians resisted the idea, seeing the group as an oppressive aspect to patient care and expressing concern about additional time requirements for "anxious" patients. There was also concern that a group might precipitate emotional disturbance, if not psychotic episodes. For instance I was warned against including a particular patient with a long history of depression for which she had been hospitalized many times. This patient subsequently chose to join the group and participated until her death.

The cooperation of the nurses was necessary. Although this staff expressed interest in the group and a desire to be helpful, initially their behavior indicated a less accepting attitude. Frequently nurses suddenly remembered to weigh patients as the meeting hour arrived. Or they would disappear when it was time to begin wheeling patients into the meeting room. However, as they began to see the benefits to patients and as I began meeting with them regularly to share appropriate information, the nurses became very supportive of the program.

Whereas the medical staff's initial resistance to the group finally gave way to approval and support, the Chief of the Service responded positively to the idea from the beginning. It was his sanction that really ensured the group's ultimate approval.

For a long time it was my feeling that as a social worker I was not associated with medical procedures and could therefore reach for and tolerate listening to feelings patients might otherwise not express or feel uncomfortable expressing to doctors and nurses. However, it is quite clear from the material I have read, the groups I have observed, and my own experience that while the social worker's strategic role and training offer her the opportunity for creative, human intervention, working with the dying is within no one professional purview (Trachtenberg; Carder and Anders, 1974; Parsell and Tagliareni, 1974). Eda Goldstein also makes this point when she catalogues various therapeutic approaches with dying patients (Goldstein, 1973). Her position reinforces my own current thinking that the dying patient is not mine or the doctor's or the nurse's. He or she is a person being treated for or dying of cancer, and jurisdictional or competitive feelings should be put aside to reaffirm the primary focus of patient care.

The procedure for informing patients of the group was as follows. Because I already knew the Clinic population from the program of 100 percent screening coverage, I initially approached these patients, explaining the purposes and procedures and extending an invitation. Subsequently, in interviewing each new clinic patient, I included information about the group as well as an invitation. Even when, much later, physicians began referring patients, I continued seeing patients before they joined the meetings. In this way the patient remained in control of the decision. Also, it was important to assess each patient's situation and needs to determine if a group would enhance or undermine coping. Patient reactions tended to substantiate the validity of this screening.

A patient's acknowledged awareness of his or her illness did not automatically mean he wished to join the group. Certainly those who were more comfortable talking openly about cancer wanted such an experience. Others, as R. Reeves (1974, p. 283) has pointed out, "have their reticences . . . and these limits should be respected." Reeves goes on to state (1972, p. 284) "As long as his [the patient's] signals are consistent, we should be content simply to be with him on his own terms."

On the other hand, patients who talked very little of their illness often did choose to join. This decision seemed to confirm that patients often use denial when it is expected of them. Sometimes, moreover, a patient who was unable to use the word *cancer* was relieved by being in a group—if only to listen—and in so doing to share the experience of sharing feelings.

Two other important factors about membership should be mentioned. The common experience of disease and a desire to talk with others ensured cohesiveness. Economic, racial, ethnic differences provided few impediments to joining.

From the beginning the group was open ended, and this format, while disruptive when new members entered and painful when members died, also reinforced the group's basic contract that we were here to talk about and use the words *death and dying,* as well as to focus on whatever other needs patients had.

Over two years, the group served 40 patients and provided a setting for the sharing of many feelings. There did emerge a pattern of basic issues that were almost always expressed in one way or another. A few of these follow. The helplessness and frustration that accompany being sick were often discussed. Patients were well aware "nobody ever stops coming to this clinic because they got cured." Often patients got tired of the treatment and expressed this despair. "When you have cancer you don't get well. So what's the use of fighting, especially when it's an uphill fight all the way?" The issue of dependency was also expressed in many ways—from the necessity of waiting for tardy ambulettes for transportation to clinic to the resentment of waiting for pain medication and bed pans.

Anger toward insensitive, rushed medical staff was also an issue. Likewise, in discussing how they had originally learned their diagnoses, some patients talked resentfully of being told bluntly or "on the run." However, patients were often protective of their doctors—perhaps fearful of somehow jeopardizing the treatment relationship if they got too angry. More global anger ("Why me?") was also expressed—often in bitter terms. It was tolerated and supported by members who well understood these feelings.

The uncertainty of chemotherapy and individual reactions to the drugs were frequently discussed. Patients compared medicines and side effects. They talked about hair loss and nausea and ways to cope with them. They even offered concrete suggestions such as how to remember to take "all those damn pills."

Another issue, recurrent because of the clinic's nature, was the depression that comes with seeing patients deteriorate and die. "You begin to wonder when it will happen to you" and "You suddenly are reminded of what you'll have to suffer before you die." These kinds of statements were very often coupled with some form of hope or a discussion of something more cheerful. This "seesaw" phenomenon, which occurred in almost every session, seems to bear out Kübler-Ross's statements about patients' needs to change the topic. "They all acknowledged that it was good to ventilate their feelings; they also had the need to choose the time and duration of this" (Kübler-Ross, 1969, p. 236).

I think it is important to mention my own reactions to leading such a group and my deep appreciation of the supervision I received around my feelings. Most difficult for me were patients' feelings and expressions of impotence and helplessness. Cancer is disastrous, and I often found myelf responding by wanting to do something concrete as a way of "undoing" what the patients had to experience. This meant that at times I would become overwhelmed, offer concrete suggestions, or be very directive of the group process. Such techniques do not really address the more basic issues of "Why me? Life doesn't make any sense." Supervisory support helped me understand this so that I did not lose sight of the group's purpose and the real work to be accomplished through the patients' experiencing and sharing these feelings in a frank, accepting setting that becomes "the most welcomed communication for many of our patients" (Kübler-Ross, 1969, p. 233).

The following is a small piece of the group process; this meeting occurred in January 1973.

The group began slowly—with lots of vague statements about the weather, feeling achey, the flu epidemic, and so on. Several patients were also quite giddy. Reaching for the underlying feelings, I commented on these two things, pointing out how in the past the group had avoided discussion by latching on to vague topics. I wondered too if there was something in particular that was disturbing, for several of them were quite silly today—and we have also looked before at what this device serves. Mrs. F. quickly responded: "haven't you seen the parade outside?" I asked Mrs. F. to clarify what she meant by parade, and she quickly elaborated that she was referring to the number of people who had come to the clinic in wheelchairs this week. Other patients chimed in, commenting about being upset by seeing so many wheelchairs. I asked if anyone could tell me why it was upsetting and what was upsetting.

Mrs. E. immediately said, "Well it's frightening—that's all. I mean after all—we might be in the same boat some day and it's upsetting to be reminded. In fact, I always hate Thursdays—I get up feeling nauseated—just knowing I have to come to the clinic."

Mrs. F. picked up on this. "I hate coming to the clinic too—but for a different reason. I feel trapped. I have to come because I have to take my medicine. So I don't have any choice.''

''Sure you do Agnes,'' said Mrs. A. ''You don't have to come—that's your choice.''

''Some choice,'' said Mrs. F. ''See what I mean. Either I come every week for medicine or don't come and die. What kind of choice is that? I wish I had the flu—then I could take my medicine, get better, and be done with it.''

''But Agnes, you don't have the flu, none of us have the flu, and that's what's so hard to accept—what makes you so angry today?'' Mrs. B. asked.

Mrs. E. said, ''Listen, I used to feel like you did—remember everybody—I was scared to death—and I was worried all the time—and I guess I was angry too like you are now, but I don't feel that way anymore—you just learn to live with it. I know that sounds impossible—but I did it.''

Mrs. F. commented: ''That's just it—I have to live with it, but it's lousy having cancer—always coming to the clinic for medicine, never forgetting and next week I'm going to Bermuda for 10 days, and you know what, I have to take my medicine with me and take it there. Who needs all this— why can't I just forget it for a week—and then I can't have liquor while I'm on the medicine—what a way to celebrate Christmas and New Year's on vacation, and my leg's acting up again—I know what that's from—I've been practicing how to dance to records and I guess I overdid it—Goddamn it, I hate having cancer.''

The group quickly picked up supportively on what Mrs. F. had put out so strongly. Several members identified having had similar feelings at one time. Many acknowledged that only with time did these feelings give way.

Then the patients helped Mrs. F. focus on ways to handle her vacation in Bermuda comfortably. One patient suggested that she drink ginger ale in a champagne glass—that way she would at least feel festive. One patient suggested that, instead of overdoing things by dancing all night the first night of her vacation, she should pace herself and thereby ensure a good time. Mrs. E., who had at one time been terribly anxious, said she had even had a drink last week—while out to dinner with her son and daughter-in-law. After all— one small drink couldn't hurt anyone. Mrs. F. listened attentively to all of these suggestions, getting a great deal of support from the interest and attention of the group members.

This session continued, but I would like to stop and look at what went on in this portion. The group began with some very heavy feelings, precipitated by the patients in wheelchairs (with my direction). Once they were helped to acknowledge and verbalize their feelings the patients were able to move on to other considerations and, in fact, were able to listen to Mrs. F. rather than remain preoccupied with thoughts of the parade outside.

Mrs. F.'s participation is an important one as well as an example of what the group can provide. Clearly angry at being singled out to be ill, Mrs. F. used the group to ventilate her feelings—and to someone other than just a well person. Had she not had such an opportunity, she might characteristically have acted out her angry feelings by forgetting to pack her medicine. The group provided support for Mrs. F.—and for each other—reinforcing the sense that others have felt as Mrs. F. does and so she is not alone—and moreover, that others have experienced such angry, depressed periods and have moved through them. Important here is that following the expression of strong, emotionally laden feelings, the group focused on the living piece and helped Mrs. F. find ways to enjoy the vacation in Bermuda. That Mrs. F. was willing to consider and accept some of these suggestions reflects the importance of her earlier sense of having been heard out, listened to by people who not only share her feelings and experiences but also are concerned about what she is feeling and how she is living with those feelings. To paraphrase Kübler-Ross, the group helps people die by trying to help them live.

This chapter has been an attempt to describe a group method for helping patients with cancer. It suggests that a group meets patients' needs for expressing feelings in a shared, accepting environment that offsets the isolation, loss of control, and depression so commonly experienced. A group also provides a setting where the resolution of problems around death and dying is enhanced. Lastly, it is hoped this chapter has illustrated the group's very important focus on the life piece—not always the dying—on the here-and-now reality of living. It is this focus—the emphasis on the patient's feelings, concerns, and need for expression—that enhances self-esteem and self-determination and ensures a dignified, meaningful life rather than one characterized by marking time.

References

Carder, M. P. and R. L. Anders. 1974. "Death and Dying—Oncology Discussion Group." *Journal of Psychiatric Nursing and Mental Health Services,* July–August.

Goldstein, E. 1973. "Social Casework and the Dying Person." *Social Casework* (December) p. 607.

Kübler-Ross, E. 1971. "What Is It Like?" *American Journal of Nursing* 71, no. 1 (January):54.

—— 1969. *On Death and Dying.* New York: Macmillan Company.

Parsell, S. and E. M. Tagliareni. 1974. "Cancer Patients Help Each Other." *American Journal of Nursing* 74, no. 4:650–51.

Reeves, R. B., Jr. 1974. "Reflections on Two False Expectations." In *Anticipatory Grief,* eds. B. Schoenberg et al. New York: Columbia University Press, 1974.

Trachtenberg, J. "Team Involvement and the Problems Incurred." Available from Social Service Department, Memorial Hospital for Cancer and Allied Diseases, New York, New York.

Additional Bibliography

Abrams, R. D. 1966. "The Patient with Cancer—His Changing Patterns of Communication." *New England Journal of Medicine* 274:317–22.

Feder, S. P. 1966. "Psychological Considerations in the Care of Patients with Cancer." *Annals of the New York Academy of Sciences* 125(January):1020–27.

20

Group Therapy with Advanced Cancer Patients: What Are the Issues?

Clelia P. Goodyear

Psychotherapy with the advanced cancer patient is a new and important field of clinical work. Much of the case material gathered from this work indicates that two of the most prevalent factors characteristic of the advanced cancer patient's struggle against death are social and emotional isolation and fear and that, despite meaningful one-to-one contact between patient and therapist, there always remains in the patient's mind the nagging question: "Is there anyone else in the world going through what I am going through?" At the same time, the therapist who sees many advanced cancer patients during any given week wants very much to share with patients case histories demonstrating that there are indeed many others waging a similar battle against the emotional and physical stresses inherent in coping with advanced cancer. Clearly, group therapy would seem to be a preferred modality of treatment for this patient population. As Yalom (1970) states:

Many patients enter therapy with the foreboding thought that they are unique in their wretchedness. . . . In the therapy group, especially in the early stages, the discomfiture of their feelings of uniqueness is a powerful source of relief.

Toward this end a group initially composed of nine females, all suffering from advanced cancer, was formed and met for 12 weeks. This chapter presents the results of that group experience in order to suggest guidelines for the formation of such groups and to present superficial observations of this particular group experience.

Purpose of the Group

It was felt that group interaction between advanced cancer patients should optimally help patients to feel less isolated; free to verbalize questions, anger, and fear; motivated to explore their present life situation in an effort to better use whatever time was left, specifically, in the area of interpersonal relationships; free to establish meaningful relationships with other cancer patients and to be able to call on them for support outside group meetings.

In addition the group ought to provide the patients with the opportunity to examine and understand the effects of constant pain, deteriorating body functions, and constant confrontation of death on the following most basic ego functions (Bellak, 1974): reality testing, judgment, sense of reality of the self in the world, regulation and control of drives, object relations, thought processes, adaptive regression in the service of the ego, defense functions, stimulus barrier, autonomous functions, synthetic–integrative functioning, and mastery and competence.

Through a better understanding of what they were feeling and what was happening to them physically and emotionally, and through an examination of past and present coping patterns, it was hoped that patients would gain some sense of control over their current life situation.

Finally, because of visible physical deterioration of self or others and the possibility of members' dropping out because of total physical disability, or because of death, it was felt that the group setting ought to provide an arena both for collective mourning and for mourning for the loss of the self.

Selection of Patients

Optimal criteria for patient selection were a life expectancy of six months to two years; no visible surgical scars; a complete awareness of an openness to discussion of diagnosis, prognosis, and medical therapies being administered; an age range of 24 to 65 years (this was to be an advanced cancer group, not a geriatric group); a male/female population; no restrictions on ethnic, religious, socioeconomic background, or marital status; a mental status limited to normal-neurotic. (Patients with latent psychosis or organic brain damage due to metastasis or a primary brain tumor were not considered.)

All patients who were receiving some form of assistance from the agency and were cognizant of their diagnosis were approached and asked if they would like to participate in a group experience related to "coping" personally and interpersonally with advanced cancer. Each patient who expressed interest was interviewed at least once before admission into the group by the group therapist, to establish motivation, medical and emotional eligibility, appropriateness of problem areas, and ability to speak of cancer and death openly.

The group began with nine members, and by the fifth week had stabilized at six members. Of the three members who dropped out, one experienced a psychotic reaction to excessive pain and fear and was referred to a private psychiatrist; one experienced severe debilitation as a result of an adrenalectomy and post operative chemotherapy; and one became frightened and dropped out without warning.

The remaining six members all suffered from advanced cancer. Five had undergone two or more surgical procedures and extensive chemotherapy and radiotherapy. The sixth, diagnosed Hodgkins IV B eight months previously, had undergone 75 cobalt treatments and was not experiencing a significant remission. The majority of patients took a variety of daily medications, including oral chemotherapy, hormone therapy, and psychotropic drugs. All were suffering from multiple symptoms, including general fatigue, which made it impossible to forget that they were gravely ill. The age range was 32 to 56.

Creation of the Group

The group met at the agency. All members were medically and financially eligible for agency services and had been receiving, before the conception of the group, some form of assistance from the agency.

It was decided that sessions would be weekly, and last 90 minutes, and that the agency would reimburse group members for transportation costs each week. Each member was responsible for arranging his or her own transportation.

Stages

The group experienced three clearly defined stages: (1) catharsis, characterized by diffuse discussion and a generalized anger; (2) indecision, characterized by pervasive anxiety and fear; and (3) acceptance, characterized by the group's aggressive attempts to explore in depth life problems experienced by individual members. During this third stage, group members felt free to confront one another and to actively separate neurotic conflicts that had characterized a life-style before the onset of cancer from issues that had occurred as a result of the cancer.

The first stage, catharsis, lasted for four sessions. During this period group members seemed compelled to verbalize all the angry and confused feelings they were experiencing. Some of this anger was projective. Members felt that well people, including family members and spouses, saw them as "repulsive" and "frightening." They felt that discussion of feelings with friends and family was "too overwhelming. They just can't take it." However, much of the anger was well based in reality but owing to social and emotional isolation it had become diffuse and irrational. Much of this anger had been introjected and was being experienced as anxiety, guilt, and depression. All members expressed fear of being out of control emotionally and intellectually and the feeling that their days were spent in attempts to flee from the reality of their illness. One group member stated: "I think the reason that I'm unable to concentrate even on the smallest, most trivial matter is that I am so busy trying to deny what's happening to me. I'm so busy denying, I can't even think any more." Another member stated: "Where the hell do you find the guts to say I'm just going to go for my treatments and not walk around feeling like the world is going to come to an end, and who can you share that feeling with? No one."

All members shared the following feelings

> Family members tend to infantalize and isolate them.
>
> There are very few, if any, people who will go "all the way" with them. As a result of multiple "crisis" even family members tend to "fade away" physically and emotionally.
>
> It is difficult to know whom to be open with. Very often the logical person such as a spouse cannot bear the emotional strain for very real reasons, for example, chronic heart condition.
>
> Loss of control is experienced in every area of life. The advanced cancer patient can no longer count on his body, even on a daily basis.
>
> Doctors are too busy and most often are interested only in the medical aspect of patient care. No attention is paid to the emotional impact of cancer and cancer therapies and their effect on the patient as a person.

The second stage, indecision, lasted for two sessions. Group interaction during this period was more focused. However, the group as a whole was permeated by a sense of fear. Members indicated: "There is a lot of fear in this room; you can smell the fear in here." Attempts to define this sense of fear brought forth such statements as: "I live with a specter, a bogeyman. He is always with me. It is a fear of the unknown, not only how am I going to die, but also how am I going to live. What else is going to happen to me?" There was also a sadness that related to loss of self. One member stated: "I feel like every day something new happens to chip away another piece of me. Pretty soon there won't be any more of me left. I can't stand it. I'm just nothingness.'' Members were angry that the ''fantasy'' that life goes on forever was no longer available to them. They expressed their thoughts about suicide and euthanasia, but all members agreed they would be unlikely to actually kill themselves. Rather, they felt that their present state of mind was ''killing'' whatever chances they had left for happiness. Members directed their anger onto any target available, including the group leader. When the leader observed that she felt it was possible, despite all the negatives in their lives, for the members to experience some positives about themselves, the group as a whole attacked the leader and stated that no positives were possible. Cancer and the fear and loss of control associated with it annihilated one as a human being; therefore, a positive sense of self could not be achieved.

The sixth session began with an active concern on the part of all members that they were halfway through the group experience. Members agreed that the group was the major physical and emotional activity of their week and that it was proving to be a meaningful experience. They agreed that ''Now I'm linked up to something. Before I felt so alone and confused,'' and that: ''I'm always so blue and depressed before I get here and I always leave feeling buoyed up.'' As the session progressed the group focused on depression and its immobilizing effects. Members expressed feelings of impatience with themselves and their depression and questioned whether or not a ''new me'' was possible. This session ended with all members in agreement: ''It's simply not possible to go on living this way. There must be something good that we can find in our lives.''

The third and final stage, acceptance, began by group members' actively seeking a redefinition of their contract with the group leader. The group expressed frustration at not being able to get at ''painful inner feelings.'' They felt that the leader should be ''pulling things out of us.'' One member verbalized the thought: ''I haven't been able to talk about what's really on my mind. I want to go deeper, but we really don't know each other that well.''

It was at this point that the group, including the leader, began to focus intensely on individual members and to define the emotional conflicts within their personal lives related to the cancer itself. Some of the issues that evolved were the following:

Grief and anger over body loss and mutilation and over inability to accept current body image.

Feeling of sexual inadequacy and impotence and the subsequent fear of abandonment by a well spouse.

Feelings of guilt over occasionally excessive dependency, both financial and emotional.

Anger at having a normal life denied them.

Frustration over a life style they had all developed—one of constantly searching for a "cure" and an obsessive preoccupation with the "self"—which occupied all their emotional strength, leaving them isolated and unavailable for family and friends.

In addition, the group aggressively tackled such practical issues as how to deal with doctors and health care. Finally, members began to differentiate between maladaptive coping patterns and emotional conflicts characteristic of themselves before the onset of cancer and to realize how these conflicts were exacerbated by the emotional and physical impact of suffering from advanced cancer. All members agreed that, before onset of the cancer, they had had many difficulties in interpersonal relationships. They felt that they were constantly behind a "facade," unable for various reasons to present "the real me." To a certain extent they agreed that with the onset of cancer they had found a "tool," a "way of getting what I wanted."

Role of the Therapist

It became quite clear at the outset that the role of the therapist would have to be one of verbally acknowledging all manifest and latent content when appropriate (Langs, 1973). Without this activity on the part of the therapist, the group, afraid of their own feelings and fantasies, would have dealt only with superficial material, remaining in Stage 1 and perhaps disbanding as a result of excessive fears and anxieties explored in Stage 2. In the same way it was necessary for the therapist to elicit and explore all fears and fantasies present in Stage 2 in order for Stage 3 to occur.

The tasks of constantly and consistently sorting out the unreality of neurotic conflicts from the reality of physical illness and fear of death, and of continually realizing that no matter how much work group members did there were many areas in which no work at all could be done, were difficult and emotionally draining to the therapist. Ultimately, each member must face death alone, and the therapist's task of continually considering this factor and her own death was often anxiety-provoking. However, for the group experience to be successful, the therapist had to confront her own death and also her feelings of anger, anxiety, and impotence at not being able to prevent death. Without this confrontation there would have been an "empathic blocking" and a slow emotional withdrawal from the group.

Secondary Implications

With the exception of one patient, by the twelfth session all group members not already receiving individual psychotherapy had requested and had begun this mode of treatment. In addition, spouses of the married patients had requested a group for themselves.

Conclusion

The implications of group psychotherapy for the advanced cancer patient are manifold and concern not only the patient but also family members and physicians. The cancer patient who has a sophisticated knowledge of his illness and who has of his own volition consented to artificial prolongation of life by any and all medical therapies faces a life experience totally unrelated to that of a well person. Body image and a sense of the self in the world are massively assaulted. The vital delusions (Bellak, 1974) are attacked, and as Eissler (1955) so aptly states: "The ego founders upon the id." As a result the patient must form new intrapsychic defense mechanisms to continue to experience satisfactory interpersonal relationships and emotional performance of maximum capacity. The group experience initially allows advanced cancer patients to come together and to discover that they are in no way unique. This realization leads directly to an eager ventilation of feelings. A sense of universality is gained (Yalom, 1970). Directly thereafter comes the necessity to acknowledge fear—both of living and of dying. Negatives such as fear, depression, and anger appear to outweigh any positive element that exists. At this point in the group experience, confrontation is crucial. Do members want to retreat into the relative "safety" of isolation and depression, or do they want to seek out positives and in so doing rejoin life? A successful resolution of this confrontation will lead to the stage of acceptance, in which members are able to realize that they experience neurotic conflicts, as well as realistic fear, related to cancer and death and begin to use the group in a more traditionally "psychotherapeutic" manner and thereby gain some understanding of their emotions and more of a sense of control over their personal lives and interpersonal relationships.

References

Bellak, L. 1974. "Contemporary Character as Crisis Adaptation." *American Journal of Psychotherapy* 28, no. 1 (January): 46–58.

Eissler, K. R. 1955. *The Psychiatrist and the Dying Patient*. New York: International Universities Press.

Langs, R. 1973. *The Technique of Psychoanalytic Psychotherapy,* Vol. 1. New York: Jason Aaronson, Inc.

Yalom, I. D. 1970. *The Theory and Practice of Group Psychotherapy*. New York: Basic Books.

21

Developing New Norms for Parents of Fatally Ill Children to Facilitate Coping

Ruth R. Boyd

When a child is dying, the excruciating pain associated with the experience is complicated by the dynamics inherent in our society. Despite recent professional attempts to lift the taboo on death and dying, it is still considered deviant to talk about death and to share the intense, often frightening affects associated with anticipatory or actual grief. Open discussions of these topics are not deemed "polite, appropriate behavior"; they threaten defenses created by denial, and such "insensitivity" and "morbid thinking" result invariably in avoidance or withdrawal from the dying and the bereaved. In general our society is characterized by an orientation of mastery over nature that seeks, as a way of dealing with its fear of death, to deny death as a naturalpart of life.

No other relationship parallels that of parent and child; in American culture, death—particularly for the white middle-class population—is associated with old age. Many parents have said that it seems "un-American for a child to die." Hence, parents of children diagnosed with fatal illness experience the fact as incomprehensible and incredible. They believe there must be some answer somewhere to the problem.

Questions arise about the doctor's competence. Is he up to date? Has he had adequate experience? The situation is so far beyond control of the parents themselves, regardless of their competence in other areas, that the sense of their own impotence and failure produces the most profound feelings of distrust, frustration, and anger, compounded by the feeling of isolation that grows as parents feel themselves increasingly more cut off from "normal" family activities and relationships and marked out as "different" from others around them. They crave empathic understanding but reject maudlin pity.

This chapter reports on the development and use of a therapeutic group for supportive treatment. The major therapeutic ingredient was its use to create a subculture, a new social reality, that freed parents of fatally ill children from some of the constraints of "acceptable behavior" required of them by the broader society and offered them a substitute support system. The co-leaders introduced and sanctioned new norms, attitudes, and values, permitting parents to face in the safety of the group what they often could not face alone or with spouses, other family members, or friends—the internal and external impact of their child's possibly preceding them in death.

The children were being treated by a Department of Hematology–Oncology in a voluntary research-oriented children's hospital, where the most common disorders were the acute leukemias and solid tumors such as neuroblastomas, Wilms tumor, and rhabdomyosarcomas. The families were predominantly white, middle-class, from the surrounding suburban areas.

In contrast to their attitude toward individual conferences with medical staff, casework help, and other supportive efforts provided within the medical setting, the parents intuitively felt that a group, with its unique properties, might provide an additional resource for help in coping with the unprecedented stress of living with a fatally ill child. They requested that such a group be formed.

Sociocultural Expectations for Parental Behavior

The parents recognized earlier than did most treating personnel that new and conflicting social and psychological problems were emerging at a time when they felt least able to handle them. The majority had internalized well the dominant norms and values of the culture with regard to taboos around death and to behavioral expectations in other areas as well, which they found increasingly difficult to meet. For example, in the face of pain (psychic or physical) one is expected to be stoic, restrained, and rational. One can accomplish all goals with hard work. Indeed, there must be active mastery versus passive acceptance when one is confronted with a problem. The external world of things and events rather than inner experience and affect are important. Significantly, independence in management of one's personal affairs, especially of one's family, had long been a value to which many had subscribed.

Hence, major sources of anxiety seem to stem from a conflict between sociocultural expectations for parental behavior and the necessary adaptational responses to the psychosocial impact of a diagnosis of malignancy in one's child. The fact of the matter is parents do not have much control over the often unique drama that begins to unfold in their lives. Work will not alter the reality of the diagnosis or the course of the illness. The nature of the disease and its treatment is such that the doctor and other medical/nursing personnel become among the most "significant others" in one's life, on whom one feels profoundly dependent. Whether or not one likes it, inner experiences and affect intrude with an intensity and tenacity often heretofore unequaled in one's experience.

Simulation techniques used in training sessions around effects of a diagnosis of cancer attest to this as well. They elicit most intense affects, quite similar to those actually experienced. In reality situations a complicated set of emotions seems to be activated, and a correspondingly complex set of responses is mobilized in efforts to adapt. Many parents maintain that the pronouncement of such a diagnosis makes them feel as if a "death sentence" is hanging over their head, followed by "a kind of solitary confinement—partly of their own making, partly imposed on them," (Koltnow, 1972) as they await the execution of the sentence.

The inferences and analogies to crime and punishment associated with death made by them are impressive. Kübler-Ross (1969, p. 2) explains that death is always associated with something bad and frightening that calls for retaliation and retribution because in our un-conscious we do not die of natural causes—we are killed. Whenever there is death or the threat of death, the malevolent intervener from the outside must be identified, so that the guilt may be placed where it belongs and the guilty one can be punished. Guilt, fear, and frequently punishment fantasies are associated affects with which parents of fatally ill children must struggle, with little or no under-standing of what is happening to them. Many have said there is never a time when one feels more isolated, lonely, and different. Emotions tend to shift, intermesh, ebb, and flow, depending on changes in the physical condition of the child. As internal resources of the isolated nuclear family erode, undermined by altered relationships to every-one in their environment (including the sick child and God), their re-ality needs and moral imperatives continue. They must live as "nor-mally" as possible, so long as there is life. Life for the patient may extend from a month beyond diagnosis to 14 years or more, as in the case of a "good responder" known to us with acute lymphocytic leukemia. There is an awareness by most parents that "death expec-tancy" should not disrupt living. The breadwinner must work; bills must be paid; the other children's needs must be met. The child with the medical problem must be cared for physically, psychically, edu-cationally, and socially. Changing medical regimens must be mas-tered. Complex decisions must be made about how much information should be made available to the child, governed largely by the parents' sense of adequacy (or inadequacy) in handling the situation and by their doubts of the child's readiness to incorporate and handle knowledge traumatic even to the parent. There is the ever-present need to protect the child as far as possible from the fear and trauma arising from unwise use of information by often well-intentioned but misguided persons to whom she/he may be exposed. One of the most critical concerns and most vulnerable areas is the attempt to maintain a viable marital relationship under these unprecedented conditions of stress. According to Koltnow (1972, p. 125), "The evidence that making a positive adjustment to life with childhood cancer is not uni-versal is painfully evident in the few studies that have been done on cancer's impact on the family. In one study, one-half of the couples

required psychiatric care. In another, marriages failed at a rate of 80 percent.''
It is these issues that a social work group may address.

Properties of Groups

Groups have rich, varied, and unique properties that are potentially supportive and growth-producing for its members. Among a group's significant characteristics are:

1. *The Here-and-Now Reality.* Goroff (1972, p. 496) states: ''The overriding characteristic of the group, from which all other properties emanate, is its here and now reality. . . . The interactions, the feelings generated, the problems solved . . . [are] a part of the being-and-becoming process for its individuals with the present having a tremendous impact on the participants.''
2. *Peer Support.* Empathic or confrontational interactional responses from peers, those with whom one is sharing a common problem, differ in quality and impact from those that may be derived from the worker/therapist. Parents of fatally ill children indicate ''nobody, no matter how empathic, can quite conceive of the experience unless he is living it.'' This sense of common experience coupled with a feeling that others care, based in part on the resultant shared understanding, can and does impact on the loneliness and isolation so frequently expressed as feelings accompanying parental experience. The group offers the individual the opportunity to become part of a network of social relationships and interactions, and this is a potent force. Goroff (1972, p. 500) notes ''the perception by the individual that he is accepted, is supportive . . . and increases skill of adaptation.''
3. *Concept of Helper Therapy.* Recognition by the individual that she/he has the capacity to help and give to others diminishes the sense of helplessness and feelings of inadequacy while increasing the capacity to accept help from others in the group. Moreover there is an enhanced feeling of strength in numbers. In a group, the individual is not alone in the face of authority, particularly medical authority; hence, he tends to be less afraid to raise legitimate issues and concerns. The issue of medical authority is inexorably tied into parental anxieties. As previously indicated, the ''sick role'' imposes an ''inferior status feeling'' of vulnerability and dependence. Impersonality in management may communicate

further feelings of inferiority to the sick and their family. Thus, a hospital system's decision to provide representatives in response to collective parental requests reflects the humaneness of the system, its respect for the parents as active participants in delivery of care, and its recognition of parents' rights and of its own responsibilities for the sick and their families. This institutionalized expression of caring results in diminution of feelings of vulnerability and inferiority.

4. *Group Norms, Attitudes, and Values.* Norms may be defined as the explicit and implicit standards for the range of acceptable behaviors allowed to be expressed in the group, stemming from the group leaders and/or members. Norms incorporate value judgments and lend predictability and regularity to a group's functioning.

In our view introducing new norms and rewards "for changed behaviors" seemed a pivotal way in which the group could impact parents' need to express their "deviancy." The "deviant" behavior of the parents, in fact, becomes the acceptable standard for behavior within the group.

Although groups have these properties and potential, groups in and of themselves usually do not become mutual-aid societies. People tend to pass each other like ships in the night unless there is an external person to harness their constructive energy, provide a structure, and offer them direction. In short there is a knowledge base and skill component required for the energizing of the properties inherent in a group.

Essentials in Group Work with Parents

There are two aspects to group work with parents of cancer patients. The first is the need for understanding the physical and psychosocial impact of cancer on the patient, family, medical/nursing staff, and the social worker. Inherent in this is the dynamics of the age of the child. In our experience, children up to about 11 years old can, with help, accept their illness and dying better than any other age group. Parents and adolescents rarely appear to move to a stage of true acceptance. Fundamental to the patient's family's needs are knowledge about the disease and its treatment, maximum relief from physical discomfort, reasons for hope, and reassurance that "significant others," in particular, will not abandon them.

Second is the need for understanding of group dynamics, process, and some technical aspects of group formation that seem to require modification for work with parents of fatally ill children.

A detailed discussion of the various aspects of group work with this population is beyond the scope of this chapter. However, we would like to comment on what we consider the basic task in any social work with parents of children with malignancies, the value inherent in use of Kübler-Ross's conceptualization of the five stages of reactions to dying, the norms that were established for the parent group that freed them to handle a variety of topics, and the findings from the two-year experience with the parent group.

Stages of Dying

Kübler-Ross's conceptualization of the five stages as coping mechanisms gives guidance in several areas:

1. In understanding how a given patient is coping at a particular time.
2. In acquainting the patient and family with the normality and universality of processes or stages that they are likely to experience. (A spouse may often be enabled to appreciate why the marital partner may be responding in a fashion unlike his own and thus avert serious marital problems.)
3. In giving recognition to the fact that a parent's unwillingness or unreadiness to participate in a group experience may be caused by the particular stage he is in.
4. In allowing the playing out of feelings, particularly anger in the group, as displacements or projections and thereby supporting their ventilation and referring them to their source.

New Norms, Values, Attitudes

Co-leaders established that thoughts and feelings concerning experiences surrounding the illness could be expressed and handled in the safety of the group. Feelings were identified neither as good or bad but as necessary and important parts of the human personality. Since people cannot help how they feel, feelings would not be criticized.

People can help what they do and, therefore, would be held responsible for behavior.

On a behavioral level permission was given for parents to laugh, cry, express anger, give "gut responses," talk candidly about life and death, scream rage, and grieve.

Great value was placed on the strength and courage it took to attend the group as a source of additional support. Correspondingly, self-recognition that an individual had gone as far as he could go and wanted to leave the group was equally valued and respected.

Finally a ground rule was set that what was discussed in the group became the property of the group for analysis and constructive work but could not be used outside the group destructively, for example, spouses using against each other something shared in the group.

Of necessity the group tested if certain behavior was allowed and considered acceptable, primarily by testing the leaders and then its members. For example, the first testing was around honesty in expression of feeling. At the second meeting, when the leader was attempting to summarize the previous meeting as a way of beginning the session, the "provocateur" in the group booed him, interrupting the worker; other members looked stunned and embarrassed. The worker acknowledged that it was a "slap" and an expression of anger. The parent denied real anger but said she needed some "comic relief." We asserted, while people shuddered, that she was saying something very important, that others were likely feeling the same, that while their anxiety was building, we were droning on and they were all getting angry. This released laughter and sighs of relief and a flood of discussion about how ambivalent people felt about engaging in the group and about the pain experienced when they come to the meeting, because it reminded them of their child's illness, something they fought hard not to be reminded of so long as the child was doing well medically. The leader acknowledged this as an understandable reaction and said we were glad they had the courage to return to share their reactions in spite of this.

Emerging consensus about the new norms was revealed in one of the early middle phases of the group when discussion centered around impact of the diagnosis on the parents themselves. A young, relatively new parent, whose child had been diagnosed at another institution, said she could not talk about it without crying. (Indeed, she wept throughout most of the meetings but attended religiously.) Mr. L., a middle-aged businessman whose youngster had been in remission for five years and off medication for one year, said he understood how Mrs. H. felt because he had cried for the first eight months after his child was diagnosed. Elaborating, he said, "I felt so badly I wanted to punch Dr. X. in the nose when he told me my child's diagnosis and that she might die. I hated them (doctors), did not trust them at first, but I eventually came to respect them as among the most competent and to feel there was no Medical Center better able to treat my child's disease." It took several more sessions before Mrs. H. could cease crying sufficiently to reveal how her child's diagnosis had been told to her. She was heartily reassured that this group setting was the place to cry. "We all do it and we all understand." Some said they held themselves all week for this one place where they could release feelings.

Mrs. H. was then able to say that, after a period of months of diagnostic work, a young doctor came to her in her 7-year-old child's presence in the hospital room and said the child had leukemia and had about six months to live. The consequences to the child and to herself were extremely bad. The group rallied around her, many members realizing fully the difference in approach at this hospital. Their understanding helped her to feel a part of the group. This was the first time the members had moved in and taken responsibility for helping another member adjust to the group in such a personal way. Significantly, months later, when this mother's child was dying, she was able to call on her experience in the group to accept that her mourning reactions were "normal."

With the establishing of the group's credibility, the following major themes and issues emerged and recurred, according to our content analysis:

1. Medical aspects of care (before diagnosis and during treatment).
2. Attitudes and relationships with medical–nursing staff.
3. Feelings of anger and dealing with anger.

4. What and when to tell the patient and siblings about diagnosis.
5. Sense of isolation, feeling of "difference," helplessness, and lack of understanding by others.
6. Guilt and punishment fantasies relating to etiology of illness, death wishes toward the sick child, feelings of relief at time of death.
7. Role of religion.
8. Alteration in relationships to ill child, siblings, spouses, family of orientation, friends, and God.
9. Jealousy and resentment of new life or well children, resulting in shame and guilt.
10. Death and grief.
11. Magical thinking with the feeling of being cursed and that the dead or witchcraft could provide answers or help; feeling of being singled out by fate for harsh destiny.
12. Universal fear that marriage may not survive strain of coping with illness and threat of loss.

Summary of Findings Derived from Group Experience

Our experience with the group revealed that, when a physician gives information on a potentially fatal illness, parents can understand only what they are ready for, owing to varying degrees of anxiety. Thus a place is needed where they can work through a continual questioning of the medical information, its implication and impact, and move toward gradual acceptance. In response to their queries about medical issues and implicit requests (in the early phase of the group, usually the second or third session) it is helpful to have the Director of Hematology–Oncology talk to them. Answers to questions submitted in advance by members of the group form the basis for the Director's discussion. Candor, with appropriate optimism regarding research and lack of defensiveness under attack, seems essential to the success of this critical area in the beginning of the group. We found the impact of this well-attended meeting far reaching, for it demonstrated clearly the hospital's readiness to discuss fully with parents their problems in understanding some of the implications of the disease and its different forms and treatments. The concern of all was that their children were receiving the most modern techniques of care and treatment. The result of knowing that these were available was most valuable. Staff observed a dramatic decrease in calls made to them, diminution of hostility in clinic contacts as the parents felt increased trust, understanding, and security with medical staff. Stress seemed to be reduced for parents and staff, freeing their energies for other tasks. In spite of these many positive aspects, some did express sadness and a "feeling of let down" because their "secret hope" was that the Director of Hematology would reveal some new information regarding a cure. Whenever they met with him or his Associate Director, this thought was a part of their "hidden agenda." Undoubtedly, frustration and criticism directed toward the hospital (doctors and other staff) were brought on by the realization that they could not offer "cure." At a later stage the parents were able to verbalize the cause of any hostile behavior and handle it.

We found the implications of the cancer diagnosis so fearful and anxiety-provoking that some parents initially could not use the word *leukemia,* and there was a superstitious avoidance of the word *death* in the initial phase of the group. For example, one parent, whose teenage daughter had been in hematologic remission for five years, could not use the term *leukemia* nor had she been able to allow medical staff to provide the patient with appropriate knowledge about the disease. Although this parent did not become a core member of the group, her limited participation allowed her to begin to use the term and permit medical staff to work with the youngster, who was questioning the need to attend clinic periodically, take medication, and undergo procedures such as bone marrow tests.

An incident that precipitated fear at first but greater understanding ultimately was the first death within the group. For the period preceding the child's death, Mrs. X. attended the sessions, explaining it was the one place she could be assured of understanding and could feel absolutely free "to be herself." She was given great support by the members, some of whom stated they knew a similar fate awaited them. Mrs. X. missed only one meeting, and though she was extremely emotional at times and thus aroused corresponding emotions in others, the group gradually came to realize that this was an experience one could live through without, as one member stated it, "becoming unglued.'' Afterward members stated that she had been most helpful in demonstrating that it was possible to live through the experience, to be able to pick up again on life, and to find compensations. The experience, if anything, strengthened the group appreciably.

Hence, these parents were enabled gradually—in the safety of the group, in a subculture that sanctioned it, and with exposure to the experiences of group members—to talk about death, examine it, anticipate it, mourn their impending loss, and still retain appropriate hope. This "living in" experience, where enormous fear, the world's shield of secrecy, and the barriers separating spouses from each other were relinquished, allowed for communication—first, via the group and then with each other. Some couples said they could hold themselves together all week, knowing this was the one place they could "let go" and cry and talk. Often spouses heard things about the other's reactions first in the context of the group. One mother stated her husband was most giving to her following the group. Serious problems arising from spouses' being at different stages and having different coping patterns, from the fallacious cultural expectation that the husband provides the "strength" in all crises, and from the fear that all parents had that their marriage could not endure the crisis were examined and at least intellectually appreciated. Through verbalization and universalization there was assuaging of guilt and diminishing of the danger inherent in forbidden thoughts and feelings, such as death wishes toward the sick child and relief at the time of death. When it was apparent that the downhill course could not be reversed, and they began the enormous struggle again to "let go of the child" (only for another remission to occur), parents were now free to say that they wished that the experience could be over. Some indicated that when friends said it was "nice" the child had been spared, "you want to kick them!" Acceptance of these feelings was given, with expressed recognition that they were in response to deep psychic pain and desire to spare the child more suffering. Where indicated, when a parent had separated emotionally from the child, direction into more neutral areas of interaction was encouraged to prevent additional reasons for guilt after the death.

With regard to religion there was movement full circle, from rage and rejection of God to, at least, an intellectual appreciation that teaching religious or ethical tenets is necessary for providing a framework for children's understanding of certain phenomena and for having hope. The leaders stressed that disease and illness are properties of all living things and that belief in God and "being good" does not necessarily protect from hardship but exists to be a strength in the face of hardship. Increased awareness of the needs of the patient's siblings often resulted in a parent's giving much neglected sibs some exclusive time.

In essence the open communication supported by the group helped to improve the quality of family life. To varying degrees the family's communication system around life and death opened up. Their reports of diminished anxiety and the ability to use terms formerly avoided superstitiously improved self-esteem and enhanced understanding and acceptance of complicated and discomforting medical information. The parents' ability to sort out and manage complex relationships with hospital staff and family members seemed to suggest change and an effective relearning process. Concurrently this parent group demanded the most from the co-leaders in handling their countertransference emotions. Because of the demonstrable improvement in the behavior of parents and patients, use of the group method was institutionalized as part of continuing service provided by the Department of Hematology–Oncology.

Technical Aspects of the Group

Analysis of the technical aspects of the group suggests, perhaps, that traditional ways of establishing and running groups may have to be modified for work with those anticipating or those who have experienced loss. Provided were a time-limited contract of eight sessions with a closed-ended group, adequate evaluation of these sessions, and a voluntary self-selection process for accepting parents into the group based on their own determination of what they could tolerate in frequency and context of meetings. As a result a "successful" group that ran for 19 months evolved. On the basis of the very favorable evaluations after the first eight sessions by 21 parents (15 of whom constituted the core group), the group was continued as then constituted and ran for nine more months. The second series integrated new parents, who were quickly socialized into the group. They were enabled to move much more rapidly from external to internal concerns because of and with the help of the "veteran parents." In the first meeting parents were certain they could meet only once monthly but soon modified it to biweekly 2½-hour sessions. Consistency of attendance is required to achieve necessary comfort with content material and peers. We learned that followup by phone or otherwise after meetings with each member of the group, particularly during the early phases, is essential to deal with the anxiety activated by the experience. Allowing parents to begin with safe external targets (medical procedures and practices and staff), in the early stages of the group as well as in each session, also seems essential to the process.

Finally, co-leaders are needed who offer a balance in style, orientation, and skill to provide a highly supportive, philosophically oriented approach. The model found most useful involved two social workers, one highly experienced in group process skills, and the other a part of the medical setting, who was equally experienced in clinical social work and work with staff, patients, and family around death and dying.

Implications for the Future

From the relatively successful outcome of this group experience and the data stemming from it, further testing of the group as a type of treatment, and as an aid in management of loss, both anticipatory and actual, seems indicated, not only for parents but conceivably also for siblings and patients. The experience also suggested that people require active assistance for at least one to two years following loss. A further implication stemming from this experience is the need for preventive community work in the form of education of children by parents about death if we are to begin to influence societal attitudes and norms in this area.

Furman (1971, p. 72) questions (and we concur) whether we can develop more healthy attitudes, impart them to our children, and influence current mores. If a systematic approach to imparting the concept that death is a part of life is followed, by the time children develop meaningful speech and fantasy life is less lively (beginning at about age two) they will be enabled to integrate this information with the other data and education they are acquiring in the world around them. Over the long term, conceivably, a generation could grow up better able to face and assist in the realities of death and dying.

References

Furman, R. 1971. "The Child's Reaction to Death in the Family." In *Loss and Grief: Psychological Aspects in Medical Practice,* eds. B. Schoenberg et al. New York: Columbia University Press.

Goroff, N. 1972. "Unique Properties of Groups: Resources to Help People." *Child Welfare* 51, no. 8 (October).

Koltnow, P. 1972. "The Family." *Proceedings of the American Cancer Society's National Conference on Human Values and Cancer,* June.

Kübler-Ross, E. 1969. *On Death and Dying.* New York: Macmillan Company.

22

Bereavement as a Normal Life Transition

Phyllis R. Silverman

Bereavement needs to be looked at from a public health perspective, not in terms of individuals but in terms of populations. Bereavement is not an illness; it is a universal reaction that touches all individuals who are connected to others. It is therefore essential to move away from the limited concepts of individual pathology and patienthood. Everyone must die, and those who survive will be bereaved. Their grief is a psychologically appropriate and healthy reaction to their loss.

We live at a time when the expression of strong feelings is labeled as deviant and regarded as symptomatic of emotional illness. Yet to be bereaved is to know great sadness, despair, and sorrow. In some cultures, people tear their hair or scratch their face until it bleeds and thus vent their strong and unhappy feelings. Most people in our society are embarrassed by such demonstrations of emotion. In the United States members of the immediate family may be given tranquilizers to sustain them during the funeral service under the pretense that they may become too upset if left unmedicated. This act implies that to be upset is bad. In actuality it may be that the beholder cannot accept the intensity of the feelings expressed. Knowledge of how to cope with grief must be made available to everyone. The bereaved cannot be "cured" of their condition; rather, they need to learn to accept their feelings and, ultimately, to accommodate to the loss. They must learn how to build a new life without the deceased, and to do this they must learn to remember the deceased while also integrating the memory of the past into the life of the present.

Bereavement can be seen as a time of transition (Silverman et al., 1974), but the knowledge of how to pass through this transition is not readily available. Mourning rituals and customs that formerly helped the individual accept the reality of loss and change have been cast aside. When the bereaved person cannot make this transition in an orderly manner, then maladaptive sequelae may develop. From a public health perspective, the concept of prevention is paramount. Therefore, we talk of trying to prevent the development of serious psychological problems in this target population. One way of doing this would be to facilitate progression through the transition for those bereaved who may not be able to do this for themselves. Programs to serve the bereaved would need to offer various types of help, having as their goal the increasing of the mourner's coping resources to make it possible for him to accommodate and change. How can this be done? Focusing on one category of the bereaved population, the widowed, has given us a model for such a program.

There are at least 10 million widowed people in the United States, with approximately 850,000 individuals joining these ranks per year. All widowed people must deal with the sense of loss, with the disbelief that their mate is really dead. They must give up the role of a spouse and, in the long run, find a new definition of who they are and how they now relate to the larger world (Silverman, 1972). For many the resources required to support coping behavior can be found within their usual helping networks. For others these networks are inadequate to provide the additional information, guidance, or support needed. An effective program must meet the needs of most people in this category or population.

What should these services offer and how should they be made available to the widowed? As mental health specialists we think of setting up agencies where people come for counseling. Typically, in any agency case load there may be one or two widowed or bereaved people, and agency workers who are not accustomed to thinking in terms of populations will say that they serve the widowed. In truth they may serve one widow, but they cannot presume that their overall program of counseling precludes the need for specific programs of a very different nature to meet the needs of most or all widowed people in their community. A typical professional assumes that he possesses unique knowledge to which only he is privy, and on the basis of this, he evaluates other people's situations to determine their specific needs. He also sees himself as having the power to heal or minister to the patient because the very source of relief or help lies in his expert knowledge (Hughes, 1958). But when the problem is part of the human condition, can anyone claim to have this special expertise (Freidson, 1970)? When the agency and its professionals provide a service, too often the emphasis is not on the substance of the problem to be solved but on what the agency and its professional staff are already trained to offer.

Special Needs of the Widowed

What are the special needs of the widowed? In the initial phase of bereavement, the period of impact when the widowed are dazed and often acting reflexively, many helpers are available. Guilt and anger may surface, but these are not the critical and practical issues with which they must cope (Silverman, 1976). Funeral arrangements must be made, financial resources investigated, and the first legal steps taken toward the settlement of the estate. Funeral directors, family, friends, and the clergyman are on the scene then to provide the assistance needed. These observers often perceive the widow or widower as doing very well since apparently he or she seems to be able to keep going. This may be an illusion. In retrospect many widows talk of not really knowing what had been going on, of behaving as if the spouse were still alive, of still being involved in the relationship, and of looking to the spouse for guidelines for decision making. Certainly those on hand to give help can serve as buffers, and the widow then only occasionally and fleetingly feels the full impact of what has happened. If all the implications of the loss had to be confronted immediately and at the same time, the system would overload and the pain would become unbearable. Gradually the complete reality of bereavement overwhelms the new widow. By then friends and family have moved back to their own lives, and now, at the time of greatest need for support, the formerly available helpers have gone (Silverman, 1974).

The widowed themselves are often deceived into feeling that all is well with their perception of events. They have faced the traumatic post-death period and have a sense of pride in the fact that they have done fairly well, until they find themselves almost literally "falling apart." Unless they are forewarned, they can view this later period as being the beginning of impending insanity. This is the time when they begin to accept the meaning of the word *widow* and realize that it applies to them. Without being aware of what is happening, they may be preoccupied with memories of their spouse and forget that he is dead. How does one remember? Does the past become prologue?

In our society the word *widow* has almost lost meaning. Does it mean wearing black and living in the shadow of life? Does it mean being assigned to an all-female society? Does it mean that there is no hope for a new life without the deceased? For example, the widow may feel that she has lost her right arm, and in any working relationship this is an accurate description of the investment it takes to make it work (Pincus, 1975). How will it be possible to reconstruct another kind of life without this relationship? The widowed need perspective, understanding, and acceptance of their feelings. It helps to know that it is normal to "fall apart" or to forget that one's spouse is dead. To change their patterns and accommodate to the new status, widows need information about the options available and role models to indicate how they can make use of these. How are these provided in a context that makes the service available to every widowed person? Help should not require the widow to become involved in new dependencies when she is trying to develop confidence in her own ability to cope. Help should vary with the particular stage of transition at any particular moment in the recovery process. The help should also be as available as a next door neighbor (Silverman, 1971).

Widow-to-Widow Program

From research done in 1965–1966 I discovered that most widows considered another, more experienced widowed person the most helpful available to them. This is understandable because other widowed people who have coped successfully with the problems of bereavement have knowledge about how to cope. They can provide role models, they know what resources and agencies are useful, and they can listen without being upset by the intensity of feelings expressed by the newly widowed. They can, therefore, serve as a bridge back to the community and are able to offer alternatives to the loneliness and isolation experienced when other helpers have departed. This kind of help is offered in the context of the mutuality of a friendship.

Every community contains widows who can function on behalf of the new widow, and they have served in this way for many centuries. In our urban, more transient societies, this kind of extended helping network is not readily available on an informal basis. Originally the Widow-to-Widow experiment, with which I am associated and which is now being copied throughout the country, attempted to capture some of these qualities in a formal program (Silverman, 1974). Today these programs are run by volunteers who are themselves widowed and who are willing to use their own experience as a resource for helping others. These volunteers reach out to the newly widowed in their own communities within a month after the death of the spouse to offer friendship and any other needed help. In many communities these volunteers work with funeral directors or clergymen who inform them when a death occurs (Silverman, 1977).

Those who participate in a Widow-to-Widow program are learning to deal with the transition as a means of preventing problems at a later date. They learn to cope, to find hope, and to look forward to a future. Bereavement changes a person for all time. One part of the transition can be the building of a different life and the finding of new ways to be involved with people by discovering new competencies. Tragedy, as it relates to oneself, is made less absurd, and the victim of the circumstance is able to help someone else.

Other groups reach out in different ways to the newly widowed.

Their active social and educational programs are announced in news-papers, church bulletins, and so forth. However, many newly widowed women may not be ready to join a club or seek out others. The outreach provides them with an opportunity to develop a new network of helpers who are available when needed. A peer rela-tionship already exists and new friendships are formed. The helping process becomes an exchange where the helper also receives some-thing. In time most widows do have a need for certain information that all programs try to offer in some type of group setting within an educational format. Advice on managing legal and financial issues, on making career changes or even on starting a career, on helping children with their grief, on raising children in a single-parent house-hold, on learning how to live alone, on dealing with loneliness, on dating and remarrying, on instituting alternative life-styles, is all nec-essary to build a new social life.

In Boston an educational conference series is part of an experi-mental program (Silverman, 1977). Similar programs have been of-fered by the Naim Conference in Chicago (Silverman et al., 1974, pp. 101–4). Each of the above-mentioned topics is the subject of a lecture, usually given by a professional who is widowed as well. These conferences extend over a five- to six-week period and include small group discussions, with the groups divided on the basis of whether or not the widow is still raising children.

Mutual help has been considered an untried method, without con-trolled studies to demonstrate its value. The same may be said about help provided by professionals.* Most studies of mental health ser-vices raise more questions about their value than they answer. But it is not an either/or situation. Mutual help is not offered in place of professional help; it is only one aspect of a helping network. More people are likely to be involved or become involved in this type of exchange than in an exchange with a mental health specialist. It is in the exceptional and not the typical situation that such a specialist is

---

* There are continuing evaluations of some of the mutual-help programs for the widowed. The most extensive is that at Clarke Institute, Toronto. This is a controlled study with an untreated population. Informal findings thus far seem to support my more qualitative case study findings.

needed. Mutual help happens whether the professional is there or not. It is really a question of deciding if the goal is to help the bereaved and to find ways of reaching most of them with the services that would be most meaningful for them.

Experiencing grief, learning to cope with it, and integrating it into one's personality and approach to life indicate that an individual is living competently. We need to work toward establishing an atmosphere in our communities that accepts this outlook and understands its importance and thereby breaks through some of the social isolation (as well as alienation from our own feelings that are often irrational) imposed on us by our rational, technological, mobile society. Mutual help is one way of encouraging people to become involved with each other, of making each individual's life experience important and valid. To delegate all helping tasks to the professional encourages individual dependency and discourages creative searching for solutions. To ensure that all who need help are reached, it is essential that professionals recognize that new helpers with other skills are needed and are involved. Otherwise we can arrive at an economically and socially intolerable situation, for the cost of maintaining professionally staffed agencies to be primary helpers would tie up too many resources and be unacceptable. The issue is how to work as partners so that every mode of help needed is used to the fullest (Silverman et al., pp. 127–33). The professional has to rethink his role and ask how he relates to and works with other helpers to provide the help necessary for a bereaved individual to cope with a normal life transition.

References

Freidson, E. 1970. *Professional Dominance: Social Structure of Medical Care.* Chicago: Aldine Press.

Hughes, E. 1958. *Men and Their Work.* Glencoe, Illinois: The Free Press.

Pincus, L. 1975. *Death In The Family.* New York: Pantheon Press.

Silverman, P. R. 1971. "Factors Involved in Accepting an Offer of Help." *Journal of Thanatology* 3:161–71.

Silverman, P. R. 1972. "Widowhood and Preventive Intervention." *The Family Coordinator* 21:95–102.

Silverman, P. R. et al., eds. 1974. *Helping Each Other in Widowhood.* New York: Health Sciences Publishing Corp.

Silverman, P. R. 1976. "Mutual Help and The Elderly Widow." *Journal of Geriatric Psychiatry,* January.

Silverman, P. R. 1977. *If You Will Lift the Load: A Case Book on Mutual Help for the Widowed.* New York: Jewish Funeral Directors of America.

23

Private Troubles or Public Issues: Explorations in the Policy Implications of Euthanasia

Burton Gummer and Diane M. Simpson

The decade of the 1960s has been referred to as the time of the "citizen participation revolution"—a period when people began to make increasingly strident and forceful demands to be involved in making the decisions that affect their lives (Bell and Held, 1969, pp. 142–75). The current interest in euthanasia can be seen as an extension of that movement, with the difference that now people are demanding to be involved in decisions that affect their deaths. In this chapter we shall explore the policy implications created by this movement toward allowing people a greater say in the conditions and timing of their deaths. The chapter is exploratory, since its major aim is to develop a framework for asking appropriate questions about this issue; it is hoped that the raising of these questions will lay the groundwork for future empirical research.

The Euthanasia Movement

The euthanasia movement is one of many manifestations in a technologically advancing society wherein there is a significant lag between technological achievements and human capacity to adapt to these changes. When we look at the advances made since 1900 toward prolongation of life, it becomes clear that medical technology has concerned itself with the quantity versus the quality of life. This, in turn, became the issue around which the euthanasia movement was organized.

Birth rates have been altered because of improved contraception devices, and life expectancy has increased. In 1900 approximately 4 percent of our population was 65 years of age and older. This proportion has grown steadily during the century, reaching 9.8 percent by 1970 (Commission on Population Growth, 1972, p. 98). The Commission notes that

Lower birth rates in the future would further raise the proportion of people in this age group. If the population should grow at the two-child rate, the proportion 65 and over would reach 10.6 percent by the end of this century. If the two-child average prevailed until the population ultimately stabilized, the proportion in this age group would level off at approximately 16 percent—a rather considerable increase in this segment of the population (Commission on Population Growth, 1972, p. 98).

With the possibility that the aged will constitute a larger proportion of the population has come increased concern about funding and programs for the care of this group. Of all groups in society, poverty is more prevalent among the elderly, particularly among minority group members (U.S. Bureau of Census 1971). The health care needs of the aged will therefore become increasingly important and costly. Increases in standards for health care are also probable. Hence, with likely change in the age composition of the population and increased standards of health care, this group will in all probability become critically significant with respect to the euthanasia movement. To quote the Commission again:

While the entire population 65 years old and over will rise 43 percent between 1970 and the year 2000, persons 75 to 84 will increase by 65 percent and those 85 years and over by 52 percent. It is among these old people that chronic conditions (including impairments and disease) increase, limitations of activity become more prevalent, and institutionalized care is more often required (Commission on Population Growth, 1972, p. 100).

At present "the prevailing image of institutional life is largely negative, and older people generally express greater aversion to it than either their relatives or the public at large" (Commission on Population Growth, 1972, p. 100). The aged constitute one of the most vulnerable segments of the population. To grow old in America is to lose status, roles, income, the comfort of family and friends, and control over the decisions regarding one's last phase of life. To grow old in America is to know the meaning of powerlessness. Simone de Beauvoir talks of old age as a reflection of the life one has lived by virtue of one's class (Beauvoir, 1972). The age at which an individual's decline begins is dependent on his class in life. The worker's decline begins much earlier than that of an individual from a privileged class. She states:

Society cares about the individual only in so far as he is profitable. The young know this. Their anxiety as they enter in upon social life matches the anguish of the old as they are excluded from it. Between these two ages, the problem is hidden by routine. The young man dreads this machine that is about to seize hold of him, and sometimes he tried to defend himself by throwing half-bricks; the old man, rejected by it, exhausted and naked, has nothing left but his eyes to weep with (Beauvoir, 1972, p. 543).

The notion that one should determine and control so far as possible the conditions under which one must function undergirds the current interest in euthanasia. This notion gained legitimacy in the 1960s and has been transposed to "death rights" now. A brief review of history may reveal some of the possible bases for current attitudinal differences.

In ancient Greece the laws of Thebes and Athens (which, we can assume, were representative of the official attitude) viewed an individual who took his own life as committing a crime against the state. The usual funeral rites were denied him or her, and he or she was subjected to other symbols of degradation, even confiscation of property (Saffron, 1970, p. 3). Saffron notes, however, that

it was not long before exceptions were allowed for those individuals who openly avowed their intentions, pleading in their self-defense a serious illness, extreme pain, or a general distaste for life. A state like Sparta, which officially encouraged the elimination of the weak and the unfit in an attempt to enhance the strength and beauty of the race, could hardly take severe measures against the aged or chronically ill who sought relief from the miseries of existence (Saffron, 1970, p. 3).

The major influence of ancient Greece with respect to euthanasia has to do with Hippocrates and the oath, the benchmark of medical ethics, although the history of medicine in Greece suggests that many physicians did not abide by the code) (Saffron, 1970, p. 6). Probably the rise in Christianity in the first three centuries A.D. was the force that had the most impact in crystallizing attitudes against suicide and euthanasia (Saffron, 1970, p. 6). What ultimately emerged was not one attitude regarding euthanasia but several within the religious–philosophical realms.

Although *euthanasia* means an easy, painless, and peaceful death, or a method of providing such a death, for many it connotes the nightmares of Hitler's Germany. Many will never forget Dr. Karl Brandt, personal physician to Hitler and key supervisor of the Nazi program for mass slaughter of mentally or physically handicapped Germans, stating, before the American Military Tribunal in Nuremberg on February 5, 1947, that "the life of an insane person is not in keeping with human dignity." About this, Deutsch states:

Dr. Brandt . . . was presenting the philosophy underlying the program which put to death at least 275,000 "lunatics and cripples" as "useless eaters." It was an act of mercy, he said, to shorten the lives of these miserable creatures. The cost of maintaining German "insane asylums" he explained, amounted to 350,000,000 marks a year—"a great price for the state to pay." A battleship could be built for that sum, he added (Deutsch, 1948, p. 281).

More chilling a tale is hardly imaginable, and yet a small voice in each of us whispers, "Could it happen again? Could it happen here?" When large segments of the population are rendered useless, unneeded, devalued—like the aged—the question takes on even greater significance. Given a work-oriented society and a depression economy, could mass panic make it happen? As one economist observed: "To the economist qua economist . . . human life has economic value only as a function of its ability to produce goods and services that are demanded by others" (Bailey, 1970, p. 281). These kinds of questions are of great import because of the emotionalism around the euthanasia question.

In England, as recently as 1970, supporters of euthanasia presented a proposal in the House of Commons "to make lawful administration of euthanasia at the request of the patient" ("Euthanasia in England," 1970, p. 463). Although it was shouted down, support for euthanasia seems to be mounting. In the United States, since the beginning of this decade, we have witnessed a considerable number of "euthanasia situations" that have received much publicity. Such publicity, as well as being informative, also contributes to emotionalism that clouds rather than clears.

A Policy Framework

The title of this chapter contains a concept developed by C. Wright Mills, that of "troubles" and "issues." This concept has proved an important device in the development of frameworks for the analysis of social policies. "Troubles," according to Mills

occur within the character of the individual and within the range of his immediate relations with others; they have to do with his self and with those limited areas of social life of which he is directly and personally aware. . . . A trouble is a private matter; values cherished by an individual are felt by him to be threatened.

Issues have to do with matters that transcend these local environments of the individual and the range of his inner life. . . . An issue is a public matter: some value cherished by publics is felt to be threatened (Mills, 1961, pp. 8–9).

With this concept as a guide one can examine a society in terms of the proportion of concerns or problems treated as "troubles" and those considered "issues." If something is considered a "trouble," then the individual affected by it will be granted a high degree of discretion in deciding on how to deal with it. If a concern is treated as an "issue," however, it is taken out of the control of the individual and dealt with in some public arena. Different societies can be categorized in terms of the ratio of "troubles" to "issues" within that society. For instance one could hypothesize that, in a country such as the United States, with its strong commitments to individualism and personal autonomy, a greater proportion of concerns are treated as "troubles," and therefore left to the discretion of the individual for their disposition, than would be true, say, in Israel, with its more collectivist orientation. For example, problems about the raising of children are dealt with privately by parents in the United States, but in the *kibbutz* these problems are treated as public issues and dealt with in a collective forum.

At first glance one would imagine that death would be categorized as a "trouble," if not the quintessential "trouble," because of its deeply personal nature and its impact on the individual. That this is not the case, however, and that death is rather seen as an "issue," is attested to by the existence, in Christian and Moslem countries and in Israel, of a range of public laws and widely held normative beliefs prescribing the conditions under which a "legitimate" death can occur. Primary among these restrictions is a generally universal prohibition against voluntary death, either in the form of suicide or of euthanasia (Gibbs, 1971, p. 272). These prohibitions are now being challenged by the various movements advocating the right of the individual to be the primary decision maker in the issue of his or her death; in Mills's scheme they are demanding that the question of one's death become a "trouble" rather than an "issue."

A major distinction between a "trouble" and an "issue" is that the former involves "values cherished by the individual" while the latter involves "values cherished by publics." A critical concern raised by the advocacy of voluntary death has to do with the nature of the public values that would be sacrificed by turning this matter over to the individual for decision. One format for addressing this question is to develop some benefit–cost model, however crude, for looking at the advantages and disadvantages, to both individual and society, of advocating public policies that would be either indifferent to or supportive of private decision making about one's death.

The Benefits and Costs of Euthanasia

Our analysis of the benefits and costs involved with euthanasia proceeds by an examination of what the potential gains and losses will be to the individual selecting such a course of action, to his or her family (or significant others), to health service providers (on the assumption that most people interested in euthanasia will be suffering from physical or mental illnesses of a chronic or terminal sort), and to the society as a whole. Again, this discussion is exploratory and suggestive and makes no claims to be a definitive listing of the critical concerns in this area. It is hoped, however, that this kind of policy-analytical framework will facilitate the raising of critical questions.

THE INDIVIDUAL

The major benefits that would accrue to the individual by a privatization of the decision about his own death would include the following (and this listing does not imply a ranking by order of importance): cessation of physical or psychological pain, the individual's belief that stress from the sufferer's illness on family and significant others will cease, expansion of the opportunity for free choice.

The major cost to the individual appears to be what the economists refer to as "opportunity costs," namely, the costs incurred by opportunities foregone. In the case of the terminally ill individual these costs would take the form of possible breakthroughs in medical science that could lead to an alleviation of the disease. For the chronically ill the costs would be expressed in possible future shifts in attitude toward one's plight, the advent of new rehabilitative or supportive services, and the like.

THE FAMILY AND SIGNIFICANT OTHERS

The benefits that the family or significant others could realize would include cessation of stress from sufferer's illness; reallocation of family resources (e.g., time, energy, sympathy, money) to other concerns; financial benefits from insurance policies, life savings, pensions, annuities.

The major costs to be considered include loss of the individual, necessitating realignments of all relationships (both within the family and with significant others); "opportunity costs," which, for the survivors, will have their expression in guilt, remorse, and recriminations over the failure to take more aggressive action to save the individual.

HEALTH SERVICE PROVIDERS
The primary benefit from euthanasia that would be realized by the health service providers is the opportunity to reallocate scarce resources (e.g., life support systems, bed space, professional's time) (Bailey, 1970). The costs involved would include feelings of guilt or failure over the patient's choice of death over trust in the ability of the health professional to effect a cure; violation of the canons of the health professions (e.g., Hippocratic Oath) (Manning, 1970, pp. 253–274); loss of opportunities to observe scientifically the progress of a particular illness; lack of incentive for the health service provider to develop more nearly adequate care facilities for the chronically and terminally ill. (Cicely Saunders suggests that the reason for the relatively minor interest in euthanasia in Great Britain as compared to the United States is the quality of the care facilities available.)

SOCIETY
From the societal point of view a major benefit that could be realized is support of the value of the individual's freedom to make choices unfettered by societal constraints. This may sound like a contradiction in terms, since what is being argued is that society will benefit by having the role it plays in an individual's life reduced. American society can, however, still be considered to be organized around the principle of *laissez-faire*, with the consequence that there will be a high value placed on activities that promote autonomous decision making (Williams, 1963 and Fine, 1964). In this sense euthanasia can be seen as an extension of the free-market orientation to social organization that characterizes much of contemporary American life.

No society, however, is organized around a single principle, and the multiple values that Americans attempt to pursue point to some of the anticipated costs of euthanasia to the society as a whole. The first of these is the erosion of the humanistic and religious belief in the sanctity of life. Both Judaism and Christianity stress the belief that life is given by a supreme being and can only be ended by being taken by that same deity. (As one observer put it, to take one's own life is to "co-opt Christ") (Personal communication with Dr. Elizabeth Lakind, Philadelphia). From the humanistic perspective life is considered superior to death under all circumstances. (The current debate about the "disengagement theory" of aging is a good example of the strong opposition of humanistic professionals to any position that advocates a retreat from life as opposed to a constant and active involvement with living.)

Another value that could be seriously affected is altruism. Care for the ill and the dispirited is a major way in which individuals can engage in unilateral giving to others. This kind of giving, moreover, is seen by many as an essential ingredient in maintaining the social bond in a particular society. A society that limits the opportunities for altruistic giving is, in fact, running the risk of producing a high degree of autonomous and alienated behavior on the part of its members, with the consequence that its members will have little capacity for entering into viable social relationships (Titmuss, 1971; Gouldner, 1960; and Boulding, 1967).

Aside from the question of the particular religious or secular values of a society, there is a cost incurred in voluntary death for any society in terms of the potential threat to the social structure if individual members are allowed to depart from it by choice. Every social system must deal with the issue of how to induce and sustain the participation of individuals in the life of the system. The mechanisms for doing this range from subtle modes of socialization and the manipulation of rewards to more overt tactics of coercion and harsh sanctions. But for any society the continued participation of individuals in that society would be seriously threatened by allowing the individual free choice in the matter of life or death (Deutsch, 1948).

The impact of a benign policy toward euthanasia or toward the overall willingness of others to continue their involvement in the social order is not a straightforward one and needs some elaboration. The individual considering euthanasia will most probably be uninvolved in social life because of serious illness. Why, then, should his or her being allowed to choose death voluntarily affect the commitments of other, healthy individuals? The answer lies in the possible normative precedents that would be established. Would a liberal policy toward euthanasia have an effect on the suicide rates? If people were allowed to choose death when faced with serious physical pain, would not others in the society begin to extend this line of reasoning to situations where other forms of "pain" had to be faced (e.g., psychological, social, or economic "pain")? In a similar vein what impact could one expect from a liberalized policy on attitudes toward drug use, since the latter is frequently seen as a device for withdrawing from the demands of participation in society? To arrive at answers to these and other questions raised in this chapter we need a strategy of research in the area of voluntary death.

Implications for Future Research

The stated purpose of this chapter was to create a framework that would facilitate systematic and rational analysis of the questions involved in euthanasia. This purpose has, we hope, been accomplished by the kinds of models employed in our discussion. The next task is to translate this general discussion into specific guidelines for research so that we can begin to answer the many questions raised in this and other papers dealing with euthanasia.

One possible line of research would be to conduct cross-national surveys to see what the experience of those countries that already have liberalized policies regarding the use of euthanasia has been. This is true, for example, in Japan. It would be important to know what the distribution of the use of euthanasia is by different segments of the population (e.g., socioeconomic status, religion, age, occupation, sex, psychological status, and the like). Attitude surveys among people not directly involved in euthanasia would have to be conducted to assess the possible impact of euthanasia on others. It would also be important to see what the relationship is between euthanasia and the suicide rates.

A second line of inquiry would be to see to what extent policies could be developed that would be responsive to the differential needs of those interested in employing euthanasia. People in acute and constant physical pain and suffering from a terminal illness cannot, from a policy perspective, be categorized with chronically ill people who have decided for other reasons that they do not want to continue living. Is it possible to develop a policy that would treat these two groups differently? Is it possible to make these kinds of distinctions when we are dealing with something as subjective as someone's feeling he has suffered enough? We hope that the kind of thinking developed in this chapter will contribute to the clarification and resolution of these concerns.

References

Bailey, R. M. 1970. "Economic and Social Costs of Death." In *The Dying Patient,* eds. Orville G. Brim, Jr. et al. New York: Russell Sage Foundation.

Beauvoir, S. de 1972. *The Coming of Age.* New York: Putnam.

Bell, D. and V. Held. 1969. "The Community Revolution." *The Public Interest* 16:142 ff.

Boulding, K. E. 1967. "The Boundaries of Social Policy." *Social Work* 12:3 ff.

Commission on Population Growth and the American Future. 1972. *Population and the American Future.* New York: Signet Books.

Deutsch, A. 1948. *The Shame of the States.* New York: Columbia University Press.

"Euthanasia in England: A Growing Storm." 1970. *America*:463.

Fine, S. 1964. *Laissez-Faire and the General-Welfare State.* Ann Arbor: Ann Arbor Paperbacks, the University of Michigan Press.

Gibbs, J. P. 1971. "Suicide." In *Contemporary Social Problems,* eds. R. K. Merton and R. Nisbet, 3rd ed. New York: Harcourt Brace Jovanovich, Inc.

Gouldner, A. W. 1960. "The Norm of Reciprocity: A Preliminary Statement." *American Sociological Review* 25:161 ff.

Manning, B. 1970. "Legal and Policy Issues in the Allocation of Death." In *The Dying Patient,* eds. O. G. Brim, Jr. et al. New York: Russell Sage Foundation.

Mills, C. W. 1961. *The Sociological Imagination.* New York: Grove Press.

Saffron, M. 1970. "Euthanasia in the Greek Tradition." In *Attitudes Toward Euthanasia.* A Summary of Papers and Discussions at the Third Euthanasia Conference. New York: New York Academy of Medicine.

Titmuss, R. M. 1971. *The Gift Relationship: From Human Blood to Social Policy.* New York: Pantheon Books.

U.S. Bureau of the Census. 1971. "Characteristics of the Low-Income Population, 1970." *Current Population Reports.* Series P. 1-60, No. 81. Washington D.C.: U.S. Government Printing Office.

Williams, R., Jr. 1963. "Values and Beliefs in American Society." In *American Society,* 2nd ed., rev. New York: Alfred A. Knopf.

Part VI

The Education
of the Social Worker

24

Teaching Death and Dying Content in the Social Work Curriculum

Rosalind S. Miller

Course content about the meaning of loss and separation in family life has been taught to social work students, probably since social work curricula were first developed. Whereas death, that final reality in the life cycle, has long been acknowledged in the classroom, there has been a greater emphasis on teaching about those human conditions that have resulted in the separation of family members through physical and emotional illness, economic crisis, social dislocation, and child abuse or abandonment. Probably not until this past decade have social work faculties, particularly those responsible for the teaching of casework courses, included specific teaching materials about death and dying—case records, tapes and films, augmented by a growing literature.

Inclusion of this content has been a slow process. The instructor's conviction about the necessity of teaching about death and dying appears to be a greater determining factor for its inclusion than a consensus by teachers that it should be a requirement within a syllabus. Like others in the helping professions, social workers need much more help in the development and refinement of their interventive skills with clients if they are to reach out to individuals who are terminally ill or to families about to experience the most final of all loss, the death of a loved one. Two preconditions are necessary if this material is to be successfully taught by the teacher and, in turn, incorporated as part of the learning experience by the student: a teacher who is more anxiety free than anxiety laden about death and dying and a student, supported by the teacher as a role model, who can be helped to examine and communicate his own fears and anxieties about death.

The Teacher/Student Transaction

The teacher brings to the classroom his years of practice skills as well as theoretical understanding and a professional value system. He also brings himself, a mature, "normal" individual with capacity, to use Freud's term, for "Lieben und arbeiten (love and work)." Erikson (1968, p. 136) reminds us that "it pays to ponder on this simple formula; it grows deeper as you think about it. For when Freud said 'love,' he meant the generosity of intimacy as well as genital love. . . ." Within an atmosphere of the "generosity of intimacy" a meaningful, trusting teacher/student relationship is nurtured; it is an atmosphere that enables the student to risk talking about conflict-- laden feelings. However, it is not the purpose either of the teacher/student relationship or the classroom situation to resolve these feelings. Rather, the student will enhance his self-awareness so that he can perform in his helping role with his client. The real learning takes place at a later time, when the student can share freely his thinking and feeling from his actual practice experiences.

The success of such practitioners and teachers as Dr. Cicely Saunders and Dr. Elisabeth Kübler-Ross rests not only in their own work with the dying but also in the atmosphere they have created in their teaching roles and in the exchange of their experiences, observations, and feelings. Kübler-Ross (1969, pp. 237–38) says, "In spite of the increasing number of students, the seminar often resembles a group therapy session, in which the participants speak freely about their own reactions and fantasies in relation to the patient and thus learn something about their own motivations and behavior."

Where the social work teacher—or the teaching physician—have a resistance to imparting this content, both may cope with their anxiety by calling into play defenses that enable them to deny the need to include death and dying material or to rationalize by claiming that such content has low priority, given all the other subject matter that needs to be covered.

Within Erikson's epigenetic framework the classroom teacher in a professional school is frequently well into his middle years or reaching into the last maturational stage of the life cycle. For those teachers in the former group, generativity includes not only concern for and guidance of their own children but also support and teaching of the student who is to become the professional of the next generation. Yet, at this maturational stage, the teacher is coping with the very anxiety-laden problems in his own life that he is called upon to teach: the care of an older parent and with it the concomitant role reversal problems, chronic illness of older family members, the death of a parent, or even the death of a spouse. For the older teacher—in spite of professional self-awareness—vulnerability may impede motivation as well as pedagogical capacity to support and sustain the student through death and dying content. For this teacher is coping with feelings about retirement and curtailing his professional activities. Preoccupation with his own health or that of his spouse, the loss of a mate, the assessment of his achievements, and feelings of failure are realistic concerns. How well the teacher has mastered his own maturational tasks will in large measure determine how well he can cope with death and dying content in the classroom, serve as a role model for his students, and teach the next generation of social workers to help dying patients and their families with empathy, a feeling of security in the execution of his role, and a conflict-free self-awareness.

The young graduate student is frequently a product of a family—and a society—that has protected him from experiencing directly the loss of a family member, a neighbor, or a friend. Home has been for "living"; terminal illness takes place in a hospital, the infirm go to nursing homes, the dead go to funeral parlors. Many students have not "experienced " death within the family unit, and those who have are frequently not actively called upon to support a dying family member. Early adulthood for these young students is filled with its own problems: role identity, academic achievement, professional advancement, and search for heterosexual support and gratification. These are tasks that require, for successful execution, the loosening of ties from the family unit and the unsettling recognition that parents, too, are advancing in years. For the older student, as for the teacher, there is a more acute awareness of, if not actual experience with, the reality of death. His anxiety is no less than that of the younger student. And in both cases professional self-awareness has not yet been developed, nor is there advanced preparation for the student's first experience of working with the dying client or for his rapid introduction to a host of client problems he faces in field work within a few weeks after beginning professional training.

Introducing Death and Dying Content in the Classroom

Until the student can recognize his own fears and anxieties about death, receive encouragement to share his feelings in the classroom, and experience from peer discussion that others feel equally vulnerable, he is not prepared to reach out to the terminally ill or to the bereaved family. Regardless of his intellectual understanding of the grieving process or his knowledge of crisis intervention as a frequent means of intervening, the success with which he is able to reach out rests upon his "use of self."

The first pedagogical task for the teacher is to help the student reach for his own feelings. Only then is he prepared to incorporate the theoretical content, "to hear" the client's communications, "to feel," but not experience through self-reference, the client's pain. To create an atmosphere in the classroom where death and dying content can be effectively taught is not an easy task.

I shall now share with the reader one approach to the introduction of death and dying content in the casework or practice course in the first semester of the social work student's training. For the past six years I have assigned students a case record in child welfare, specifi-

cally foster care, and have requested that they read the first six pages
and come prepared the following week to talk about the case on the
basis of questions I give them as preparation.

At the following session I begin by asking the students, "How
come these three children have been in a foster home for the past
year?" Silence follows. A student reaches for the record; others fum-
ble through the pages; after a couple of minutes a hand goes up.
"The father had to work and couldn't keep the kids." I wait. There's
more rustling of pages, students consult each other, and eventually
someone will volunteer, "Oh, yeah, the mother died." By now,
other students have found the same sentence in the opening paragraph
on the first page of the record. Here we learn that after a prolonged
illness the mother is cared for in the home during her terminal phase
of cancer. At the mother's death the children are between the ages of
three and eight.

I ask the class what it must have been like for these kids as they
saw their mother ill and then witnessed her death. Response to this
question varies; frequently students will volunteer some theoretical
comments about the effect of a loss during the oedipal period, or observe that there was role strain among family members, or share
some knowledge about foster care as a poor alternative to keeping the
family together. I suggest we can think about my question—how the
children felt, but in the meantime I show them a film.*

For the next 18 minutes we watch how a father and his two children cope with the problem of a mother's terminal phase of cancer.
We see a lovely but obviously very ill woman recently returned from
the hospital lying on her bed, cared for by a supportive, affectionate
but distraught husband who stoically copes with his feelings but who
is totally unable to talk to his children about their mother's imminent
death. We watch the father as he vacillates between his feelings of
anger at his daughter, who hostilely confronts him to know why
mother isn't better, and his feelings of frustration toward his son,
who fights with his friends, withdraws to his room, and refuses to

* "A Special Kind of Care," prepared by Cancer Care, Inc., of the National Cancer
Foundation.

visit with his mother in her sickroom. Supported by the social worker, the father is helped to grieve, to cry, to talk about his sorrow and distress. Then painfully, hesitantly at first, he reaches out to each of his children. With his capacity for love and understanding and their need for each other he helps them face the impending death of the mother. Aided by the father, the children reach out to the mother, and each member reinforces the family bonds.

With the window shades still drawn, the lights out, I help the projectionist remove the film equipment from the room. In the darkness soft crying is stifled, eyes are wiped, noses are blown. The lights are turned on, I am back in my chair, and we are where we were 18 minutes ago. There is a stony silence: some red-eyed students look to each other; some gaze at the floor; more Kleenex is found; and one or two stare hard at me, communicating their hostility that I dared to do this to them.

Having found a comfortable seating position, I look at them, conveying as much support as I can, and wait for someone to break the silence. This can take several minutes. There is no urgency—there is time to reflect and time to restitute.

How the silence is broken varies from year to year. If the initial comments relate to intellectual content, I acknowledge the speaker with an affirmative nod and continue to respond but nonverbally. The comments, usually very short, are probably motivated as much by the student's need to break the silence as by the wish to discuss the content. My nonparticipation is obviously calculated. But my experience has been that if the discussion is about the film or if intellectual content is pursued, the student's affective responses, when they finally come, are diluted.

Sooner or later a student will risk himself with an affective response. "How can I help others when I can't control my own feelings?" is a frequent opening observation. My verbal response encourages him to continue and signifies that this is the content I wish him to pursue. My empathic response supports him and helps give the other students permission to contribute to the discussion. They do respond. The response is self-referential, some of it quite dramatic. A young lady recently said, "Maybe as I sit here, my father knows my mother is desperately ill, but he hasn't told me." Some share that they have never experienced the death of a loved one. There may have been a death in the family, but they were too young to partici-pate in the last rites. Or they recall questions about death that were not answered by their parents. When death has been experienced, students share with each other familial attitudes as they perceive them. Some feel that they were expected to internalize their feelings and respond stoically, as the father in the film had at first. Others recall the cathartic release provided by the wake of the Jewish memorial period of shiva. Some students remain sad and through their tears say they cannot understand why they are reacting with so much feeling since they have never experienced loss by death. Other students concur and relate to their unspecified anxiety. There are also the participant observers, those students who do not become verbally engaged but who will reflect upon the experience, presumably at another time.

The Teacher's Role in Affective Response from the Students

Although the content of the discussion is self-referential, the teacher must be aware that the purpose for eliciting this material is not thera-peutic. It is important that the instructor be in control of the discus-sion, encouraging the student to share his feelings on the one hand, while reaching for the content to be learned on the other. It is a deli-cate balance in which the relevance of earlier content needs to be reinforced and deepened for the student's understanding as he deals with his own feelings in relation to this new material. Enough time must be provided in the session (in this case 2 hours) to enable the in-structor to incorporate the teaching material. It would definitely be contraindicated in this learning situation for the instructor to termi-nate the discussion by allowing only the affective material to come out.

Many teaching points flow from the discussion. The student can quickly see how his self-awareness and his "use of self"—content discussed earlier in the semester—are enhancing attributes that facilitate his practice skills within the mutual exchange between worker and client. Students who have been working at their agencies with terminally ill patients and bereaved families are able to share their experience in the classroom. The instructor should always reach for this type of content for illustrative purposes because it helps the student see how he may begin to separate his personal involvement from his professional commitments, a learning experience that is ego enhancing.

The student begins to see that self-awareness does not mean the elimination or resolution of feelings about loss or death and dying. He learns rather that, the more attuned he is to his feelings, the better he is able to move from self-reference to understanding a human condition to which he can bring technical knowledge, helping skills, and an empathic understanding in a way that allows him to be involved with clients but separate from their pain. The student should then be encouraged to make a broader application of this point to clients who experience, if not loss and death of a loved one, problems of deprivation, isolation, and loneliness.

Reaching for the affective response in a classroom situation, as described above, does not mean that the student is now emotionally equipped to work with dying patients. As with all learning, reinforcement of this content must go on in the classroom as well as in the field through both years of training. Unless this happens, the student will, unfortunately, get the message that death and dying content is necessary to learn only if one decides to practice in medical settings.

Teaching Death and Dying Content

Death and dying content is highly cathected material. But for most students enough of the "available" feeling about this anxiety-laden topic has been tapped to allow them to begin to learn the technical material that needs to be taught.

Early reading assignments, such as Freud's "Mourning and Melancholia" (1917) and Lindemann's "Symptomatology and Management of Acute Grief'' (1944), enable the student to distinguish between grief as a normal response to death and morbid behavior, which is pathological. Other content elaborates on the grieving process, the identification of the range of behavioral responses to loss, the defenses used, and the coping mechanisms and adaptational patterns to look for in the resolution of grief and in restitution.

Each year there is increased, rich bibliographical material available to help the student learn about management of the dying patient, work with bereaved families, affective responses to grief, and the religio-social factors related to death. Whereas it is not the purpose of this chapter to review this literature, the breadth and quality of material available have substantially helped in teaching this content and resulted in some excellent written work by the students. Although it is also encouraging to see increased numbers of students participating in conferences, particularly in hospitals, on content about death and dying, it is also true that social work students struggle alone in their work with dying patients when doctors refuse to discuss either with the social worker or the patient the nature of the illness, even where there is evidence that it is diagnostically and dynamically indicated to do so. But in either case all this content is available for classroom use, particularly through case presentations by the students which, again, allow for the integration of the theoretical material and the practice experience. The overly zealous student, bent on "telling" the patient about his condition, needs help about how he assesses the facts he has from the patient, the physician, and the team to determine *differential* interventive strategies. The role of the social worker on the interdisciplinary team, the worker's relationship with the physician and nurse, and the hospital's policies on patient care are all salient teaching content.

Deepening the student's theoretical knowledge about the family system has particular relevance in teaching about death and dying. The quick assessment of the family unit, its homeostatic balance, the response to crisis, the identification of family roles, the awareness of role reversals, the range of coping activity, the assessment of family strengths and· vulnerabilities—all need to be explored with the student, who is then helped to identify the necessary skills for intervening quickly. The student needs to understand how to help the family, not only to cope with financial problems because of skyrocketing medical costs or because of the problems when the head of the household, now terminally ill, has been the primary wage earner, but also to help family members support the dying by visiting and encouraging communication, if only by their presence at the bedside.

Nor should the focus be only on the hospital. Death and dying content has relevance for social workers, regardless of where they practice. Family agencies, child guidance clinics, and mental health settings have always worked with clients whose problems are related to earlier unresolved losses or crisis situations where there is impending death or recent death following an illness, accident, or suicide. In child welfare, the illustration given earlier, familial breakup and placement of the children after the death of a parent are well-known problems. The school, settlement house, camp, and residential settings are community agencies where the social worker should be attuned to the youngster's struggling with unresolved feelings of grief following the loss of an immediate family member, a grandparent or relative, a friend or a neighbor, a teacher, or a pet. Facilities for the aged, golden-age clubs, and nursing homes are also social agencies where workers practice and need to bring their understanding and skill to working with the aged, the ill, and the dying.

Throughout the life cycle, in every maturational stage, death is part of the human condition. And so it seems ironic that social work students are exposed to a wide range of human problems affecting some part of the population but are given very little content about death and dying, the one task that affects everyone. Perusal of schools of social work curricula will quickly confirm this observation. An elective course in death and dying begs the issue, for many students will not choose such an elective. Rather death and dying content must be integrated into the practice courses as well as into a range of electives. How today's student and tomorrow's professional practices is determined by those who teach him.

References

Erikson, E. 1968. *Identity: Youth and Crisis*. New York: W. W. Norton and Company.

Freud, S. 1917. "Mourning and Melancholia." *Complete Works,* Standard Edition, 1953. London: Hogarth Press.

Kübler-Ross, E. 1969. *On Death and Dying*. New York: Macmillan Company.

Lindemann, E. 1944. "Symptomatology and Management of Acute Grief." *American Journal of Psychiatry* 101:141.

Selected Bibliography for Students

Goldberg, S. B. 1973. "Family Tasks and Reactions in the Crisis of Death." *Social Casework* 54, no. 7 (July).

Goldstein, E. A. 1973. "Social Casework and the Dying Person." *Social Casework* 54, no. 10 (December).

Foster, Z. P. 1965. "How Social Work Can Influence Hospital Management of Fatal Illness." *Social Work* 10, no. 4 (October).

Glaser, W. 1970. *Social Settings and Medical Organiation*. New York: Atherton Press.

Hamovitch, M. B. 1964. *The Parent and the Fatally Ill Child*. Duarte, California: City of Hope Medical Center.

Hinton, J. M. 1967. *Dying*. Baltimore: Penguin Books.

Koenig, R. 1968. "Fatal Illness: A Survey of Social Service Needs." *Social Work* 13, no. 4 (October).

Morrissey, J. R. 1966. "Death Anxiety in Children with a Fatal Illness." In *Crisis Intervention,* ed. H. Parad. New York: Family Service Association of America.

Proceedings of the Fourth National Symposium, *Catastrophic Illness in the Seventies: Critical Issues and Complex Decisions,* Cancer Care, Inc. of the National Cancer Foundation, 1971.

Schoenberg, B. et al. 1970. *Loss and Grief: Psychological Management in Medical Practice*. New York: Columbia University Press.

—— 1972. *Psychosocial Aspects of Terminal Care*. New York: Columbia University Press.

Weisberg, L. M. 1974. "Casework with the Terminally Ill." *Social Casework* 55, no. 6 (June).

25

Teaching a Social Work Perspective on the Dying Patient and His Family

Eda G. Goldstein

I am a psychiatric social worker who is trying to find a meaningful way, based on my clinical experience, of teaching social work students to deal with dying patients and their families. As a practitioner in a large teaching hospital I define the casework task by my boundary function. I find myself at the interface between clients with human needs and a vast, insensitive system of medical care services. In my work with a dying woman and her family (Goldstein and Malitz, 1974), a case involving a prestigious voluntary hospital, a city facility, and an excellent psychiatric setting, I became enmeshed in a network characterized by the stereotypical denial and avoidance of death and dying attributed to health professionals. It was clear that the value system of our society, with its emphasis on youth, productivity, and the future, reinforces the lack of resources and care given to the dying. It became my job to work with a family who had little ability to negotiate their own internal needs, let alone the needs of the dying member, and who desperately needed concrete and emotional help from the professionals with whom they came in contact. I was anxious about death but imbued with a desire to be of help; I had little formal knowledge and training about working with the dying, and I searched for a theory to guide me. Finding none, I was thrown back on using human relationships with the client and hospital staff as a means of helping a woman cope with death.

As a teacher of social work students who have the same desire to be of help, who share a similar lack of knowledge and skill and the same societal values and anxiety about death, I need to define my task in teaching them about death and dying. They face clients and institutions that reflect the bureaucratization of death, the lack of openness and humanness in the care of the dying, and the helplessness and despair of dying patients and their families. Instructing them in the use of relationships is critical but not enough. Social work embodies values, knowledge, and skill, and if we want to use the potent tool we have in education to prepare social workers who are "at the crossroads of life . . . on the scene of the natural life event [that makes] help available and more possible" (Reynolds, 1974), we need to be clear in our teaching about what we value, what we know, and what we can do so that we can mobilize our students' use of themselves and transform it into the therapeutic work.

The following discussion stems from my experience in teaching a section on death and dying as part of a course on human behavior and the social environment to social work students at the master's level.

Essential Elements

There are three essential elements in the approach I use. It is based on what Carel B. Germain has called "an ecological perspective"—a view emphasizing the creative capacities of man, the process of growth and adaptation, the therapeutic potential of life events, and an individualizing role for social work services with an emphasis on understanding all the transacting forces in a person's total life space and on intervening in ways that promote growth in the system (Germain, 1973a).

VALUES
The first crucial element and the one with which I begin my classes is a value position. It may still need to be articulated in the face of sev-

eral generations of social work education dominated by a deterministic Freudian theory that sees people as bound in the present by unconscious conflicts rooted in the distant past. Other theorists in the psychoanalytic tradition (Erikson, 1950, 1959; Hartmann, 1958) write that life is infinitely more complex and dynamic—that growth and the potential for change do not stop at a prescribed age, even in an individual with serious intrapsychic struggles. Not all of a person's energy needs to be bound up in conflict. From birth to death—throughout the life cycle—there are identifiable phases that have mutually adaptive tasks for the individual and his environment. Successful resolution of these tasks strengthens adaptation and identity. The potential for growth and change is as intrinsic to adult life as to childhood. Whereas task mastery in later phases is dependent on earlier ones, the relationship is not simple or deterministic. The interplay of contemporary events and needs is crucial, and at any given critical phase, when the personality is more fluid, an individual can resolve previous difficulties in mastering current tasks.

The value position inherent in these writings of the ego psychologists is one that sees people as capable of growth and change throughout life because of the natural process of life and the dynamic interplay between an individual's phase-specific needs and environmental supports. This view is buttressed by those authors who are loosely termed "crisis theorists" (Parad, 1965; Rappaport, 1970). Grounded in ego psychology, they have shown how individuals not only have developmental crises but also face crises associated with role transitions (e.g., marrige, parenthood) and traumatic events (e.g., illness, death). They have described the potential for adaptive change available to people at these critical points throughout life. Germain has pointed out that, when one views the demands on coping resulting from what Toffler has described as the "transience, novelty, and diversity" of our contemporary existence, it should be clear that critical points abound in our lives (Germain, 1973b). Perlman (1968), Meyer (1970), and others have emphasized that, because clients seek social work assistance during such crucial moments in their lives, we as social workers are optimally positioned to be catalysts of growth.

In trying to articulate this value base to social work students in the

1970s who are eager if not desperate for a noncynical authority to tell them that they can make a difference and can help, I am asked: "But how can someone grow if they're dying? What can I do? What can anyone do?" These questions prompt a discussion of the value statement inherent in them—that the prospect of death is overwhelming, terrible, final, and, in short, the worst prospect with which anyone can be faced. In fact it is so total that, even though one might live with the knowledge of impending death for days, months, or even years, it must destroy all chance for meaning until it occurs. The students concede that we deal with death through avoidance and fear because we all face the specter of the certainty of its occurrence with its host of "terrible" meanings. Yet they assume our societal view is the only one and the correct one, allowing our culturally imposed anxiety about death to keep us from examining how people die, what their needs are, and what the needs of loved ones are. It is not clear to them that we may keep ourselves from getting close enough to our subject to gain the knowledge we need to be of help.

At this point the students begin discussing more fully what death means in our society and why we deal with it through avoidance. This usually has three aspects: (1) a highly theoretical discussion of our societal emphasis on youth, activity, productivity, and the future and a comparison of our society's values to those in other cultures and subcultures of our own society; (2) a discussion of how our medical services and other services, particularly to the aged, embody these values; and (3) a more emotional discussion in which the students begin relating personal, familial, and professional experiences providing important observations and information about how real people—dying patients, family, and hospital staffs—cope with death and about their own difficulties in knowing how to be of help.

The original value position thus sets a process of discussion in motion that moves from a semiphilosophical, theoretical discussion to one in which the students begin drawing on their own experiences in the light of what is being discussed. The class atmosphere grows intense but also reflects the students' heightened readiness to learn something that might be used to help dying patients and their families. One senses that the students are also seeking to master their own fears of death. While conscious of the latter motivation my goals at this point are to mobilize the students' active involvement in the material and to further their grasp of knowledge and principles about the subject so that they can use these in their work with clients. I believe that engaging the students in the way I described is essential to their learning. Either remaining aloof from the material or attempting to get emotional involvement too quickly would not be fruitful. The intellectual concepts alone lack the reality and humanness so essential to moving the students from their avoidance of death into meaningful work with clients, and yet an approach to the emotionality of the subject does not have proper respect for the students' struggles with the subject. The students have a wide range of ways of coping with upsetting subject matter, and this needs to be appreciated, particularly with regard to death and dying. Why? Because, more than any other subject, death has become a topic for repression (Group for the Advancement of Psychiatry, 1965) and touches off powerful feelings. What is gratifying is that students respond to this emotional but controlled atmosphere with a remarkable interest and quest for knowledge. With the avoidance momentarily suspended it is as if the students are now free to search for knowledge with which to deal with their anxiety about death.

KNOWLEDGE

The second crucial element then in this approach is imparting knowledge about dying patients, their families, and the ways medical services and social work manpower can be used to meet human needs. This begins with a redefinition of death as a phase of the life cycle—a biopsychosocial stage having identifiable tasks for the dying person, his family, and social environment. It is conceptualized as a crisis point for all those involved in which certain tasks can be mastered that allow for growth in all concerned. The class focuses on understanding what dying patients experience: their loneliness, isolation, loss of self-esteem, multiple physical losses, anticipatory grief, and mental and physical pain. It studies the range of coping (e.g., denial, hope, despair) available to the individual. It views the family's vulnerabilities when a member becomes ill and the helplessness, loneliness, despair, and grief it experiences. It identifies the family's need for concrete services and help in planning for the dying and the survivors. The lens is turned to the needs of organizations such as hospitals for maintaining efficiency, morale, teaching and research responsibilities, and commitments to service, often in the face of minimal financial resources. It looks at the professionals in such places who have their own administrative sanctions, their own needs to defend against death, and their own loneliness, grief, and despair in dealing with the suffering of dying patients and their families. In sum the focus is on all the forces in the life space of a dying person and on an attempt to individualize them and identify the coping demands that the crisis of death brings about, in the hope that we can better understand where and how to intervene.

When we view what each part of the system experiences, it becomes clear that the individual, the family, and the hospital all have certain tasks that should be mutual but in reality are generally in opposition. Dying persons and their families thus need to do grief work. One part of this may require that all share the angers, hopes, and pains brought about by the crisis of death. Yet those closest to the dying person are often the least able to tolerate this intimacy because of the anticipated pain involved. The question becomes how to promote this sharing necessary to successful coping. Similarly, both patient and family may need to plan for a lengthy terminal illness or for children left behind, but how are they to achieve this if accurate information is withheld by the medical staff? The class is asked to think in terms of this notion of mutuality in analyzing the transacting forces in the total situation so that appropriate interventions can lead to more successful task mastery and thus strengthen all involved.

Students also share numerous anecdotal, sometimes emotional, experiences as an idea mentioned in class stirs a personal association. They consistently appear adept at controlling how much they feel comfortable with sharing. A poignant example is the following:

The class was discussing whether a dying person knows he is dying. The debate became heated and divided. Mr. B. began recounting how he had been called home from college because his grandfather was dying. Mr. B. was admonished not to tell the grandfather the true nature of his condition, since he was convinced he had a minor illness. Mr. B. faithfully kept the secret though he found this difficult. He knew he would never see his grand-father alive again and felt overcome with love for him that he felt unable to share because it would seem strange. Mr. B.'s kid brother was also called home from boarding school and was instructed in keeping the grandfather's illness from him. He went in to see the grandfather just after Mr. B. and blurted out: "You look awful! I don't want you to die." He became fright-ened when he realized what he had said, but the grandfather heaved a sigh of relief saying, "Finally it can be said aloud." He and the grandson remi-nisced the rest of the afternoon. He died during the night. One of the students who had voiced the opinion that people don't know they're dying and shouldn't be told was moved by the story and asked Mr. B. if he was upset about not having told his grandfather the truth. Mr. B. thought and said, "No, I think we really knew we were sitting together for the last time even if we didn't speak it. I did what was right for me."

There are students who find it difficult to be tuned in to the class atmosphere. They remain silent or ask many questions about the do's and don'ts of working with dying patients and their families. They require the space they need to deal with the material. What is curious is how many come to me right after class or within weeks and talk about how meaningful the class was to them. They have usually been students who have had traumatic episodes with death.

In my experience, the use of personal experiences to supplement theoretical discussion has not posed the hazard of stirring up the students in ways detrimental to them, but it has resulted at times in the discussion's becoming diffuse. For this reason I find it useful to introduce a case history (Goldstein and Malitz, 1974) of a woman dying of cancer that illustrates almost all of what the discussion so far has dealt with: (1) the specific emotional needs of a dying woman during her terminal illness; (2) the emotional and concrete needs of her family; (3) the inadequate way the hospital services were orga-nized to deal with the woman and her family; (4) the range of ways the woman, the family, and the hospital staffs coped with her termi-nal illness; (5) the specific ways in which social work intervention was used in the total situation, along with the serious limitations in the approach chosen and the obstacles encountered.

Of particular significance for the discussion is that the case illustrates how a woman who had serious emotional problems before development of her terminal illness nevertheless coped with her death with a bravery, strength, and sense of purpose that had previously been absent in her life.

In addition to focusing discussion I introduce the case material at this point for two other reasons: the readiness of the students to assimilate it and the need for a bridge to the method component of the class. Initially I distributed the material to the students before the class but found three patterns, none of which seemed useful: (1) Students who were ordinarily conscientious did not read the material; (2) many of those who did read it became overwhelmed by it; and (3) some of those who read it wanted to spend the entire class discussing the case and my experiences, since it was clear I was the social worker involved. I should add here that using one's own material has problems associated with it both for the students and for the teacher. It seems to me that the major asset in doing so if it is well selected and if one is able to objectify it is that it is real. It also propels the teacher into an honest discussion of practice issues with the students.

This material is meant not to further discussion so much as to consolidate it and help the students integrate their learning around an actual situation. This case embodies the redefinition of death as a crisis with which all concerned may or may not adapt with mastery. Because a social worker was involved in a case in which many different systems had identifiable needs to which social work might address itself, it neatly introduces a discussion of social work interventive strategies.

SKILL

The third and last aspect of the teaching approach I am discussing addresses the skill component of work with a dying person and his family. But neither the class nor this chapter is meant to provide a manual on social work technique. Rather, I am concerned with developing a perspective from which different strategies can emerge. This perspective does not confine itself to a social casework model alone. At its best the social work process it envisions is a facilitative one that sees the therapeutic task described in Bandler's life model

(1963): "First we must identify and help remove the blocks and obstacles . . . second we must identify the progressive forces with which we can ally ourselves and which, at the appropriate time, we can mobilize." These progressive forces are not confined to the individual on the one hand nor to the environment on the other. Rather there is a fit between the person and the environment that can be strengthened in the service of "producing growth-inducing and environment-ameliorating transactions," (Gordon, 1969).

The first task is the assessing of all of the resources that exist in the client's total life space to determine where to intervene to promote task mastery and growth. The social worker faced with work with the dying person and his family should ask: "Given the needs and resources that exist in the total situation I am faced with, how can I go about setting in motion a process that will have positive effects for the system I am working with?" The answer to this question will vary depending on where a professional happens to be in a particular system. A family therapist outside of a hospital setting and a social caseworker on a medical ward may see the same family situation. The former may focus on helping the family deal with their grief and the insensitivity of the hospital staff. The social caseworker may attempt to help the hospital staff become more sensitive to the needs of this particular family. The underlying assumption in both situations is that something positive can be mobilized. Similarly two social group workers may define the same situation differently, depending on whom they see as the target of their interventions. One worker may seek to overcome the isolation, loneliness, and hopelessness of dying persons through providing them with a group experience in which they can gain support from openly sharing their fears. Another may seek to overcome the dehumanization and discouragement of the medical staff by providing them with an opportunity to discuss the frustrations and anxieties inherent in their work in a setting of mutual support. Again, the aim in both relates to promoting a more adaptive fit between the individual and his environment.

As with any other area the specifics of the interventions must be geared with dying persons and their families to the strengths that the clients possess as well as to an appreciation of the forces that block successful coping. Having decided where to intervene, one should proceed with the following questions in the forefront: What are the tasks that I know this individual, family, group, or organization needs to accomplish to strengthen its ability to cope with the crisis at hand? How do they identify their needs? What means are at my disposal to allow the client to move forward in identifying and mastering the tasks at hand?

In attempting to make these abstract notions more real to the class, it is again useful to draw on case material to illustrate many of the points raised. The material I use describes an individual casework process in which a woman is helped to cope with her terminal illness through the use of the casework relationship. As such, it is defined narrowly, not addressing itself to helping the family or the hospital staff. It is gratifying that by this point in the class the students are able to pinpoint all the areas in the case that might have been addressed given the perspective in which the subject has been cast. Those who began the class thinking there was nothing to be done with a dying person and his family have become the prime advocates for ways in which all the people involved in the case could have been helped. They draw on the particular method or body of techniques with which they are familiar to provide the specifics of intervention strategies they suggest.

It is difficult if not impossible to evaluate accurately the effects of a class, especially when one is teaching it. We have all had the experience of thinking we have "gotten through" to our students, only to discover that it was an illusion. The active involvement of the students in a class is desirable but not synonymous with good teaching. Beyond the highly subjective feeling I have that these classes on death and dying have gone well is the fact that a large number of students each semester seek permission to substitute a research paper on this subject for the final paper in the course. These papers, in addition to reflecting a scholarly command of the subject matter, consistently express the following sentiments:

This paper has been very meaningful to me. I was fearful initially about writing it but was so moved by our class discussion that I felt I had to learn more. . . . When I began this semester I thought I would never be able to work with dying patients—that I was too soft. Somehow from our class I began to realize that professionalism does not detract from being a person and that one does what one has to—to help another. . . . As I wrote this paper I began feeling more comfortable with all my feelings about death and should occasion arise in my work will venture to try out what I have learned.

Summary

In summary I have been describing a teaching perspective on the dying person and his family that encompasses the three components—value, knowledge, and skill—necessary to such work. The approach has been used with master's level social work students as part of a course on human behavior and the social environment. The classes have been a gratifying experience in which the students allow themselves to experience rather than avoid the anxiety involved in the subject of death and use it to learn. Perhaps one final point needs to be made in this connection. Our students also have the capacity to grow and change as part of their educational experience. Our task is to mobilize that potential.

References

Bandler, B. 1963. "The Concept of Ego Supportive Therapy." In *Ego-Oriented Casework*, eds. H. J. Parad and R. Miller. New York: Family Service Association of America.

Erikson, E. 1950. *Childhood and Society*. New York: W. W. Norton and Company.

——— 1959. "Identity and the Life Cycle." *Psychological Issues* 1, no. 1.

Germain, C. B. 1973a. "An Ecological Perspective in Casework Practice." *Social Casework* 54, no. 6.

——— 1973b. "Social Casework." In *Goals for Social Welfare 1973–1993: An Overview of the Next Two Decades,* ed. H. B. Trecker. New York: Association Press.

Goldstein, E. G. and S. Malitz. 1974. "Psychotherapy and Pharmacotherapy as Enablers in the Anticipatory Grief of a Dying Patient: A Case Study." In *Anticipatory Grief,* eds. B. Schoenberg, et al. New York: Columbia University Press.

Gordon, W. E. 1969. "Basic Constructs for an Integrative and Generative Conception of Social Work." In *The General Systems Approach: Contributions Toward a Holistic Conception of Social Work,* ed. G. Hearn. New York: Council on Social Work Education, p. 7.

Group for the Advancement of Psychiatry. 1965. *Death and Dying: Attitude of Patient and Doctor* 5, Symposium II, p. 648.

Hartmann, E. 1958. *Ego Psychology and the Problem of Adaptation.* New York: International University Press.

Meyer, C. H. 1970. *Social Work Practice: A Response to the Urban Crisis.* New York: The Free Press, pp. 158–161.

Parad, H. J., (ed.) 1965. *Crisis Intervention: Selected Readings.* New York: Family Service Association of America.

Perlman, H. H. 1968. *Personna.* Chicago: University of Chicago Press.

Rappaport, L. 1970. "Crisis Intervention as a Mode of Brief Treatment." In *Theories of Social Casework,* eds. R. W. Roberts and R. H. Neww. Chicago: University of Chicago Press.

Reynolds, B. 1974. "Between Client and Community: A Study of Responsibility in Social Casework." *Smith College Studies in Social Work* 5, no. 1, pp. 5–128.

26

Helping the Social Work Student Deal with Death and Dying

Helen Cassidy

In preparing students for effective practice in the professions it is necessary to cover a range of subjects that provides the awareness needed when similar problems are encountered in later, real-life situations. All students in the health professions need preparation for dealing with death and the responses to grave diseases and illnesses that can lead to the termination of life. This calls for understanding of the feelings experienced by the patients and their families and the complementary responses evoked in the students as they confront these emotion-packed situations, possibly for the first time ever or at least very likely for the first time in a relationship in which they carry a professional role. This is the area covered by my presentation, which concerns work with a group of seven second-year graduate social work students in a general hospital as they handled case situations of dying patients on the cancer wards and the pediatric intensive-care unit.

This chapter reviews a modest attempt to help students look frankly at their experiences and their reactions in life–death situations. The objective of the exercise was to help the students toward knowledge of their own personal reactions and to develop sufficient self-awareness about handling the problems of death and dying to place their feelings within their conscious control. In developing this theme, the presentation focuses briefly on the tasks of professional education, relates to the meaning of death and dying in our culture, determines what is involved in learning the role of professional helper in life–death crises, and speculates on how these experiences can be encompassed in the total learning situation so as to achieve better integration for the individual student and a higher level of ego mastery.

The actual approach used with the student group in question was a retrospective one whereby they were asked by reflection and analysis to scrutinize their own responses to the cases of terminal illness assigned to them for service and to suggest measures that might have been built into the learning situation to better prepare them to meet the problems. They were given a written questionnaire that asked them to review their experiences with patients facing death and with their families, determine what emotions were evoked or reactivated if they had in the past suffered personal losses by death, consider how they handled these painful reactions, and suggest ways in which the learning situation might prepare them better to meet the demands.

Students were asked either to respond in writing or be ready to participate in a discussion on the topic. All participated in the seminar. They seemed free to articulate reactions and, as if by doing so and sharing with peers, to gain a new perspective on self. Before describing the results of this small study, a review of the subthemes mentioned earlier may help to place the outcome and recommendations made by the students into the broader context of the total problem.

The Tasks of Professional Education

There is no question but that young adults preparing themselves for professions must make certain adaptations in their personal outlook and affective responses to carry through productively the new behaviors called forth in the role transition. A growing body of material concerns the adult learner and the factors that can be useful in the process of socialization into new roles with accompanying expectations. In reviewing adaptational problems of the medical student, Renee Fox (1957, p. 208) focuses on the young medical student whose uncertainty about his own inadequate knowledge and skill for the tasks confronting him are compounded by the insufficiency of the current body of medical knowledge. So his concerns in life–death situations are a mixture of his imperfect mastery of available knowledge, the actual limitations of medical knowledge itself, and the confounding problem, at his stage of learning, of distinguishing between the two. Pressure is frequently on him to adapt a manner of certitude, for that is the cultural expectation of the doctor role—the one who can offer stability in a world of confusion and unpredictability. Within this framework the medical student may find that his attitude toward death may be compounded even beyond normal dimensions as he attempts to achieve a balance between the expectations inherent in "the role of physician and those which inhere in the role of student" (Fox, 1957, p. 241).

Theorists of adult learning state that, for effective learning to take place, the integrity of the ego must be protected. The individual is free to learn and will learn if he has the intellectual capacity and aptitude and if that knowledge and skill are timed to his powers of assimilation (Towle, 1954, p. 84). The integrative capacity is defined as the capacity of the ego to withstand and master pressure and to screen out those stimuli that overtax the assimilative powers. It is one easy step from successful discrimination and screening out to that of making maladaptive concessions in admitting to consciousness those stimuli that are overwhelming. Hence, it is characteristic of the student confronted with demanding tasks to seek, out of his self-dependence and need for survival, knowledge of "what to feel and think and how to act" (Towle, 1954, p. 93). The integrative task is heavier where the intensity of affect is heavy. In many areas the student social worker—like the medical student—is called upon to understand and help people whose experience is beyond his own. His emotional development, readiness to deal with reality, and ability to deal with interrelationships and to think and act for himself and apart from others all figure into the integrative capacity of the ego (Towle, 1954, p. 110).

The Meaning of Death and Dying in Our Culture

The tasks faced by professional educators are staggering as they attempt to help students prepare themselves for life roles that incorporate the emotional demands of such a dimension as the confrontation with death. Our Western culture has traditionally not offered much support to the educational push. Too often there is more disdain than reverence for old age and its ills; society is much more preoccupied with pursuing pleasure than with the grim fact of death. However, despite this attitude, the last decade has shown remarkable changes so that the search for "what is real" has surfaced in a frank look at death and its meaning. Other than the poets in their continuing search for universals, theory about death and dying has been slow to emerge on the professional front. Now the subject is almost popular! Along with some faddist preoccupation with death we are currently surrounded by a professionally healthy search for truth via serious study and research.

The attempt to analyze and arrive at basic principles has afforded a dimension of new knowledge in both the public and professional domains. Much is being researched and written to afford a theoretical entrée into a realm calling for intense affective involvement and resolution of feelings and personal reactions. With sufficient theory developed for backup and an attitude among young people that seeks out knowledge about death, there is a more favorable climate for students to gain the experience of working with terminally ill and dying patients and to integrate their encounters into their personal and professional armamentarium. Kübler-Ross's work and Glaser and Strauss's *Awareness of Dying* are examples of the high professional caliber that is now on the scene, but other work and articles on the subject abound in the professional journals. So one might agree that the tide is with the topic and the educator's job is a little easier since the phenomenon of death is an idea whose time has arrived for consideration and review on the public scene.

Learning the Role of Professional Helper in Life–Death Crises

Students for the most part are young, and death can have almost a remote, even nonthreatening meaning for them. Many have not had any personal experience with dying people. If they have had, it is likely to have been a grandparent or older relative rather than an immediate family member. In the process of their becoming professional persons who plan to work in a medical setting the reality of dealing with death is very real and something that the serious student knows he must come to grips with in a way that will make the confrontation professionally and personally encompassable and that will give him some sense of beginning skill and mastery in meeting the crisis and doing a humanly and professionally responsible job.

A tenet of the social worker's role is to meet the patient where he is, assess his strengths and weaknesses, size up his capacity to meet the crisis, and determine how much support must be offered. The social work student is free of the life–death responsibilities ascribed to the doctor's role. Hence the terminally ill or dying patient does not represent a personal threat to the social worker's skill or sense of adequacy as might be the case with a physician. The social worker's only job is to help the patient and provide some satisfying human experiences even in this final stage of life. The concomitant responsibility of the student worker in this phase is to be the outside arm of the medical setting in forming the link with family, helping them through this experience with whatever attendant conflicts, struggles, differences, or grievances the threat of death of the family member may tend to exacerbate.

To meet the situation with equanimity and honesty, to use himself as constructively as possible, and to incorporate this personal–professional experience so that it helps him deal with other, similar experiences are the teaching–learning goals. The range of personal and professional needs must be met simultaneously because in this highly charged human situation they cannot be separated fully. One must respond with all the humanity possible even as he absorbs the shock of the experience and its meaning to him and as he gains some gauge of the impact of sharing the experience of another's death.

Integrating the Experience of Working with Death through Preparation of the Student

The student must learn the role of professional helper and find out how to use himself and his human investment in life crises. As he experiences the impact, he determines what aspects of self he has to reckon with. Since the whole idea is to perform a professional function effectively, the student's capacity to know himself and what he must do and how he must handle his emotions and responses to give the service is significant. As this particular group of social work students analyzed the range of considerations that came into their purview in working with patients and their families in life–death situations, they listed the following points:

1. They found themselves filling the roles of comforter and nurturer and engaging in the "mutual pretense" behavior wherein student and patient were operating outwardly at the level of nonrecognition of death as a reality while inwardly both knew the truth and were aware that the other did also.
2. They found most difficult the "nothing to do" phase and the long silences that often ensued in their visits. They recognized that, because their own anxiety was the problem, they had to control this. Once they were successful, satisfaction gained through standing by and engaging with the patient on the level of his need was all that was necessary. The continuity of seeing and relating to the patient was most important in view of the feeling of desertion often experienced by dying persons when medicine can offer nothing more and medical personnel try to avoid them. Touch contact or a meaningful glance may be all that is needed.
3. They came to recognize the need not only to help the family through recognition of death and the phases of grieving but also to help each member in terms of his past relationship with the patient. Included here is the help in anticipatory grief as a preamble in cushioning the actual event of death and the importance of families' experiencing the reality of death as a first stage in engaging in their grief work. This may be of

special significance in cases of sudden deaths or deaths that occur when the family is not present.

4. They learned to sense the individual responses of patients to their current situation as a direct relationship to those things that had meaning for them in life, for example, the hostility and disgust of the fastidious man to whom grooming and appearance were paramount in the face of his physical deterioration; the shock and heartbreak of the young girl whose head was shaved and who lost her boyfriend in the trauma of a brain tumor and its sequelae.

5. They observed that death as a specific moment in time can be peaceful and reassuring. However, any reference to survival expectations in specific time measurement should be avoided by physicians, since families tend to attach significance beyond the broad parameters intended by medical personnel and either express disappointment that the end has not come or experience a reactivation of hope beyond any reality. In all situations the need for a kind of "hope" on whatever level was viewed as essential in keeping patient and family going until the end.

6. Students need to experience, recognize, and hence be able to subjugate to conscious control their own feelings about the person and the event. As with the individual reactions of family members, students will not identify in their own experience a universal response to death. It will vary with the patient and the quality of the student's relationship to him. One sensitive student pointed to her "anger" at one patient whose own deprived life had caused her to establish a provocative and trying relationship with the student in constantly testing her. Although this patient made it difficult for someone to like her, the student stood by this lonely and unhappy woman, went beyond the call of duty in trying to meet her needs, and provided possibly the one meaningful contact she had in her final weeks of life. Having expected to be called by the woman's father when death neared, she learned of the event only in the obituary column of the newspaper. Anger and guilt, frequently in the same company, had to be reckoned with. The same student felt "hurt" that she was on her weeklong semester break when a second patient died, and she could not be reached despite attempts made by the family. This was a patient with whom her relations were warm, satisfying, and personally rewarding. Both patients were given the student's best professional service. Her response to each and the emotions evoked by their deaths were very different.

7. All students handled their own feelings by giving the best service of which they were capable. The "doing" helped them to handle feelings as well as to perform the required services. In discriminating the difference between involvement in personal experiences with death and

with these hospital patients (in whom the students' investment had been intensive over this final period and the service had possibly covered a long time span), the obvious difference was that personal memories and family ties were not involved in the service cases. However, the human relationship deriving from an intensive investment did make for a common denominator with the personal experiences.

8. Since service is the acceptable professional outlet for defusing the emotional experience, security in knowing hospital routine and proceeding with assurance are important.

9. In similar fashion, understanding the body of theory about death and dying is important in supplying the professional knowledge base and theoretical rationale. In the end it is likely that most social work students will resort to sublimation as a defense. For example, students recalled that the technical activities and achievements provided the solace that counterbalanced the sadness. A mechanical activity such as this helped in integrating the experience and getting back to the daily work with other patients, some with similar prognoses.

10. Students summarized their responses by stating that each had finally to handle it himself/herself. How the sublimation can be effected is the question. While one said she "left her work at the hospital" each evening to avoid "going nuts," another was able to express her grief and let it come through. All agreed that the essential ingredient is self-awareness and knowing how one must deal in these areas of filling the professional role in a trying situation.

The student group was asked to suggest an educational program that might prove a useful preface to an assignment of working with patients nearing death. Although this discussion did not lead to a particular plan outlining specific course content, the following thoughtful and timely suggestions emerged:

1. Materials such as the Kübler-Ross books and tapes should be used before students have an assignment that requires them to deal with death. As one student stated, "When you know what's 'natural,' then you don't consider everything that happens pathological."

2. Various audiovisual aids would assist in making the experience more real by emphasizing the vicarious aspect and demonstrating another's approach to the situation. If the patient is willing, taped interviews would help peers in seeing how another met the problem.

3. Role playing might be useful in achieving similar ends and afford more security in handling. This again would "spread the risk and share the

benefits'' of collegial experience since a great fear is ''whether I will make a difficult situation worse through my own ineptness.'' Although each situation is unique and each student's response the result of the unique chemistry of this particular human interaction, the panorama of types and kinds of experiences would be helpful in identifying specific responses, techniques, and so forth.

4. ''Know thyself'' is the final answer. There is no substitute for self-awareness. However, self-awareness is insight, and the process can be enhanced by conscious learning. ''Knowledge makes him free to use his intuition, whereas, without it he may be fearful and uncertain'' (Fox, 1957, p. 34).

Summary

The student social worker, like other professionals in the medical setting, must learn to deal with death and dying. To engage in a productive helping process with patients and their families amid the grief, sorrow, and crisis aspects attendant on the death, the student must become aware of his own reactions, know his own feelings, and be willing to plunge into self-scrutiny as a preface to development of insight. Each student will benefit by analyzing his responses in given situations. There is no educational preparation that will meet all these needs and make him fully ready for the experience. However, there is a body of knowledge and there are certain educational devices that will offer him a kind of preparation that can reduce his insecurity and enhance ego integration and mastery, a most important consideration in adult learning.

References

Fox, R. 1957. "Training for Uncertainty." In *The Student Physician,* eds. P. K. Merton, G. G. Reader, and P. Kendall. Cambridge, Mass.: The Commonwealth Fund, Harvard University.

Towle, C. 1954. *The Learner in Education for the Professions.* Chicago: University of Chicago Press.

Additional Bibliography

Aldrich, C. K. 1963. "The Dying Patient's Grief." *Journal of the American Medical Association* 184, no. 5 (May 4): 329–31.

Aring, C. D. 1968. "Intimations of Mortality: An Appreciation of Death and Dying." *Annals of Internal Medicine* 69, no. 1 (July):137–52.

Field Learning and Teaching: Explorations in Graduate Social Work Education. 1968. Proceedings of a Symposium, Tulane University School of Social Work, New Orleans, Louisiana.

Glaser, B. G. and A. L. Strauss. 1965. *Awareness of Dying.* Chicago: Aldine Publishing Company.

Kübler-Ross, E. 1969. *On Death and Dying.* New York: Macmillan Company

Meisel, A. M. and M. H. Hand. 1965. "Reactions to Approaching Death." *Diseases of the Nervous System* 26 (January):15–24.

Wahl, C. W. 1958. "The Fear of Death." *Bulletin of the Menninger Clinic* 22 (November): 214–23.

27

The Dying Professor as Death Educator

Lois Jaffe

I am a dying social work professor who has been teaching graduate seminars on methods of intervention with the dying since I was diagnosed as having acute leukemia in 1973. My method is to create an intensive thinking and feeling classroom experience whereby students of various helping professions have an opportunity to interact over a 15-week period with someone who is terminally ill. It is a unique case study approach to understanding the anxieties, fears, hopes, and concerns of someone facing death, her significant others, as well as her caregivers.

By involving myself, my spouse, the medical team, and other individuals experiencing loss and grief, we offer an opportunity to tease out from the particular and unique the broad general reactions that all human beings experience in facing death. My goal is to provide a chance for potential caregivers to get in touch with their own death anxieties and to resolve some of their feelings about time limits, separation, and loss in this in vivo situation so that they can work more effectively with the terminally ill and their families.

Most teaching approaches to death education are based on the assumption that, if the professional helper is to work with the terminally ill and bereaved, then his profession has the responsibility of helping him face his own death and that of others in advance of that confronting experience. My own particular approach is based on the further assumption that small losses should help us get ready for larger ones, that gradual separations better prepare us for abrupt and final ones, and that some grief makes possible the better handling of much grief. It is based on an additional assumption that the raw experience of a constant dying in the midst of full, rich living is the ground from which meaning about life and death can grow and mature (Jackson, 1974).

These assumptions regarding the ability of the terminally ill person to become teacher to those who may and do attend to the dying and their families are based on a great deal of empirical research done by Glaser and Strauss (1965), Feifel (1967), Hamovitch (1964), Kübler-Ross (1969), and others who have found that caregivers often avoid the dying patient and his family unless they have come to grips with their own fears and anxieties about death and dying. Moreover, because of the invisibility of personal dying as a result of a natural or disease process in our contemporary society, most people grow up never having witnessed a "personal death," for 80 percent of people who die today do so in hospitals or old-age homes. Consequently not only does there seem to be an absence of knowledge of how an ill person should handle his dying, but also there appears to be an uncertainty about how others who care for him should act or what they should say.

There is further empirical evidence that the most effective death education from a student's point of view is one that combines didactic and experiential learning, the most meaningful input coming from those who speak from personal experience (*Ars Moriendi Newletter,* 1974).

Genesis of My Involvement

What brought me to these assumptions and my subsequent teaching of death and dying? It all began on the day I was told of my fatal illness after being hospitalized on April 13, 1973. Interestingly this was the day after my last social work methods class ended for that semester. Sociologist David Phillips (1969) has found that people who are about to die seem to hold onto life until after a significant event takes place to which they look forward. I did indeed seem very close to death that day, for it was the end of a long week that had started with the sudden appearance of black and blue marks all over my body, followed by bleeding gums and aching teeth, and culminating in a bone-weary fatigue that I had never before experienced. After a visit to our family internist I was immediately rushed to the hospital, subjected to a battery of examinations and laboratory tests, and told the following morning that I had acute myelomonocytic leukemia, with a statistical prognosis of a year to a year and a half to live. But I was given hope that, with an immediate, aggressive attack on the leukemia cells via a combination of potent chemicals, blood transfusions, and platelet replacement, I might have a chance for remission that would enable me to return to a normal life for however long that might last. I was told that every individual reacts differently, and so there really could be no predictions about how I might fare.

Although it is true that the one thing that concerned me most during those harrowing first seven and a half weeks in the hospital was simply surviving the constant bouts of infection, nausea, chills, fever, and anxiety, the second thing I came to fear most was the threat of abandonment. Everywhere around me on the hematology unit I saw dying patients whose relatives and friends gradually deserted them, or who would come and leave quickly, guiltily protesting that they could not stand to see a loved one suffer or lie dying. I saw the newer nurses and interns and some residents devastated by deaths they were helpless to prevent. Even some of the more seasoned doctors would often appear aloof or brusque and uncaring in their rush to get their daily contact with dying patients over, as if fearful that their physical contact with death might somehow engulf them also. I saw dedicated, skillful nurses who were chronically left with the "blood and guts" issues of attending to a constant range of patients' physical and emotional needs, only to experience the "burn-out" syndrome after a few weeks or months, simply because they had had no previous preparation for facing death with this kind of intensity or any outlet when it did come. And so many would leave the unit, often when their patients needed them most. Although my social work colleagues would drop in daily to see how I was faring, no one asked if I or my husband or four children might want to talk about the process we were undergoing. They later told me they assumed because I was "professional," I would have asked for help if I or my family needed it. It never occurred to them that, when one is that sick, it rarely occurs to one to ask for anything that is not proffered by means of someone else's initiative.

When I returned home and back to full-time work, I faced another kind of isolation and abandonment. I found that some friends and a few colleagues avoided me. They would dart into doorways, cross the street, or avoid eye contact in order not to encounter me. Although I thought that they were really avoiding their own death anxiety, I began to confront them head-on with, "Hey, you're avoiding me. Can we talk about it?" Inevitably I got the same response: "I just don't know what to say. How in the world do you talk to someone who is dying?" I began to realize that it was not mere death anxiety that deterred them; they were simply unrehearsed in interaction with the dying, not unlike someone on a first date who wants to make significant contact with the other but just doesn't know how.

The idea began to take hold: I wanted to teach a seminar on death and dying. After all, I had been teaching social work methods classes for several years and had used case examples constantly from my own ongoing practice as a therapist and student field instructor at a community mental health clinic. Why not teach from my own "case example" now, as well as from the multitude of other examples I keep encountering every five weeks when I must return to the hospital for a five-day course of chemotherapy? Also, my own teaching style is predicated on a combination of cognitive, affective, and behavioral approaches, for it has long been my belief (supported by a great deal of research evidence) that effective teaching should provide modeling of these three elements of thinking, feeling, and doing to maximize learning and change (Carkhoff, 1971). Why not take this newest life experience and incorporate it into a cognitive framework so that I might better transmit it to others?

I began to read voraciously on the subject and began extending my contacts with terminally ill patients and families on the hematology unit as well as at the community mental health center where I worked. A curious thing began to happen. I found my own fear of death and the process of dying gradually diminishing. I discovered it became easier to talk to my husband, my parents, my children, and my friends about what was happening; I found that a freeing process began to take place with a release of newfound energies.

In my readings I was amazed to find that studies have revealed that five times as many people who lost a close relative died within a year of bereavement as compared to the death rates in matched age control groups (Rees and Lutkins, 1967). I read Martin Seligman's report (1974) that, in a recent British study of 4500 widowers during the first six months after their spouses' death, there was a 40 percent higher death rate than the expected mortality rate for their age group. In pursuing my interest in family therapy, I discovered from one of Dr. Murray Bowen's teaching tapes that, according to his research findings in his therapeutic work with families facing death, the "emotional shock wave phenomenon" that seems to occur after a death in the family appears to kick up a "cluster" of more emotional disturbance, accidents, illnesses as well as deaths than occur in non-bereaved families. He has also found that, where there is an open communication system around a family member's impending death, this emotional shock wave phenomenon is less likely to occur than where communication about death is closed. These data pointed more and more to the need to take the wraps off the death taboo in our culture and in my own life.

All these converging insights convinced me that, in using my own experiences, thoughts, and feelings about facing death, I might begin to open more personal communication about death anxieties and model an open style of dying, and, in addition, I could help myself to better confront my own fears and trepidations through a desensitization process that would in some ways parallel my students' continuing experience with myself and others who encounter death. I realized this might be a rather risky venture, for it would require considerable ability to preserve a certain amount of cognitive mastery and distance while being emotionally caught up in the necessarily intense process of dying. Still, I knew I had some knowledge and skill in understanding myself and other human beings that had accrued from my years of professional training and clinical experience. But more than anything, I wanted to attempt to bring the various threads of my life together in some authentic, meaningful way so that my impending death could become a vital part of my life.

It might properly be asked, "What about the impact of this intense encounter on your students, most of whom have not yet had direct professional experience in intervening with the dying? What kind of trauma might this create for them and how would you separate your own personal needs from your professional role as educator to preserve the necessary boundaries between teacher and student? More important, what would happen if you became critically ill in the middle of this process and died? Then what?"

These are the questions I myself have been pondering and trying to resolve as I have attempted to use myself creatively in this educational endeavor. I realize that currently in death education circles there is a great deal of controversy regarding the use of the dying professional as teacher. What I would like to consider in the remainder of this paper are the conditions under which this linkage between life experience, classroom teaching, and work in the field can be successful, as well as the possible pitfalls in such an attempt. The course has now been taught twice, many changes having been initiated as a result of our first effort; we have learned from experience.

In examining some of the educational issues involved, I would like to share my personal odyssey in this teaching–living–dying process, as well as the curriculum content, observations of, classroom interaction, and evaluation data, to consider the efficacy of using the terminally ill professional as one of many teaching approaches to death and dying.

When I told a few faculty colleagues that I was interested in teaching such a seminar, I was astounded at their overwhelmingly affirmative reaction to the idea. The associate dean in charge of curriculum planning told me that a very bright and competent second-year graduate student, a married woman and mother in her late twenties, had talked with her faculty adviser about wanting to design a curriculum outline and teach a seminar in death and dying as part of her independent study program in pursuing a master's degree in the specialized area of health and mental health. Although the student had been reading extensively in death education and had worked with dying patients in her field placement in the university's teaching hospital as a medical social worker, the curriculum committee felt that it would be inadvisable for a second-year student, no matter how competent, to shoulder the sole responsibility of teaching a graduate-level seminar. Since her ultimate goal was to become a death educator in higher education, the committee felt it would be a good experience for her to co-teach the seminar with me so that I could assist in the teaching, role modeling, and mentoring. I could teach "from the inside looking out" and she could teach "from the outside looking in" in respect to the terminally ill.

This seemed an ideal answer to my quandary of not wanting to leave students hanging in midair if I should have to be hospitalized during the 15-week course of the seminar. I did not know the student in question, and I was not quite certain how it would hit her. Needless to say, it was a less than ideal arrangement for her. First of all, understandably, she was hoping she could be in total charge of her own course, since she had worked long and hard to research this whole field; she had thought through and put together a commendable course outline; and she did not relish the idea of having to take what she felt might likely be a "back seat" in teaching with someone who had the obvious "edge" of having taught well and successfully, by student and faculty appraisal, for several years and who had the benefit of being able to "tell it like it is" from a patient's viewpoint. Yet she perceived that she would probably not be permitted to teach the course by herself and that this might be the most realistic accommodation. Although we were able to talk around these various issues, an uneasy truce emerged between us as we began to plan for course content and process.

Description of the Course

I suggested we follow the thrust of her outline as submitted, which was broken down into four content areas: (1) ethical issues pertaining to death and dying; (2) suicide intervention and prevention; (3) the meaning of death to one who is dying, his family, and his caregivers; and (4) loss and grief. We agreed that, since this was the first time the university was offering such a course and since there might be a great deal of apprehension about what would take place, especially when the word spread that a terminally ill person would be co-teaching, we should proceed slowly, using a gradual desensitizing approach. Betsy * would be primarily responsible for the didactic material of the first two content areas of ethical issues and suicide, giving her a chance to jump in and get her feet wet by more or less teaching on her own, and I would act as a resource person to her and the class. By the middle of the course the class should be emotionally prepared to deal directly with encountering people who are facing death, loss, and grief. I would have the primary responsibility for this third section on the meaning of death, with Betsy acting as resource person; then we would team-teach the final section on loss and grief.

We agreed that the seminar should be limited to 20 and that no audits or guest attenders be permitted so as to insure confidentiality, group cohesiveness, and an open and progressive sharing of thoughts and feelings. We believed the best way to help students integrate didactic material with their feelings about death was to proceed at first from lectures that could sensitize and familiarize them with the language of death. Then we would introduce films and experiential exercises for at least half of each class session, after the first two lecture-discussions, to enable students to get in touch more easily with their own gut reactions. This would be followed by guest speakers with personal experience in working with the terminally ill and their families, beginning with a clinical psychologist who was working in the emergency room of the university hospital with suicide attempters, followed by a psychiatrist who would speak about psychiatric

* Mrs. Elizabeth Clark, M.S.W., my co-teacher.

implications of impending death and would also share his experiences in working with the elderly who are nearing death.

We then would shift from dialogues with people who worked with the dying to dialogues with the dying and bereaved themselves. This series would begin with my own personal experience of going through Kübler-Ross's five stages, with the meaning my own death had to me, and with what has and has not been helpful. My husband had agreed to follow up my presentation with his own experience of the five stages and what others have done to help and/or hinder. After this, members of the medical team on our hematology unit would discuss issues of "who, what, when, and how to tell" regarding diagnosis, prognosis, and relationship issues between the patient and his caregivers.

In considering the area of loss and grief, we felt by this time the class could handle an encounter with a young couple whose 10-year-old son had died of leukemia the year before. To dilute some of the intensity following this session, we next asked several clergy representing various faiths to discuss their interventions with the dying and bereaved and the differing religious beliefs and cultural practices that have helped people face death. We would then conclude with someone whose husband had died of a heart attack and who had had to face all the vicissitudes of sudden death and widowhood. By encountering the terminally ill and the bereaved directly, the students would have a chance to practice their interviewing skills in a relatively safe environment. The final session would be left for evaluation, feedback, and wrap-up.

In implementing this plan, some rather dismaying as well as gratifying reactions occurred the first time around. My co-teacher and I felt we had adequately planned for a desensitizing process to occur. However, in the first class session, my mere presence and the acknowledgment of my terminal status and my brief reasons for co-teaching the course were enough to raise the level of anxiety to a high pitch. Owing to my own uneasiness and the fact that my partner was prepared to proceed with the didactic, "desensitizing" ethical material as planned, these anxieties were not adequately dealt with and continued to exacerbate until midterm, when my direct encounter with the class was scheduled. This approach was changed the second time around, as we shall see.

The idea of introducing films on ethical issues after two sessions was a sound one. We started off with "Who Should Survive?," the Shriver Foundation film, photographed at Johns Hopkins, regarding the birth of a mongoloid baby with intestional atresia and the agonizing dilemma of the parents who must sign surgical consent papers if the baby is to survive. The couple determined not to sign, and the film shows the medical staff's reaction as the baby is left to starve to death in his hospital crib for more than two weeks as an intervention act of passive euthanasia; then a panel composed of a variety of professionals discussed the ethical issues involved. This was a stirring film that enabled students to begin to combine their thinking and feeling capacities to work through their own value conflicts regarding euthanasia, genetic engineering, abortion, and other ethical issues.

Kübler-Ross's audio- and videotapes were a good preface to preparing students for a dialogue with those facing death and grief. Murray Bowen's excellent teaching videotape on "The Family Faces Death" was a most enlightening discussion and demonstration of the "emotional shock wave phenomenon" following death when a family's communication system is closed, as contrasted with an open system concerning death. The use of videotape showing a parent group of children with cystic fibrosis led by a social worker at the university-connected Children's Hospital pinpointed the importance of shared grief and professional interventions during crises. However, after the personal dialogues between the class and myself, my husband, the bereaved parents, and the widow, films were perceived by the students to be artificial and too distancing.

Experiential exercises were initiated after the initial use of films, but pacing became a problem. As mentioned previously, I began my section on the meaning of death and methods of intervention with the dying with a sharing of my own personal experience. By this time the anxiety had mounted for the class, in spite of my heretofore peripheral contributions, and my own anxieties were at a high pitch. Could the class—could I—handle the emotional impact? Although I had no trouble getting through my experiencing of the five stages and the meaning that death had come to have for me, I can see in retrospect that I had trouble encouraging and allowing free-flowing questions and discussion for fear these would get out of hand. This must have been my unconscious reason for following my presentation with an exercise intended to get class members in touch with their own feelings about their own death.

So without sufficient airing of the anxieties my own presentation stirred, I had them make drawings of their own perceptions and fantasies regarding their own deaths. Although all students participated and found this exercise profoundly meaningful, only a handful of the class was willing to share their drawings, thoughts, and feelings with the others. Too much intensity had been allowed to build in one session, and this created problems that flowed over into subsequent sessions.

The spillover manifested itself when several students came to Betsy and me with anxieties about their handling the forthcoming encounter with the bereaved couple, both of whom were professional colleagues of mine, who had faced the death of their child. My co-teacher and I consequently determined that we needed to cut off all ensuing speaker–classroom dialogues after one hour's time and use the remaining class hour to debrief and air all reactions regarding what had occurred the hour before.

The next session following my presentation was the dialogue between the class and my husband. Here they began to feel more at ease, although still a bit clumsy, in practicing their interviewing skills while dealing with most sensitive areas. During the debriefing session, we brought up the fact that several students had expressed concerns about their uneasiness over interacting with the bereaved couple who would be experiencing an anniversary death reaction. As the students began to discuss the pros and cons of their coming, which reflected their own underlying death anxieties, the class finally agreed that they would be willing to assume the responsibility for posing sensitive and tactful questions if the couple could assume the responsibility of choosing to come, having been forewarned of the class members' apprehensiveness. When the session finally arrived, the couple poignantly placed themselves across from each other as we sat around a table as a group, and they talked to each other throughout the session about their remembrances and their current pain. They both cried openly and appropriately, as did most of the class, and when the class seemed unable to go further with them, I came in with supportive comments and questions to ease the intensity. It was the most trying of all sessions for everyone. Yet the students were able to witness how, at peak moments of pain, two people were able to talk to each other about their profound sadness as well as their remembered joys and were able to move from strength to strength. The pathology the students had feared turned out to be an experience in rediscovered emotional health for both themselves and our guests.

Our next session featured the head nurse and chief resident from the hematology unit where I was a patient, discussing the vital issues of how to handle the "moment of truth" with patients who face death. At this time there was no social worker who was a regular member of the unit team, and consequently a worker rarely saw dying patients unless called in for consultation, usually around discharge planning. During the class hour the team was asked why a social worker had not been included as part of the staff who would automatically see the dying patient and his family. The answer was that a worker would be welcomed if she or he could be on the unit consistently, but that had not been the experience of the team. It was implied that social workers did not appear to be comfortable handling the emotional issues of death and dying in that setting. Betsy, who was doing her student field work in that system, said, in effect, "Amen." My husband had also commented previously to the class that he would have welcomed talking to a male social worker about his grief at the time of my first hospitalization, but none were available in the system, and indeed, no one had offered us any specific assistance with emotional or social problems involving our crisis situation.

Word immediately got back to the hospital adminstration that, allegedly, my co-teacher and I had denigrated the social work staff and had aided and abetted the nurse and resident in doing the same. The director called my dean to tell him of this affront, demanding a written apology from me. I was totally unhinged and unprepared for this turn of events. I immediately recognized our mistake in not having invited a staff social worker to come to that session, even if she were not a regular part of the team. But more than that, I began to have some understanding of how traumatic talking about death issues can become to the systems involved. I heard rumblings that other professionals in the city had heard I was teaching this seminar and felt it was a "sick" thing to do. The course, the first of its kind at the university, had apparently created all kinds of tremors everywhere.

The dean and associate supported my ability to handle this situation in whatever way I deemed most feasible. I immediately called the director of social work service and spoke with her and then with the entire social work staff. I was interested in what obstacles they perceived to be standing in the way of getting social work help for the dying and their families on the hematology unit and in what could be done to deliver the kind of services we all agreed were needed. Their answer was that nursing seemed to feel this was their "turf" and in the past had allegedly deterred social workers assigned for consultation to the unit from being more active. I suggested that the director request a meeting and air these grievances, since the team seemed most open for such help at this juncture. They did meet and a regular social worker was assigned to the team who now assists in all medical rounds and continuing help with the terminally ill and their families. As a result of our classroom encounter with hospital personnel, the hospital system began to change. Patients and their families were perceived as being a "population at risk" that had an automatic right to help, if they so desired. The hospital system gained, and Betsy and I gained in knowledge of ourselves and in more open communication after having experienced a system's attempt to dilute some of the intensity from unresolved problems "within" by "triangulating" others from outside the system.

The rest of the course was easy sailing. This latter crisis and its process were shared with the class, who began to understand better and appreciate the problems of service delivery in a large hospital complex in relation to the dying. I invited the head of the hospital's social work service staff to share with the class some of the problems and proposed resolutions around these issues from her perspective.

All the information coming in until now had been from the patient, his family, and direct caregivers' points of view. Now all of us were better able to appreciate the concerns and stumbling blocks from an administrator's point of view. The seminar ended on this note, after having had a session with a panel of clergy who skillfully and dramatically highlighted death and grief issues and ways in which the clergy might be helpful as part of the hospital team.

This experimental seminar had been alternately frightening, exhilarating, debilitating, rewarding, frustrating, and revitalizing. We had anticipated some of the range of these intensities and had suggested, as an assignment option, that students might want to choose a class partner with whom they could spend a designated amount of time each week during the span of the course, wherein they could exchange ideas and feelings about their reactions. Each partner was to write up the other's views and feelings. We felt this would help afford them a constant sounding board that could get them through some trying moments, as well as clarify cognitive issues. Another assignment option was choosing a range of concepts covered in the course that they could apply to an analysis of death and dying, suicide or grief, described in any book of fiction or nonfiction we had listed. Then they were asked to describe how they as a social worker, friend, or family member would have intervened. Other options included writing about a personal experience related to suicide, death, or grief, and the critical issues involved, or a paper about a specific ethical issue covered in the course and the writer's personal belief system and rationale for it.

Most of the students this first time around played it safe in their selected assignments and chose to discuss their reactions to works of fiction. As a safeguard against too much emotional flooding, we had offered conferences throughout the term for any student who wished to talk privately. A few students shared deeply felt experiences in their papers having to do with working through old or recent griefs. Practically all of these term papers necessitated private therapeutic conferences that we initiated for the most part, because we began to see that several people had been harboring very conflictive feelings that were never expressed in class discussion and often were not brought into sharp focus until the students sat down to write. Only four students paired up for verbal or written exchanges.

The written anonymous student evaluations at the end of the first course were highly positive. As anticipated, the speakers with personal experience were those most highly valued by the students, and many of their open-ended comments spoke about the course as having changed their lives in most profound ways. Paradoxically many wrote that it gave them a feeling of being intensely alive. The vast majority valued the seminar as the highlight of their university experience, feeling it had been the most personally and professionally meaningful course they had taken. Several referred to their difficulty in accepting a second-year student, their peer, as teacher. However, they grudgingly admitted that they eventually came to respect her considerable knowledge and expertise. Also, by the time the course ended, Betsy and I had very much come together as a teaching team, and it was reflected in the growing group cohesiveness toward the close of the seminar in the spring of 1974.

Over the summer I began to move into working with cancer patients and their families at the community mental health center in the town where I lived. As part of our consultation and education program there, I began to consult with hospital teams and nursing schools, church groups, high-school classes, and other mental health clinics. My remission continued, along with my periodic five-day stays at the hospital, where I interacted continually with patients and staff. All these experiences gave me a chance to tease out the many common elements that exist among the terminally ill and to appreciate the multiple cultural, religious, and personal variables that made for idiosyncratic differences.

The Second Year

By September I was ready to tackle another seminar in the dynamics of death and dying. Betsy had graduated and was now ready to teach her own course in the school's continuing education program, so I had to look for someone else to share the responsibility of the class with me. This time I was determined it should be out of mutual choice and for the right reasons, not out of pragmatic accommodation.

As luck would have it, one of my closest friends and faculty colleagues asked if she might sit in on my class to tape record each session and write down notes about class process, because she felt this might be helpful for future faculty who might be interested in teaching the course. I told her that, if she sat in, I would like her to be a participant-observer, contributing to class discussion at any point where there might be a need to dilute intensities or to clarify issues and process. Her observations and a relistening to the tapes could, moreover, help provide feedback and perspective for me after class each week. Her participation turned out to be a boon for all concerned. Her uncanny sense of timing in class and her sparse but sensitive and incisive comments always seemed to come at the most propitious moments. Follow-up student evaluations agreed that her presence was invaluable, and one student lovingly referred to her as "your sister who sits there emphatically in the corner." Because I had the prime responsibility throughout of conducting and relating to the class, the issues of group involvement, attachment, and ultimate separation and loss evolved much more naturally and productively. However, it was her presence and selective participation, as well as her astute interventions and our after-class debriefings, that best enabled me to preserve the emotional and cognitive control of the material so necessary when dealing with personal experience.

Another contrast to the first year was my decision to include a variety of students from other disciplines while still keeping the seminar small, although by this time we had to turn down dozens of our own students and growing numbers from other departments. At least a third of the classes were students of psychology, medicine, nursing, counselor education, and the ministry. It is my belief that interdisciplinary instruction leads both to a more vital cross-fertilization of ideas and to a greater appreciation of professional skills and talents from other disciplines and prepares students for a team approach in working with the dying. This proved to be one of the most enriching aspects of the seminar; everyone learned to talk a common language with an absence of jargon.

A third change was to modify our previous desensitizing approach and deal with students' death anxieties head-on in the first session. The anxieties were there, and the sooner they could be talked about and shared, the more open to learning everyone could be. Instead of starting off with ethical issues, I began by sharing my own death anxieties and my own narrative about how and why I had come to teach the course and about how my own anxieties have abated the more I had come to accept death as a natural part of life. I talked about how death images evolve in each of us developmentally and about the various life images and symbolic immortality we come to possess as an antidote to those anxieties. After free-flowing discussion, I had them fill out Kübler-Ross's *Questionnaire for Institute On Understanding the Dying Person and His Family*. This is a sentence completion form that includes such suggestive phrases as "I was first confronted with death at the age of ____ when ____ died"; "My reaction was ____"; "When I think of death now, I think of ____"; and so forth.

I then divided the group into triads, and each threesome shared their completed sentences with each other, which enabled them to experience the possible developmental bases for their own current death anxieties. As the small groups then merged into a larger group, they were able to see the common elements in each of their unique experiences. The bubble of fear was thus burst in the first session, and the class of separate, frightened individuals began to coalesce as a group almost from the very beginning.

Small-group interaction was continued during each of the sessions on ethical issues as students were urged, after a presentation of didactic material and after various ethical positions had been delineated on the board, to draw value continuums for themselves relating to euthanasia, abortion, and genetic engineering. Students had to place their initials on each value continuum line representing their stance in relation to a specific ethical position and explain to their small-group members why they took the position they chose. Again the sessions would close with large groups participating and comparing various group responses.

The course followed the first year's curriculum format fairly closely; it was the process that had changed. Because I was so much more comfortable with my own dying and had experienced so fully the vitality of rearranging priorities and of focusing on quality rather than quantity, on depth where there could be no length, and on having had so many soul-satisfying months of being able to tend to my "unfinished business," I was no longer so anxious about "getting it all in." There was more time for emotional ebb and flow and opportunities for modeling a style of dying characterized by full, rich living. The debriefing sessions conducted after every guest speaker's talk permitted honest, open sharing to emerge. Students began to feel more comfortable with their varying ranges of emotional responses to class material and with their recognition that not everyone responded similarly to highly charged material.

The dialogue between my husband and myself in one of our class sessions modeled dimensions of a marital relationship to which students rarely had been exposed: how "gallows" humor can be the saving grace in a continuous dying; how the longer a wife is in remission, the easier it may be for her to reach acceptance, but the harder it becomes for the spouse to think of letting go.

The session with the hospital team had wrought tremendous changes. This time the social worker came as part of the team. They all spoke eloquently of the need to become genuinely involved with their patients to help them. They spoke movingly of their struggle to preserve professional boundaries and not to "burn out" in the face of constant death. The class confronted them with why they had not taken the initiative to start group meetings on the unit for patients and their families so that a patient support system could supplement their own. This pushed the team to initiate more changes in the system, and as a result of the class interactions, the team went back to the hematology unit and initiated weekly group meetings. In addition they were intrumental in bringing in a psychiatric consultant for weekly sessions wherein patients or their spouses are interviewed before house staff, doctors, nurses, and social workers so that the staff can get a better appreciation of what the patients feel about the treatment and what it feels like to be dying. There were no tremors in the hospital system as a result of this year's encounter. On the contrary the hospital administrator thanked us for helping with the changes that had been slowly wrought.

The most painful session this year as last followed the class dialogue with a bereaved father—of a 19-year-old son who had died three months previously. His profound love and painful loss stirred recognitions in the students that soon they, too, would have to separate from me and deal with my loss. In the debriefing session several students wept and begged that those who wished might continue meeting as a small group after the class ended. I then told the class that during the week three students had talked with me about this possibility and that I had immediately slipped right back into "denial" and said what a great idea I thought this was and I would be happy to be on hand when possible. But as soon as I had left them, I realized I had reverted to "child time," to that magical, omnipotent thinking that I had infinite time left. And so I told the class that, if they are to learn what it means to face death, separation, and loss, I could not help them by buying into child time. The course is limited to 15 weeks, just as life is time limited, and I would hinder rather than help them if I perpetuated the fantasy of an unending relatedness by continuing to meet. To love is to lose and to be able to let go, whether it be our family, friends, or clients.

They continued to grapple with their intense feelings and finally resolved that they must face the class's ending in three more sessions. The manner in which they resolved it is perhaps best reflected in the following verbatim transcript from the class tape, spoken by a young ministerial student:

I felt toward you a little bit like I did when my mom made oatmeal cookies in the kitchen and you could smell them all over the house. What I've been struggling with is that there are just so many cookies on the sheet, and as much as your life style has been to invest yourself as if there is no end, my struggle in this whole class has been how close do I come to the sheet. . . . You've only got so many cookies left and as your time gets shorter, you're going to have to make more and more shrewd decisions about who to give cookies to. I just appreciate being able to see the cookies and to smell them.

In their struggle to separate and let go, students discovered a large learning in this small ending of their lives. They realized that, even in close relationships, people go through the "five stages" at different times and in varying intensities on their own emotional timetable.

They learned that they could experience an event deeply and yet have the ability to step back and examine what was occurring—an invaluable experience for the practicing professional.

The seminar ended three sessions later with a presentation by a former student, her husband, and four young children about how they had come to talk about death as a result of last year's seminar and about how it had helped them face the death of their dearest family friend. It was an example of modeling how a family with children ranging from ages seven to twelve could talk openly about death and the meaning it had to each of them. The class debriefed and then ended with a party celebrating life.

The quality of the student projects undertaken as assignments reflected the difference in class process the second time around. Only one student wrote a paper based on a work of fiction. The vast majority handed in tape recordings of dialogues between themselves and their parents, spouses, lovers, or closest friends. The modeling had taken hold. The remainder wrote stirring papers about personal experiences, with an amazing amount of creativity reflected in original poetry, prose, and songs that often accompanied their projects. Students used individual conferences selectively throughout the seminar as crisis points occurred. These individual sessions were handled therapeutically and educatively. Consequently there was not the snowballing of anxiety at the end that had occurred the year before. In the first seminar, moreover, insufficient attention had been given to group process. The second seminar ended on a rather serene, albeit bittersweet note. The university's teaching evaluation team rated the course in the highest percentile ranking of classes currently being conducted, based on the students' anonymous evaluations.

I am no longer teaching the seminar, wanting now to "just be" for awhile and not have to "do" as concertedly as before. Betsy is now teaching the seminar in continuing education where I just recently appeared as a guest speaker. The "vibes" between us and the rest of the class were incredibly good. I believe we have gotten to this point because of our own hard-won experience and because American society in general is becoming more comfortable and open about death. We all reflect that shift.

Summary

In this chapter I have examined the pros and cons of using the dying professional as death educator. I have also examined the differences between team teaching and using a participant-observer with clearly defined roles so that the modeling process of dealing with genuine sorrow over separation and loss and ultimate endings can be dealt with more effectively.

I also have indicated some of the most significant factors that enabled me to preserve the emotional and cognitive control of the material so necessary when dealing with personal experience, with particular emphasis on the sensitive interventions of a participant-observer. However, my implications go beyond death education. I believe that institutions could maximize their teaching potential by building on the idiosyncratic life experiences of their faculty. Curriculum planners could assess the strengths of faculty members by looking at those who have lived with physical disabilities, those who have had certain illnesses, and those who have experienced divorce, child rearing, old age, and so on and then permit faculty members to teach about these content areas. Obviously, to be a good teacher, one needs more than life experience. One needs to translate life experience into meaningful action, incorporate it into self, and then put it into a cognitive framework with some empirical feedback so that this feeling-thinking-doing process can become growth-promoting for others as well as for oneself. The allegations that "once we are professionalized, we are too distancing" or the opposite that "if we teach them intense life experiences we are too involved" could be disproved if only we could link up the one with the other. It is from these very linkage points that we can all learn and grow, for however long our time may last.

References and Additional Bibliography

"Ars Moriendi." 1974. Article on course evaluation sponsored by Ars Moriendi at Scheie Institute, Summer, 1973. Philadelphia: *Ars Moriendi Newsletter* 2, no. 1 (March).

Bowen, M. "The Family Faces Death." Videotape, University of Virginia Medical School, Richmond, Virginia.

Carkhuff, R. R. 1971. *The Development of Human Resources*. New York: Holt, Rinehart, and Winston, Inc.

Feifel, H. 1967. "Physicians Consider Death." Paper presented at 75th Annual Convention, American Psychological Association, September.

Glaser, B. G. and A. L. Strauss. 1965. *Awareness of Dying*. Chicago: Aldine.

Hamovitch, M. B. 1964. *The Parent and the Fatally Ill Child*. Los Angeles: Delmar.

Jackson, G. E. 1974. "The Dying Patient and His Family: The Role of the Clergy." (Unpublished, June).

Kübler-Ross, E. 1969. *On Death and Dying*. New York: Macmillan Company.

Lifton, R. J. and E. Olson. 1974. *Living and Dying*. New York: Praeger.

Phillips, D. P. 1969. "Birthdays and Death." Paper presented to the American Sociological Association, San Francisco, September.

Rees, W. D. and S. G. Lutkins. 1967. "Mortality of Bereavement." *British Medical Journal* (October): 13–16.

Seligman, M. E. P. 1974. "Giving Up On Life." *Psychology Today* (May).

Index

Compiled by Lucia A. Bove

Contributors

Arthur Arkin, M.D., Department of Psychiatry, Montefiore Hospital and Medical Center, Bronx, New York

Hilda C. M. Arndt, Ph.D., Professor and Chairperson of Specialization in Services to Individuals and Families, School of Social Welfare, Louisiana State University, Baton Rouge, Louisiana

Rachel Rustow Aubrey, M.S.S., ACSW; Adjunct Associate Professor of Sociology, The City College of New York; Staff Psychotherapist, Columbia University Health Service, New York, New York

Delia Battin, M.S., St. Luke's Hospital Child Psychiatry Clinic, New York, New York

Lucia Bove, Editorial Associate, The Foundation of Thanatology, New York, New York

Ruth R. Boyd, ACSW, Assistant National Executive Director, Educational Services, Girl Scouts of America; formerly, Chairperson, Human Behavior Department, Howard University, Washington, D.C.

Sharol Cannon, R.N., M.S.W., Director, Life Service Center, Phoenix, Arizona; Psychiatric Social Worker, Child-Adolescent Treatment Unit, Arizona State Hospital, Phoenix, Arizona

Helen Cassidy, Ph.D., Professor of Social Work, School of Social Work, Tulane University, New Orleans, Louisiana

Jean E. Collard, M.A., Instructor in Clinical Social Work, Department of Neurology, College of Physicians and Surgeons, Columbia University; Director, Social Services, Neurological Institute, Columbia-Presbyterian Medical Center, New York, New York

Grace Fields, M.S.S., Director of Social Service, Blythedale Children's Hospital, Valhalla, New York

Rev. John Freund, C.M., Director of Theological Field Education, Department of Theology, St. John's University, Jamaica, New York

Erna Furman, Cleveland Center for Research in Child Development; Case Western Reserve School of Medicine, Cleveland, Ohio

Irwin Gerber, Ph.D., Administrator, Department of Neoplastic Diseases, Mt. Sinai School of Medicine, New York, New York

Leon H. Ginsberg, Ph.D., Commissioner, West Virginia Department of Welfare, Charleston, West Virginia; Dean (on leave), School of Social Work, West Virginia University, Morgantown, West Virginia

Eda G. Goldstein, Ph.D., Assistant Professor, Hunter College School of Social Work; Supervisor of Research, Social Service Department, New York Hospital-Cornell Medical Center, Westchester Division, White Plains, New York

Clelia P. Goodyear, C.S.W., New York University Graduate School of Social Work (part-time faculty); Private Practice, New York, New York

Mittie Gruber, M.A., M.S.S., Professor, School of Social Welfare, Louisiana State University, Baton Rouge, Louisiana

Burton Gummer, Ph.D., School of Social Administration, Temple University, Philadelphia, Pennsylvania

Lois Jaffe, M.S.W., Associate Professor, Graduate School of Social Work, University of Pittsburgh, Pittsburgh, Pennsylvania

Jordan I. Kosberg, Ph.D., Associate Professor, School of Applied Social Sciences, Case Western Reserve University, Cleveland, Ohio

Austin H. Kutscher, D.D.S., President, The Foundation of Thanatology; Associate Professor, School of Dental and Oral Surgery, Columbia University; Associate Professor (in Dentistry), Department of Psychiatry, College of Physicians and Surgeons, Columbia University, New York, New York

Lillian G. Kutscher, Publications Editor, The Foundation of Thanatology, New York, New York

Sylvia Lack, M.B., B.S., Medical Director, Hospice, Inc., New Haven, Connecticut

Nathan Lefkowitz, Ph.D., Assistant Professor, School of Public Health, Columbia University, New York, New York

Larry Lister, D.S.W., Associate Professor, University of Hawaii School of Social Work; Director, Social Services, Leahi Hospital, Honolulu, Hawaii

Gary A. Lloyd, Ph.D., Professor and Dean, Graduate School of Social Work, University of Houston, Houston, Texas

Jean Markham, M.S.W., Hospice, Inc., New Haven, Connecticut

Barbara McNulty, S.R.N., Home Care Service, St. Christopher's Hospice, London, England

Phyllis, Mervis, M.S.W., C.S.W., Preceptor and Senior Social Worker, Department of Neoplastic Diseases, The Mount Sinai Hospital, New York, New York

Rosalind S. Miller, Ph.D., Associate Professor, Columbia University School of Social Work, New York, New York

Ben A. Orcutt, D.S.W., ACSW, Professor, School of Social Work, The University of Alabama, University, Alabama

Mary K. Parent, D.S.W., Associate Professor, School of Social Welfare, Louisiana State University, Baton Rouge, Louisiana

C. Murray Parkes, M.D., D.P.M., FRCPsych., St. Christopher's Hospice, London; Department of Psychiatry, The London Hospital Medical College, University of London, London, England

Elizabeth R. Prichard, M.S., Assistant Professor of Clinical Social Work, Department of Medicine, College of Physicians and Surgeons, Columbia University; Director, Social Services, The Presbyterian Hospital in the City of New York, Columbia-Presbyterian Medical Center, New York, New York

Mary C. Schwartz, M.S.W., School of Social Work, State University of New York at Buffalo, Buffalo, New York

Irene B. Seeland, M.D., Associate in Clinical Psychiatry, College of Physicians and Surgeons, Columbia University, New York, New York

Phyllis R. Silverman, Ph.D., Director of Research and Evaluation, Mystic Valley Mental Health Center, Lexington, Massachusetts

Lee H. Suszycki, M.S.W., ACSW, Department of Social Services, The Presbyterian Hospital in the City of New York, Columbia-Presbyterian Medical Center, New York, New York

Diane Simpson, M.S.W., Social Work Supervisor, Division of Public Welfare, State of New Jersey, Trenton, New Jersey

Alfred Wiener, M.D., Department of Psychiatry, Montefiore Hospital and Medical Center, Bronx, New York

Marion Wijnberg, M.S.W., Associate Professor, School of Social Work, State University of New York at Buffalo, Buffalo, New York

Columbia University Press / Foundation of Thanatology Series

Loss and Grief: Psychological Management in Medical Practice
Bernard Schoenberg, Arthur C. Carr, David Peretz, and Austin H. Kutscher, editors

Psychosocial Aspects of Terminal Care
Bernard Schoenberg, Arthur C. Carr, David Peretz, and Austin H. Kutscher, editors

Psychosocial Aspects of Cystic Fibrosis: A Model for Chronic Lung Disease
Paul R. Patterson, Carolyn R. Denning, and Austin H. Kutscher, editors

The Terminal Patient: Oral Care
Austin H. Kutscher, Bernard Schoenberg, and Arthur C. Carr, editors

Psychopharmacologic Agents for the Terminally Ill and Bereaved
Ivan K. Goldberg, Sidney Malitz, and Austin H. Kutscher, editors

Anticipatory Grief
Bernard Schoenberg, Arthur C. Carr, Austin H. Kutscher, David Peretz, and Ivan K. Goldberg, editors

Bereavement: Its Psychosocial Aspects
Bernard Schoenberg, Irwin Gerber, Alfred Wiener, Austin H. Kutscher, David Peretz, and Arthur C. Carr, editors

The Nurse as Caregiver for the Terminal Patient and His Family
Ann M. Earle, Nina T. Argondizzo, and Austin H. Kutscher, editors

Social Work with the Dying Patient and the Family
Elizabeth R. Prichard, Jean Collard, Ben A. Orcutt, Austin H. Kutscher, Irene Seeland, and Nathan Lefkowitz, editors